9/27.2022

For Julie

have a wonderful pilgrimage
of life ☺.

Tons of Love
Petra

Encounters

on the road

to Jerusalem

by

Mike Metras and Petra Wolf

Second Edition

Pilgrimage Creations

2015

ISBN: 978-1-329-32894-5

Second Edition

Published by Pilgrimage Creations

www.WorksAndWords.com
www.WalkingWithAwareness.com
Woodstock, Illinois 60098 U.S.A.

Printed by Lulu.com
December 2011

Second edition printed by Lulu.com
July 2015

From inside:

...I don't like 'peace walks,' but in fact this is really a peace walk because we are, by experience, saying, 'this is a peaceful place. There are problems and there are bad things, but this is, by far, a peaceful place. A lot of times in the media you read about the bad guy.... But that bad guy is only one out of 100,000. That leaves 99,999 who are great people."

On 6 August, 2010 on the web journal I report, "When will we return to Arles? Today we don't know when or if we will. Our time here in the dry, fresh air will tell us. We'll decide when it is time to decide."

The shaman tells Petra, "The big things happen because of the small things. Meeting people and talking and sharing life and passion and love stories, all these are small things but we never know what kind of seed we are sewing. The world changes with the small things."

The bird is back standing near the body as soon as we leave. The life of the opossums will soon be transformed into life for that bird and his companions. There is nothing we can or should do. The cycle of life shows itself clearly.

So it takes us a few extra days to get to Santiago as we sit out some rain days here and there along the way. We will neither melt nor freeze. Be patient, listen, feel, and learn. That's what this pilgrimage is all about anyway.

What is an extra day or two in a pilgrimage that will ultimately take two years?

The Katy is hot and humid. It's misquotes and no wind. No, it's not "no wind"; it's a 2.5 miles-per-hour (4 kph) wind at our backs so the result is no wind as we walk forward at 2.5 mph. But the Katy is also beautiful. Trees, fields, cliffs, and the Missouri River line the path. Everything is green: green trees, green grass, green weeds, and green moss. The sky is deep blue with puffy clouds—when it isn't raining.

"People don't want to take the time any more. Town-to-town boats haven't been [on the Mississippi] for several years. People want to quickly see many places instead of enjoying a few leisurely."

Contents

Introduction

In January 2009 we began walking east from our home on the central California coast. On Christmas Day 2010 we walked past the birthplace of Jesus in Bethlehem. Our pilgrimage was over.

This book tells the story of our encounters with people, places, animals, sun, wind, rain, snow, roads, and paths as we walked across North America and southern Europe to Jerusalem. It also tells the story of our encounters with our own joys, doubts, fears, and ecstasies. It is the story of living 23 months on the road, of trusting the Universe to provide what we needed when we needed it.

This book is a communal work with our intertwined thoughts, concepts, and words throughout. Both Petra and I write in the first person but the context usually tells you who is writing a particular paragraph. [So you can see when you get to the bottom of this page it is Mike writing this. Other places are usually as easy to determine.]

Headings mark every 500 walking miles (800 kilometers) as you read through the book. That's 38 walking days at our average of 13 miles (21 kilometers) per day.

We thank all the people we encountered along the road for their hospitality, gifts, spirit, and encouragement. They were an unexpected addition and support to our pilgrimage. They often buoyed us up when our energy and determination were flagging. We seldom walked away from an encounter without renewed energy and enthusiasm.

We invite you to walk with us now as you read through the eight seasons we spent walking (and sometimes riding and flying) more than one third of the way around the world.

Petra Wolf and Mike Metras – December 2011

Introduction to Second Edition

This second edition corrects several minor errors and omissions, expands some descriptions, and adds stories in a few places including Aurora, Illinois, Salon in Provence , and in Jerusalem left out when we first published this book.

Petra Wolf and Mike Metras – October 2014

Petra walking the western Mojave Desert.

WINTER 2009

The first steps

We are cleaning the last corners of our rental home in Paso Robles, California, getting ready for a 9:30 inspection. The doorbell rings at 9:15. It is Marie ready to check us out.

"You are 15 minutes early." Petra protests following her German logic that meetings are to happen only at the exact scheduled minute, not before, not after. "I still have things to do."

"That's OK. You can do them. I can do what I need to do without getting in your way." Marie replies calmly.

We have a few clean-up tasks to do yet. Otherwise we are ready to go. In half an hour Marie says, "It looks fine. You should get your whole deposit back." Though Petra feels there are still too many streaky windows, we are relieved the test is over.

Marie says, "I'll take the keys and you are free to go." So we put our last pieces for storage on the driveway. She locks the doors and leaves. We are homeless, sitting on the driveway waiting for our friends Rose Marie and Helmut to pick us up and transport our last few things to storage.

Petra sits waiting for Rose and Helmut. We are ready to put our remaining goods in storage, have a coffee, and get on the road.

Though a surprise, the early banishment from the house gives us a chance to sit calmly a while and say our good-byes. Petra goes to the back yard. Two humming birds we often saw in the flowers fly up and hover in front of her one at a time and look her directly in the face as if to say good-by.

Why

Hardly are we at home with a way of living
And cozily settled in, than drowsiness threatens
And we are ready to leave,
Feeling like we are held by some paralyzing trap.
  - from Herman Hesse, **Stages**

Why the walk? We like to walk. We like walking long. We like walking in straight lines, not in circles. And it is certainly a long, if not so straight, way from California to Jerusalem. Why that particular path?

Neither of us is new to walking. We both have walked most of our lives. We met on the Camino de Santiago in 2003; Petra had walked alone from Germany. We have walked parts of it again as well as the Via de la Plata from Seville to Santiago.

Move forward to January 2007. We are on a pilgrimage walk from our home in Germany over the Alps and down the Via Francigena to Rome. We stay one night at the convent of the Sisters of St. Vincent de Paul in Sienna; Sister Ginetta signs us in and stamps our credential. As we give Rome as our destination, she asks, "Are you on the way to Jerusalem?"

It shocks us. So matter-of-fact. We stand with no answer.

She adds, "After all, Rome is only a stop along the road to Jerusalem." We have surely casually thought of walking to Jerusalem but never so concretely that we would attach it to this walk to Rome, especially to make Rome only a stop along the road to Jerusalem.

The thought incubates. When we get to Rome we walk a day toward Jerusalem beyond Rome along the ancient Via Appia with all of its ancient graves. The seed was planted and germinated.

A couple months later we hear of a couple who have walked to Jerusalem from their home near Munich. Petra is working near where they live. We visit them and talk for several hours about their pilgrimage walk through Greece, Turkey, and Syria. Their book's title tells of their ordeal, Lang ist der Weg nach Jerusalem (It's a long way to Jerusalem). They are happy they walked though they had many hardships along the way.

In November 2007 we move to the United States and are looking for a place to live in California. We attend a seminar on building yurts at a lighthouse Bed and Breakfast (B&B) near San Francisco. A guy who walked across America is also there. We exchange stories. A seed for walking across America is planted.

Fast forward into the late spring months of 2008. We are walking five miles a day in the hills and along the river in Paso Robles, California, now our home town. That adds up to an impressive 1,825 miles (2,950 Kilometers) a year if we had walked it every day. But it's in circles. We come back to the beginning every time. It's much different than walking from Paso Robles to, for example, Boonville in central Missouri, more or less the same distance when you string out those five miles back-to-back for a year. We long to connect the dots not to walk in circles.

Moving forward again, I'm sitting at home in Paso Robles on a 104-degree (40-C.) afternoon in late July 2008 wondering why we are here. We cannot go out in mid-day. We don't feel part of the culture and community. At the same time it sure is nice go only 20 miles (32 kilometers) over the mountain and down to 70 degrees (21 C.) on the Pacific at Cayucos. We have been trying to get seminars and slide shows going and nothing is gelling. California is not all we had thought it was going to be for us.

In late July, Petra is out teaching a walking class with one student. Walking across America and the pilgrimage to Jerusalem are wandering the back of my mind. Then I say to myself, "Why not?"

When Petra comes home, I ask her, "Why don't we stop talking about walking and walk ourselves? Why don't we walk across the U.S. and when we get to the other side just keep going and finish that pilgrimage to Jerusalem."

She stood silent. I added, "Besides, we've been telling others that anyone can walk from his or her front door in North America to Santiago de Compostela. Let's show them."

She thought a while longer and then said, "Yes, let's do it."

So why walk a third of the way around the world? In December, I post the following reasons on our web journal, WalkingEast.com

> After less than a year in California, we're homesick for the unknown again. But why walk? We like walking. We like the lure of the next horizon. We like living every day differently, in a new environment. We'll walk to meet those along our way. We'll also walk to experience the joys and adversities that make our lives stronger and more whole as we live through them. We'll walk to feel the warmth and strength of the sun, the gentle pushes and heavy blasts of the wind, the heat of mid-day, and the cold of late night. We'll walk to live fully our pilgrimage of life day by day as we take each step along the way.

> On a mundane level, even after so short a time, our house in California is confining; it demands much of us. That's nothing new; many other people have similar feelings and do nothing about them. But we want to do something about it. We want to leave it, to end our lease, to sell many things, to store what's left, and to walk away from the house. We realize we didn't have to take care of it. We don't have to pay rent, gas bills, water bills, garbage bills, car insurance, electric bills, internet bills, phone bills, taxes. We don't have to buy gas for the car. We know we can spend our time better than sweeping the sidewalk, the kitchen floor, or the back patio or vacuuming the living room, our offices, and the bedroom. We can no longer believe it is reasonable to water grass in this semi-desert where growing cacti is a lot more reasonable. We're ready to leave all of those goodies at the every-night cost of having to find a new motel or camping spot, of having to cook over an alcohol stove or eat in a restaurant, and of daily finding a path and daily walking it [Little did we know what we were getting into with these latter tasks!].

> We know we can find a place to stop someday. But we're heading to Jerusalem on a year and a half odyssey, a year and a half pilgrimage in the pilgrimage of our lives. We

know that when the way says stop, we will stop [though we didn't always listen closely]. But until then we're ready to walk and learn from the road, to meet and learn from new people, to see new lands, to cross horizon after horizon, to celebrate life in its many forms, and to learn from ourselves. We aim to live with what we are carrying. Whatever else we will "need," we know the road, the Universe, will provide. If they don't provide it, we don't need it. We aim to have only those small pieces we truly need and no more.

The bottom line is that we walk because we are walkers, we love to walk, and we want to walk. Now with the walk in our face we are a little apprehensive. But for that very reason we are excited to face it. We have conceived it. We have given it birth. Now we will live with it to see where it takes us. We are ready to learn from our child as much as we fear it and look at it with awe.

We want to learn who we will become after walking so long. We want to be open to whatever the Universe has prepared for us. We don't know what will happen. We don't know the answers to all the whys. If we knew all that, there is probably no reason to go.

In the end, the journey is the destination. We can only see why we are walking when we walk, when we are done with the walk, and maybe a long time after we are done with the walk.

The Plan

We're planning to walk from California to Jerusalem. We plan to take a little less than a year to walk across North America. We don't want to walk in the deserts in the summer or the mountains in winter. To keep it to one year, we have to arrive in New York City not too long after the beginning of December to avoid snow. We know that we can walk the country east of the Rockies any time from March to December. Assuming all this, if we want to walk America in one pass we have to cross the western third before late March or early April. That means we have to cross the southwestern desert in the winter. We estimate a window for departing between 1 December and 1 February. We pick 16 January.

In Europe we plan on walking up Portugal and across northern Spain, southern France, and northern Italy. From there it could be down Italy or down the Dalmatian coast through Croatia, into Greece and Turkey, and finally by either Cyprus or Syria to Israel and Jerusalem.

Ultimately our pilgrimage takes us into 11 states: California, Arizona, Nevada, New Mexico, Colorado, Kansas, Missouri, Illinois, Iowa, Wisconsin, Michigan, and New York. And we pass through ten countries: The United States, Canada, Portugal, Spain, France, Belgium, Germany, Italy, Egypt, Jordan, and Israel.

The maps in the appendix (p. 329) show the route we follow.

Exploratory walks

When we conceive this pilgrimage walk we have no idea what it will be like walking on American roads. We have walked a lot in Europe but not in America. So we set off on several one-day, exploratory walks.

We walk to Templeton and take a bus back to Paso Robles, our home. Then to Atascadero, the next town south, and take a bus back. Then to San Miguel the next Mission north and take that bus. This pilgrimage is also a Spanish mission walk.

The interior of the Mission La Purisma Conception in Lompoc.

After the 10-mile (16-kilometers) San Miguel walk, we begin a new tactic. We drive to Atascadero, where we have already walked and walk to our next destination over Cuesta Mountain to San Luis Obispo. We then take the bus back to Atascadero and drive home. On this day we find an alternative to the road—over that mountain. We are also practicing looking for alternatives (shortcuts and just alternatives to road walking).

Another day we drive to San Luis Obispo, walk to Arroyo Grande and return by bus to the car and drive home as before. We continue along the Camino Real, the route connection the string missions the Spanish established in the late 1700s. We walk to San Miguel, San Luis Obispo, La Purisma Conception, and Santa Inés during nine days until we are 132 miles (241 kilometers) away when we get to St. Inés in Solvang. After those nine days, we feel we have a handle on American roads and shortcuts and are ready to weigh anchor and set out walking without the security of the house any more.

The total mileage of the walking pilgrimage includes these 132 miles from San Miguel to Santa Inés that we walked to get used to the American walking environment.

Back on the driveway

So we sit now in our driveway ready to go. Our friends Helmut and Rose arrive after half an hour. We deposit our things in storage and stop for a coffee in a café we have never visited before. We wish we had discovered it earlier, especially so when we return 17 months later and find that it has gone out of business.

By noon Helmut and Rose leave us at the bus station and we are alone ready to begin our walk. It's around 72 (22 C.) and sunny, a beautiful sendoff. As we get on the bus, tears flow, tears of excitement. Everything is done. We are free and ready to start. Yes, there are more than a few tears.

We move forward the 132 miles (214 kilometers) we already walked. After four local busses with transfers in San Luis Obispo, Santa Maria, and Lompoc we arrive in Solvang in the evening and book ourselves into the Solvang Inn.

In Lompoc, Petra rushes into a local store and buys a windbreaker while we wait 15 minutes for the next bus. That's one fast buy.

St. Inez Mission in Solvang.

The first full day

We begin walking the next morning, 16 January, on my 66th birthday. The weather is beautiful as we walk along two busy highways. Most shoulders are wide except for a few miles where we brush arms with the speeding cars.

Petra walks in new construction south of Solvang on our first day.

We spend the first night in our new tent at Cachuma Lake, a Santa Barbara County park. As part of our dinner, we have a soup from a plastic bowl, you know: add water, cover, and let sit. Not a very momentous thing, but we save our bowls and use them for a long time as we walk. In fact, Petra still often uses hers more than five and a half years later, calls it her "5,000-mile cup."

Over ambitious

The next day is ambitious, over ambitious. We hope to make it all the way to Santa Barbara, 24 miles (38 kilometers) over the St. Ynez Mountains. For some reason I was thinking in kilometers as I planned the route and 24 kilometers (14 miles) is truly doable. Sometimes brain cells get crossed.

Our walk along Hwy 154 is hectic with a lot of speeding traffic and sometimes tight shoulders. But we branch off onto the old route of the road, Old Stagecoach Road. It winds around and under the new highway and its huge concrete-arch bridge. We meet, Kevin, a local out walking. He tells us 46 have jumped to their death from the bridge in its short existence since 1965, a black cloud over a pretty addition to the the landscape.

Along with the tens of motorcyclists and tourists, we stop for a hamburger at the Cold Springs Tavern, a historical landmark on Stagecoach Road. After clocking only around 150 miles (243 kilometers), we tell those near us that we are heading for Route 66 and walking to New York and afterward Jerusalem. No few of them look at us a little skeptically. We don't have enough miles under our feet yet to be taken seriously. That will not happen until we are out of California.

We leave the bikers and trudge on up to the pass. I feel like I am using my last strength. We walk four miles (6.5 kilometers) down realizing more and more as we go that we will not make the Santa Barbara Mission before 6:30 pm. We hitchhike and get a ride with the second car. They are also walkers and realize we must have miss-calculated as they have done before too. They give us a ride to the front door of the mission. We arrive just in time for 6 pm dinner after a very warm reception. Because of our pilgrimage to Jerusalem the people at the mission give us our evening lodging and meal as a present. Thanks for the ride and for the evening at the mission.

The next day we walk through Santa Barbara to the ocean and follow bike trails to Carpentaria. It is a long 13 miles (21 kilometers). Our feet are bothering a lot. Petra thinks it's the load because when the backpack is off she can walk without the pain. I am beginning to agree. We haven't got accustomed to the weight yet. The distance is also a factor. We practiced carrying our loads six miles. The second six is doable. But we accept that a third six or even a part of it is still too much. In time we will get back to our old 18-mile (29-kilometer) level we

Petra in front of the Santa Barbara Mission.

did some days on our Germany-to-Rome pilgrimage in 2006-7.

Rest on a beach

After a day in a motel, we move across town to a state park on the beach. We'll stay here a couple nights to rest. We begin to find each other and see a wonderful walk in front of us slowly unfolding. We sit in a campground at the Pacific in Carpentaria listening to the surf just over the dunes separating us from the sea. We readjust to our new lives as walkers and pilgrims before heading east again toward the distant Atlantic. After three days walking and now two days resting here to realign ourselves from the get-the-house-done-busy-busy mode, we chill a bit and feel more openness between each other and for the walk. We have started.

It feels like we are on our honeymoon, like we are on a honeymoon with the walk. We are nervous. This is new and exciting. What will we learn from the pilgrimage and this new relationship living 24/7 together for months?

Our new tent in Carpintaria and it's about to be vandalized.

Our tent

As we prepare for the walk, we know we want to camp along the way. But our old tent is heavy, much heavier than we want to carry. We are planning on carrying everything. Our carts only come as an afterthought after we are on the road almost a month.

We search the Internet and came up with a tent weighing 2.2 pounds. It's made of parachute material and boasts that it can withstand 160-mile-per-hour (260-kph) winds (like the winds on Mt. Everest). We aren't foreseeing winds like that but we like its weight. The tent also meets our needs for warmth in desert winter nights. It has double sides with an aluminum reflecting barrier against the heat and cold.

Soon we have a sporty new tent set up in our back yard to test it out. It's as light as advertised. At 12 feet (3.6 meters) long and six (1.8 meters) wide, it holds us and some gear well on many rainy nights.

Frustration

But all is not serene. The second afternoon in Carpentaria we come back after a beach walk and find a *hole in our brand new tent*. Frustration! We are so proud of that tent and now it has a hole the size of a grapefruit. A squirrel must have smelled the food inside and gnawed his way in. We get out the repair kit that came with the tent and fix it with little effort beyond a lot of whys and how can we let it happen. Our tent has received its baptism!

The telephone rings one day on the beach. A reporter for the Northwest Harold, in Woodstock, Illinois, asks to interview us. Woodstock is my long-time home town and I have several relatives there. Someone tipped off the newspaper. The phone is almost dead so our first interview on the road takes place over the phone in a park toilet, the only place to plug in the phone. His article is the first of many interviews we give as we walk across America (See p. 343).

As we tell the campground host we are planning to walk to Ojai, she says, "The road is narrow and has no shoulders and, besides, it's steep. Go along the coast. The highway isn't that bad. You'll like it." And so we get our first advice from a local on the best way to go. We will listen to and follow much advice like this in the coming months. Most of their suggestions turn out to be sound.

Petra savors one of her last walks on the Pacific.

We stop for a picture on the Pacific just west of Ventura.

Ventura

We walk to Ventura the next day partially on the highway but six or seven miles along the beach, feeling the Pacific for the last time for a while. It has always been a dream of mine to walk along a beach and not walk back. We do it today. The weather is beautiful and we are in high spirits.

As we enter Ventura it starts to rain and rains most of the night. Many homeless people live in Ventura. When we set out the next morning a couple street people, seeing our backpacks and thinking we are one of them living on the street, ask us, "Did you find a dry place to stay last night." "Yes." In fact, we stayed in a dry motel.

From Ventura, we walk a laser-straight road 13 miles (21 kilometers) to Santa Paula through orchard after orchard of lemons, oranges, and grapefruit. Rain threatens most of the day but we only have to take out our umbrellas once for a half hour shower.

The next day we leave Santa Paula with our umbrellas open and keep them that way for the first couple hours. The rain is never heavy, but it drizzles off and on all day. After walking through the poorer, run-down part of town, we walk a stretch of the busy Cal 126. The mostly wide shoulder makes the heavy traffic bearable. Eventually we veer off on an empty side road. From it, we enter the back side of the campground where we are planning on staying tonight, the lushly forested Kenny Grove Park. But it's closed. We end up in Fillmore in a motel as the rain returns. On the way we stop in Starbucks for coffee and receive two pieces of pizza from two young ladies we talk with for a while.

As we walk along the highway in the midst of thousands of Sun-Kist orange trees, I begin to think about people driving by us walking. Do they see us and think we have nothing? Do they see us as indigents? Then I realize that many of those driving by in their big cars probably don't even own them or the houses they are living in. Each passer-by plausibly owes several thousand on his/her car and several tens of thousands on his/her home. That makes them thousands in the hole. We have no car or house and money in the bank. They are much closer to the poverty line than we are.

To tell those passing us we are not indigent, that we are walking with a purpose; we created our flag, the flag on my backpack here. See page 332 for details on the flag.

Petra has foot pain and has to put ice on them for the first couple weeks of the walk. Then the pain goes away. Her big toe joint bugs her also. I often have foot pain at night but it is gone by morning.

People often ask us, "Why are you walking?" Each time someone asks, we ask ourselves again also. The answer coming up these days is that we want to feel who we are after walking a very long time, after walking for a year. Tomorrow's answer will be different.

Cold Camp

East of Santa Clarita, California, on a canyon road leading up to Palmdale, we are the only ones camping in a new KOA Campground. They have just emptied their pool. It is damp and cold. Petra cooks supper on our alcohol stove and I am in bed before seven. I am COLD. The water from that pool and the 24-degree (-4 C.) air make the evening quite unpleasant for me. But the new tent makes life better than it would be with the old one. We get up to a cold morning the next day and are quickly walking to warm up. It is old hat for Petra who has camped in the cold before. And now she is getting used to cooking on the road again. Enough camping for a while until it warms up a bit.

Our first desert

The next day we walk beautiful mountain roads and some not so beautiful ones on our way to Palmdale. The wind pushes us a lot. Just after noon we pass the edge of the village of Acton. A restaurant catches our eye. We eat two of the best and cheapest pork chops that we have seen in a long time. I hope I can remember just where that place is because I want to return the next time I am anywhere near.

We drag ourselves into Palmdale late in the afternoon and take the first motel we see. We're really tired. Mistake! Malhi's Inn is on its last leg. Its beds are like rocks. We don't like it. They won't give our money back. But we survive and learn to be a bit more observant before paying. (See "Ideal inn" on page 178.)

Today we opt for a rest day, our first in seven days. We find a new motel on the east side of town and settle in. I think my apprehension for our looming first desert crossing demands that we wait a bit. But we'll survive it. And we will flourish.

Petra says her feet are doing fine now—at least up to 18 miles. They finally have adapted to her new shoes. Mine are doing well likewise. Sometimes we have to give things time. One thing for sure: our 6-mile (9.6-kilometer) practice with full packs was not the same as walking 15 miles (24 kilometers) in one day.

An Israeli journalist emailed responding to our Woodstock Harold interview saying he wants to interview us when we get to Israel.

Sister says no

As we leave the motel in Palmdale, the man behind the desk says, "Head southeast for Pearblossom. They have a motel. There's nothing else to the east."

But yesterday Petra called the Carmelite Sisters in a monastery near Lake Los Angeles. The sister said we could stay with them. So we head straight east into the western Mojave Desert trying to ignore our apprehension of the desert.

We walk straight roads turning at right angles now and then to keep us on the path to the Sister's place. As the afternoon draws longer and we get tired, we see more than one place where we can set our tent. But we have an invitation up the road.

At one place late in the afternoon we see what looks at a distance like a nice multi-story motel with a gas station in front. Maybe we can just stay there. But as we arrive, we see a movie crew. The "motel" is a movie set. The director, an Austrian, says they are about to break up for the day, "I can give you a ride to a motel." We decline saying we have a place down the road another hour or so.

We arrive at a closed gate at the monastery around six. It's already dark. The days are short in January. I turn on the cell phone only to get a voice mail saying we cannot stay. I call and the sister calmly repeats that we can't stay. Petra takes the phone and protests. The sister says she will come to the gate.

When she arrives, she says, "I was wrong to assume that you could stay. My superior overruled me and said no. Some people from the drug-troubled Lake Los Angeles to the north have come in the past and were difficult to dislodge. You know, we teach kids during the day. We can't have adults being around with the kids there." Security, you know.

She says, "You can camp along the road here in front."

"We cannot, not with these big lights and all the stickers in the grass. They'll puncture our tent."

Then she said, "I could ask some neighbor if you could set our tent in their lawn."

"No, we do not want to do that." *How would the neighbors say yes when the sisters are saying no?*

We have no place to go. If we would have heard the message earlier, we could have stopped in several places to set up tent. But setting up a tent after dark with all these stickers is pretty much out of the question. I give the nun one of our cards with the WalkingEast.com website and she retreats to the monastery to see if she can come up with some solution for us.

We grumble about our difficulties, trying to figure a way out. Petra says, "Let's get out of this situation. We need a reset. Don't push the sister to stay."

The sister returns and says, "If you had given us your web site earlier, we might have been able to let you stay. But you have to go now. If you don't want to camp here, we can give you a ride into Lake Los Angeles."

We take the ride getting out at a gas station and general store. The sister gives us a bottle of water and a big bag of mixed nuts. We eat those nuts for a couple weeks afterwards. They are great. Thanks.

Our first angel

In the store we asked Tonya, the woman behind the meat and salad counter, "Is there a motel somewhere around here?"

"No, but there's one in Pearblossom, nine miles south of here."

"Wow! That's too far to walk now. It's already seven. Where can we get a cab or a bus there?"

"There isn't any. But if you want to wait until I'm off at eight, my boyfriend is picking me up and I can talk him into giving you a ride." Our angel.

We eat in the Mexican restaurant next door while we wait an hour. When her boyfriend, Ed, arrives, we squeeze into the back of his small car along with our backpacks and we ride south and west. [Get it, *west*, not east.]

We thank Tonya and Ed as we get out at the motel, the very same one last night's motel owner suggested to us this morning. It took a rejection by the Carmelites and a ride from our angel in Lake Los Angeles (The Angles) to get us here.

The redirection to Pearblossom sets us up for a long visit with the Vietnamese woman running the six-room motel the next morning and a detour to St Andrews monastery for a relaxing evening camp among the trees the next night.

After our camp in the woods, we continue our walk east over the Mojave. We discover the California Aqueduct. The footpath along the aqueduct is flat and without traffic, an ideal route for us. As night falls, we set up our tent just off the path away from the water.

At one or two in the morning a van stops. "What are you doing in there?"

"Sleeping." We both answer almost together through the tent.

"Do you know you are not allowed to sleep here?"

"No," though I suspect as much.

"I'm not going to make you pack up and leave. But make sure you are gone before 7:30 when the next check car comes by or they will take you in and fine you."

We thank him and are packed and on the road by 7:00.

Last night we tried to get water from the canal with a string and a bottle. It didn't work. We have a filter to purify it. So we start walking in the morning with a seriously low water supply. Petra spots a house without a fence—a very unusual thing for California. "And there's a water facet next to the garage. Let's get some water."

I protest. It's early Sunday morning, too early to wake someone.

"Let's just take some water." We do and no one comes out. I'm relieved. Thank you to the fenceless owners.

Gift of the desert

We have light backpacks for this pilgrimage, less than two pounds. But even with that I am carrying just over 30 pounds (13.5 kilos) and Petra 25 (11.4 kilos) as we leave Paso Robles. With food and water the weight probably fluctuates four pounds more and less as we walk.

That weight is manageable. But we are now in the western Mojave Desert and about to face several more days of desert, days we will have to take extra water at 8.3 pounds (3.8 kilos) a gallon (3.8 liters) and extra food at its weight. We are beginning to feel the wear of carrying just what we have day after day.

To make things worse, five days ago I went out after dark in Palmdale looking for water (or was it O'Doul's). I tripped on a raised curb in the middle of the road between the traffic lanes. I went down clobbering my head and twisting my back. I have been feeling it since. My pack is getting more than a little uncomfortable.

Encounters on the road to Jerusalem

We have been walking the western Mojave. It is full of garbage. Full. Paper, plastic, metal, cars, bicycles, plastic, paint, tires, and more plastic. In places the plants compete with the rejects of mankind.

As we walk north toward Silver Lakes, Petra steps off the dirt road into the desert and comes back saying, "I have something to carry your backpack." She's pulling a doll carriage, a miniature baby carriage.

We stand it up and look at it. "Yes, it might work."

I strap my backpack to the carriage and begin to push it. It's a little clumsy, but it works. I change the harness so I can pull it. It's a little better that way. It's working!

I walk it the rest of the way into Silver Lakes. My back begins to feel better.

As we leave three days later, Petra's backpack is on the cart. She straps her walking stick to the handle so she has a more convenient handle and can push as well as pull it.

Mike with Petra's new cart — the gift of the desert.

In the next few days we alternate using the cart, one hour Petra and the next me. And it becomes clear that pushing our goods is a lot better alternative than carrying them on our backs. We decide to get another cart. I look in Barstow and reject what I see including an inexpensive wheel chair in a second-hand shop (I first think I can use it in our camp at night too, but it's too heavy).

Finally I find a baby carriage, a bicycle trailer, in a Wal-Mart in Kingman, Arizona. It has a wheel to use in place of the connection to the bicycle.

We figure that taking the load off our backs allows us to walk an extra three to five miles as we cover the long distances in the west. And that says nothing about avoiding joint pain on this long walk.

Petra's cart, truly a gift of the desert, lasts all the way to New York though we repair it many times. I push my cart all the way to Arles, France, though I replace two broken axels before getting there.

Besides the physical cart, the desert also gives us the gift of the Joshua tree with its deep routes that sustain it when water is scarce. It reminds us of the spiritual roots we must set down to carry us through dry times. We need spiritual back-ups drawn from those deep routes to live our lives well.

Silver Lakes cafe

We walk into Silver Lakes, a town created from the desert, three concrete-lined lakes surrounded by houses in a sea of sand with a golf course in the middle. This is a place you find only in California or Arizona. It looks like a neat Danish village as we walk in from the south.

We find a room on the golf course, the only hotel in town. It is so spacious and so less expensive than we expect that we stay for three nights taking a rest after two weeks on the road.

As we walk around the thirty-something-year-old town the next afternoon we happen on a coffee shop. As coffee is on our mind, we walk in. Three or four are sitting around one of four tables.

"What can I get for you?" asks one woman.

"Two coffees."

"What brings you to Silver Lakes?"

"We're walking through on our way to Jerusalem." Now you have to realize that this place is remote—many miles from the nearest main road and many more miles from Jerusalem.

"Really? That's interesting. We were just praying for peace in Jerusalem." She tells us she is the pastor of a church in Barstow and runs the coffee shop on the side. They get together in the café every week to pray for peace. It is a coincidence that we, who are walking to Jerusalem, come in just as they are praying for Jerusalem.

We drink our coffee and talk a couple hours about our walk and her work. As we talk, I notice a card on her counter announcing a chiropractor. That fall the other night crossing the street twisted something in my back. I am still hurting.

"I have never been to a chiropractor in my life. I'm not sure I'm ready to have my back cracked. I'm a bit afraid."

"I can call him," she offered. "He's very good. He'll come and work on you right here in the café."

Petra encourages me to have a try.

I give in. In a few minutes Dr. Craig comes in with a table and sets it up in front of the counter. He asks me questions about my injury and has me lie face down on his table. He keeps talking, raises the center of the table with a clack, and gives my back a quick shove in the middle. My stomach breaks away the table as my back gives a bigger crack than the table. He does it again before I can protest the shock.

Strangely, I feel better. Maybe it's not strange. Maybe that's how chiropractors do their thing. He has me stand up and pulls me apart in the back and tells me he was done.

He offers to come to our hotel tomorrow and give me a follow-up treatment. In the meantime I should take Advil as an anti-inflammatory for the next few days and all will be well.

After his follow-up cracking and back stretch he wishes us well.

Before we leave Sally's, she asks us to stop the next morning as we leave town. As we stop, her husband makes us breakfast and sends us on our way with sandwiches for lunch. She wishes us a good walk to Jerusalem and says they'll be remembering us during their weekly prayers for peace in Jerusalem.

Thanks to Sally, her husband, and Dr. Craig for their warm welcome in the still cold desert.

Walking through history

This is a good time to look at another aspect of this walk. We are walking through history as we walk east.

As we planned our pilgrimage we realized we would be walking through history starting in modern California and ending in 4000-plus-year-old Jerusalem.

In California as in other states we walk through the most modern city streets and commercial malls. We also walk the Camino Real of the late 1700s and early 1800s. This was the California that became a state shortly after the Mexican War as gold was discovered in 1848 bringing thousands west. We meet the spirits of those Indians, missionaries, and prospectors as we walk east.

In southern California, Arizona, and western New Mexico we think little of history beyond old Route 66. But arriving on the scene in 1926, it was late in coming and was officially gone by 1985, superseded by Interstate 40. It only existed 59 years. Most of the commercial buildings along its route are in ruins or simply no longer there. And while many miles of its pavements are covered by I-40, many are not, and its entire route lives on in nostalgia.

The Native Americans of Arizona and New Mexico endured so much grief since the 1700s from first the Spanish, then the Mexicans and the Americans. Much earlier history, going back to before 1000 A.D., is told in the pueblo villages of several Native Americans groups.

In central New Mexico the Spanish Land Grants take us back to the 1700s. But as we follow the Santa Fe Trail through New Mexico, Colorado, Kansas, and Missouri we are again back in the 1800s, 1821 to 1879. We walk with merchants who walked our pace, 12 to 15 miles (19.5 to 24.5 kilometers) a day, merchants who carried goods to and from Santa Fe on the Mexican frontier. And we feel the hoofs of the horses carrying the U.S. soldiers to Mexico to fight the Mexican-American War in 1846 to 1848.

The 1800s in Kansas also remind us of the U.S.-Native American wars; of buffalo herds obliterated, annihilated almost to extinction;

of native Americans killed in the thousands with survivors herded into ever smaller compounds culminating in the Wounded Knee massacre; of European immigrants surging into first cattle land and then fenced-in farm land.

By Kansas City and western Missouri we reach the early 1800s when people were leaving for the northwest coast and later for California.

Farther east we are in 1803 with Louis and Clark exploring the new Louisiana Purchase for President Jefferson. As we read historical markers about Lewis and Clark, we walk along the path of a recent causality of progress, the Missouri, Kansas, and Texas Railway, which ceased existence in the 1980s. It's now the Katy Trail, a 225-mile (365-kilometer) bicycle trail following its route along the Missouri River.

Marquette and Joliet priest-explorers of the 1600s meet us at the Mississippi near St. Louis. In Nauvoo we run into John Smith and the Mormons of the 1840s. Farther north it is the Blackhawk Native American wars of the 1830s and the new canals and trains of the mid-1800s. And there's Chicago, only a small fort (Ft. Dearborn) on a river lined with wild onions (chi-ca-go) in 1832.

Michigan, the cradle of the car industry of the early 1900s, also goes back to fur trading times and the French and Indian War (really French against the British with Indians fighting on both sides) of the 1700s.

Ontario brings both the French and the British of the 1600s and 1700s and Upper Canada of the early 1800s. They too subdued their native populations putting them on reservations, though they did it a little earlier than we did. We walk through Queenston where the British, Canadians, and Mohawks held off the Americans in the War of 1812 at the Niagara River.

As we arrive at the Erie Canal we are looking solidly into the 1600s and 1700s. We are pushing the early 1600s and even 1500s with some of the early European settlements. Of course, the Native Americans were there much earlier.

As we walk into New York City we don't know then that an Italian, Giovanni da Verrazano, discovered the island for the French in 1524 and named it Nouvelle (New) Angoulême. Michelangelo finished the Sistine Chapel ceiling only12 years earlier. The Dutch renamed

New Angoulême New Amsterdam 90 years later in 1614. When the English won it from the Dutch in 1664, they renamed it New York. Our Declaration of Independence was still 112 years away.

Though modern things are everywhere across America, the earliest European-American history of each place (except New Mexico) is earlier the farther east we come. The East has many more layers than the West. We are walking back through layers of history as we walk east. In Europe and the Middle East culture after culture has in turn overran its predecessor. We bunch many migrations, changes, and altercations under terms like Modern, Renaissance, Medieval, Roman, Greek, Hebrew, Arabic, and Egyptian histories. All those and many more paths intertwine and overlap where we walk.

Route 66

When we decide to walk through Arizona and New Mexico it doesn't take long to realize that old Route 66 is our route. Everyone has sung about it. We walk some of what is left of "Main-Street America," the "Mother Road." It was the main road from Chicago to Los Angeles from the time it was inaugurated into the National Highways System in 1925. Though its exact route changed several times, at the start it ran 2451 mi (3945 kilometers) connecting the main streets of American towns along the way. Most vacationers, to say nothing of truckers and dust bowl down-and-outs, traveled its route. In 1985 after Interstate 40 (I-40) replaced it functionally, it was decommissioned.

Many remnants of the road remain. Route 66 nostalgia bugs routinely travel most of them. We decide to walk 66 knowing the heavy traffic will be on I-40.

Backpacks in a truck?

We join Historic Route 66, as it is known in California, east of Silver Lakes and south of Barstow. It's cold and the forecast calls for several days of rain. We expect little or no wood for warming up and drying out. The prospect of several days in a row—without a shower and a place to warm up—gets through our thick heads and says it is time to travel a little on wheels. What faces us makes us realize again why cross-country walkers appreciate a support van. We are not ready to do that though it will happen when my brother joins us in Flagstaff, Arizona.

We don't want to take a bus and rush down I-40 to Needles so we rent a U-Haul truck (no cars are available this Friday afternoon in Barstow). We put our two backpacks in the back of the 14-foot (4-meter) truck and spend a slow one and a half days following historic route 66 stopping every 15 miles (24 kilometers) at each place we would have camped had we walked. In the end, the two motels we thought were functioning are not. That means we would have had to camp eight days in a row had we walked. The only relief would have been at a park in Goffs.

In addition, we would have had to carry water for three days at one point. We have only our backpacks and the tiny doll carriage, little room for all that water. It would have been more of an "expedition" than a walk had we chosen to walk. It's a good decision to drive. We are not in survival camp mode. We are here to enjoy the walk. Today we enjoy the slow ride and stop at the Bagdad Cafe (from the movie with the same name) and at several places along the road including Amboy and Goffs. All these places are important to walkers but only tiny dots, totally unimportant to those who drive along I-40 and totally bypass these old, once important places.

We return the truck in Needles at a closed lot the next morning and take off walking north. The sun is hot and the wind cool and light.

Paperclip repair

Just after noon the wheel rolls off Petra's new cart. A C-clamp holding the wheel broke or fell off. I walk a half a mile (1 kilometer) back to a gas station to see if they have a C-clamp. No chance; but they do have a couple paper clips. I bring some back, slip the wheel on, open the paper clip, and wrap it a couple times around the C-clamp race. The wheel is as good as new. It feels like the old days when my dad used to say, "All you need to repair a Model T is bailing wire and a pair of pliers."

As the day goes on, the weather changes. The northeastern sky gets darker and darker. The clouds slowly fade out the sun. We are headed for Oatman, across the valley and up the mountain toward now black clouds. We begin to look for an alternate target.

The Moon River Campground, an RV Park, stands at the corner where we would turn east. Maybe they have a camper to sleep in because we're not ready to camp in the rain. Suzie, the woman running the place says, "I'm sorry, but we have no RVs for rent." Then she adds, "But if you want to wait till I'm off in an hour and a half, I can take you up to the Avi Casino a few miles from here."

Avi Casino

We checked the Avi Casino out last night on the Internet. With the storm lurking, it suddenly is no longer as out of our way as it appeared then. We wait wandering Suzie's little store. I buy a stocking hat that I have several months before losing it as I lose two or three others along the walk.

When she gets off, Suzie takes us a few miles down some dirt roads and over a bridge on the Colorado River into Nevada. A huge complex of buildings, parking lots, lawns, and palm trees are arrayed before us. The desert is invisible here.

She lets us off at the main entrance. We park the "gift of the desert" in front. It's a bit surreal walking into this fancy place with our cart parked at the entrance and decked out in our walking clothes. We pass slot machines and ask for a room at the hotel desk. "Our standard room is $18 a night. But it looks out on hotel walls."

"And what else do you have?"

"Our deluxe room is $36."

"Can we see a deluxe room?"

She gives us a key card to a fifth-floor room. We walk into the room and are hit with a wide view of the Colorado River and the valley and mountains beyond. Yes, we'll take this room over one looking at the hotel wall. Who needs a TV with that view?

We rest in luxury, eating well in the inexpensive restaurant and playing a few slot machines. It's Petra's casino introduction. She takes to the slots and even finds one that someone has failed to cash out. When no one returns we cash it out to the tune of $30.50.

On the second day it rains heavily. It doesn't hurt us. We enjoy sitting watching storm after storm crossing the desert and mountains just beyond our room's window.

The third day brings sun. We take a taxi back to the trailer park and continue walking east. This is our one and only venture into Nevada.

Oatman

We walk east across the valley and rejoin Route 66. As we approach Oatman, Petra takes a primitive trail along some power lines. The trail takes her to the far side of the town. I arrive three quarters of an hour before she does. We almost send out a search party for her. In fact, someone does drive down the trail looking for her. In the end she comes in along with the power lines a mile beyond the town. We are happy to be reunited.

Oatman is a "ghost town." This ghost town is actually a stage that, in spring, summer, and fall, plays to tourists complete with street "gunfights" every day. Thousands visit yearly. Ever since Paso Robles, people have been telling us, "You have to see the donkeys in Oatman. They're everywhere." We see none.

We stay in a cabin in Oatman. Owner, Jim, bounces us along two-rut paths as he shows us around town in his pickup. He tells us a lot about Oatman before showing us our cabin and then buying us a beer in the saloon. Thanks, Jim.

The next day we walk 66 along a winding path over the mountains. One time it was considered so dangerous that tourists hired locals to drive for them. The route takes us to Cool Springs. a refurbished gas station. But Richard, the operator, not only offers us a wonderful place for our tent but also gives us canned food from his kitchen. We were expecting a store but there is none.

Petra cooks noodles from Richard at our home in Cool Springs.

Though it's a cold night, we sleep warm enough in our tent. When you retire at 7:30, it's a long time to lie on the ground even with the good mats. But in winter we can do little else. In the morning we are ready to get up early even though it's near freezing.

Throughout the night we hear donkeys baying in the desert. They are here instead of in the streets of Oatman. It's nice to finally hear them even if we don't see them.

In the morning we walk 20 miles (32 kilometers) across a vast sloping plain down and then up to Kingman. Huge snow-covered mountains almost circle us as we walk. Sizes are so large in the desert. Petra comments often that it's hard to judge distances. She thinks something is two miles (3 kilometers) away and it is as many as five miles (8 kilometers). I have similar perception problems though not quite so extreme. We feel small in the greatness. Then I remember how much of a speck the whole world is in the Universe.

We are short on food. We have only an orange, 25 or 30 strawberry bars (like Fig-Newtons) Jim gave us as we left Oatman, and some chili-flavored peanuts we got while driving from Barstow to Needles. But four miles (6.5 kilometers) before Kingman along the road near I-40, a mobile hot-dog stand appears. We each have a foot-long hot dog, Coke, chips, and a pre-Valentine cookie. Petra says, "I'm not usually hot on hot dogs and Coke, but hunger is the best cook."

Valentine's Day

It's Valentine's Day. We start it in a very unromantic truck stop. "Hun, you *are* in a *truck stop*," implying, "Forget it, Hun" is Petra's answer when she asks for some orange marmalade for her toast instead of the grape and mixed-fruit jelly in the bowl on the table.

We have been walking for almost a month. It's 40 miles (65 kilometers) to the next motel in Truxton. That's too far on a short winter day—or on a long summer day for that matter. So before starting our walk, we pack our brand new push cart and buggy into the trunk of a taxi and ride the first 23 miles (37 kilometers) northeast to Hackberry, an aging general store along the road.

We take out the bicycle- trailer-now-backpack-cart we bought yesterday in Kingman and get ready for its maiden run. But first, what's this store with all the "junk" sitting around?

A car more aged than the store stands rusting in front of a sign announcing "300 miles [486 kilometers] desert ahead." Another rusted sign announces that this once was a Greyhound bus stop. Inside a dog, the "famous" Max, lies on a couch next to a Klondike stove. I don't know what he is famous for. It sure isn't for moving fast.

Outside we wander the "antiques" setting around the store and pose in front of a cow skull and our new cart for a couple pictures. Then we set off walking.

In a couple hours we walk past the small village of Valentine, Valentine on Valentine's Day. It's a photo opportunity and a kiss but little else.

We're in Valentine, Arizona, on Valentine's Day with our new carts.

We are climbing gently all day. It is getting colder. By mid-afternoon, snow lays on both sides of the road. Snow on the desert is a first for us. We aren't particularly cold though the wind is blowing lightly. We are well bundled up with coats, scarves, and long johns. We walk forward along Route 66 through wide-open desert.

A motel on its decline

It's getting late in the afternoon as we come over a hill before Truxton. A few houses, a gas station, a motel, and a couple horse corrals spread out in the snow ahead of us.

We push our carts through ankle-deep snow as we enter the motel driveway and make our way to the entrance. The unplowed parking lot is empty. A woman near 70 meets us at the door. "Yes, we have a room. You can have Number One in the front."

"But we don't want to be close to the noise of the road." Petra said. This proves to be an unfounded fear since there is almost no traffic on the road at night.

"Ok, you can have Number Three instead. Both are $55"

"Can we see Number Three?"

We cross the snowy driveway to Number Three and go in. Unclean is not the word. It looks like it hasn't been cleaned for ages. The dust is thick on everything. If we were not walking we would leave in a second. But the next town is eight miles (13 kilometers) away, at least three hours walking. We have no choice. It's almost dark.

I go back to the office and ask the woman, who has been working here since 1972, to see the other room, adding, "It's almost like you are taking advantage of us since we are stuck here" She said nothing as she gives me the key to Number One.

"By the way, when does the restaurant open?" I asked pointing to the closed café in front of the motel.

"Oh, it will be closed for a while. The pipes froze the other night and they have no water. They have to fix them before they can reopen." It is clear that they are not going to open any time soon.

"Is there another restaurant here in town?"

"No." Oops, where are we going to eat? We were depending on that restaurant to feed us. Someone back in Kingman told us they had eaten here so we expect to do the same tonight. Not all information we get along the way leads us to something useable.

Back across the driveway I join Petra already looking into the windows of Number One. We walk in. It's cleaner, not spotless, but passable. Petra, who loves to have the windows open at night, will have no problems with getting fresh air tonight. The crank-out windows are warped so even when they are latched they let a big crack of air in. Another window has been broken for a while. Someone fixed it with masking tape that has long since dried up and left the half-inch (2 cm) crack fully open from top to bottom.

As for the rest of the room, everything was well worn but useable. The bathroom sink had a great bonus, a marble-topped counter for the sink. That will be the surface for our cook stove.

First we walk half a mile back up the road to a Gas station-mini mart and get some noodles that Petra will mix with the spices we carry with us. She also is enamored with a huge single pickle in a plastic package. She buys it but we don't eat it that night. In fact we carry it for better than a month before eating it. It wasn't worth the effort.

Back at the motel, I find three bricks to sit the pan on for cooking. Our little alcohol stove sits between the bricks. We are traveling with just the burner. We gather supporting stones every time we cook. Soon we are eating dinner.

I look out the window. It's almost dark. A big neon sign announces the "Frontier Motel and Restaurant" and a "Vacancy" sign glows red under it. No one else arrives that night.

We sleep well. Our Valentine's Day was a bit like a toast sandwich: rough bread on each side (an ancient truck stop and an old motel) with sweet jelly in the center (the walk past the village of Valentine and through the snow).

Stopping for a rest on the way up out of Truxton.

The next day in the Hualapai Native American hotel restaurant in Peach Springs, Petra is delighted with her first Native American fry bread and stew. And the tea is really hot. Do only Native Americans have really hot water?

Petra likes her tea like it is in Germany, *hot*. And *hot* means 212 degrees, boiling. Not many restaurants serve tea water that way in the U.S. It comes out somewhere between 150 (65 C.) and 170 (76 C.) most of the time. Tea doesn't brew at that temperature. I don't like it that cold either. It's a theme at every place we stop for breakfast tea: the water has to go back to get hot. The first hot tea to arrive without being resubmitted didn't land at our table until here in Peach Springs, Arizona, 477 walking miles (772 kilometers) into the pilgrimage. We celebrate.

Winter is still with us as we stay at the Grand Canyon Caverns motel the next day. The crisp air made walk here a joy but the motel has to scratch to find a room without frozen pipes. It is a good place even though the pipes are frozen in our room the next morning. The people in this Arizona desert do not plan for a hard freeze in the winter.

We leave the Grand Canyon Caverns motel the next morning walking down the road scrunching in newly-frozen, wet snow on the shoulder. We walk gingerly slipping every few steps. I guess that the ice will be gone by noon. But before it leaves, the snow on the juniper desert looks a lot like snow in brushy land in the mid-west. Take away the sand and the land looks quite similar. The snow ends in a line with snow on one side and sand on the other, at almost noon.

500 mi. (810 km.) – February 17, 2009

Seligman

We arrive in Seligman after walking 25 miles (40 kilometers), our longest day in our 42 so far. We jump into the first motel we see. Though tired and sporting sore muscles and feet bottoms, we feel quite well for such a long walk.

Seligman is a few streets along I-40 in the middle of the Arizona desert. But it is a special town with a special street. The street is the Historic Route 66. The town is dedicated to 66. Everything attempts to attract the Route 66 enthusiast: period cars, old buildings, and curio shops packed with Route 66 memorabilia. The desert around offers only sand, piñon, and juniper trees.

Main Street Seligman complete with Edsel and manikins.

The second day we move to the Canyon Lodge in the center of the town's "action." The motel's rooms are each decorated in adifferent Route 66 motifs: cars, railways, motorcycles, desert. We spend a few hours sitting on the second-floor, front porch watching the curious world of Route 66 pass. An Edsel, the short-lived 1958-60 hope of Edsel Ford, sits across the street. A bright red, 1959 El Camino truck sits a few spaces to the right. A red, tear-drop camper trailer hangs on its bumper. They are parked in front of a strip of curio shops.

An El Camino sitting across from our Seligman motel.

In the afternoon we wander the shops. License plates from around the world crowd the walls and rafters of the Delgadillo Memorabilia Store. We leave our card to be put somewhere in the tens of books of business cards. The place is quiet. A bus arrives and a torrent of tourists flows into the place. Everyone is walking, talking, pushing, and picking up and buying things. Then in ten minutes they are back on the bus and it's quiet again. No leisurely browsing for them. We linger. The barber here, Mr. Delgadillo, spearheaded changing the status of 66 from defunct into a historical route many years earlier.

In late afternoon we stop in at the J & R Mini Mart and café and strike up a conversation with owner Rick. We leave at 7:30 after long conversations and Thai vegetables. In addition to supplies, we also have two new coffee cups and some foot-massage rubbing oil, gifts from Rick. When I forget my hat Rick brings it to me at our motel room. Thanks Rick, we enjoyed our evening with you.

Seligman is a transportation town. Route 66 nostalgia is clearly in your face. But another "industry," the railroad, the Burlington Northern Santa Fe Railway uses the town as a crew-change and crew-rest place. Our motel owner tells us that when times are good, over 150 trains go through town in a day. Many crews stay in his motel. But these days this economic indicator is pointing down with only a hundred or so trains a day.

Petra walks up out of Seligman, the bowl of trees down in the valley. Two days earlier we walked around the far ridge and down the road into town. It's cold enough for that scarf against a light wind blowing from the north. The Route 66 traffic has left this old route for the more convenient I-40.

Our longest day

As we get ready the next morning, I think about the 24 miles (39 kilometers) to Ash Fork, our next stop. Then we add a mile to that even before we leave town. We backtrack half a mile for breakfast.

On the edge of town we miss a sign and add another mile, as we backtrack again and drag our carts up a steep embankment and through a field to get to the correct road. They made an overpass so cars could safely pass without stopping out here in the middle of the desert where the traffic on Route 66 is not exactly heavy.

As we follow old 66, we come to a place where they shunt the road onto I-40, 66's replacement route. A path continues but the signs clearly tell us to take I-40. I saw this a few months earlier as I scouted the route by car. Last night while talking with a Seligman storeowner, I asked about it. He assured us we could take the old route into Ash Fork. "I have done it often with my 4-by-4."

So we follow the old route passing a sign saying, "Dead End." The surface is still paved in many places. We learn later that they abandoned this section in 1952 in favor on one farther north. We even crossed an old bridge with a tree growing out of a corner of the bridge guardrail and a "US 66" shield on an abutment.

But the surface deteriorates until we reach a railway blockaded by a fence. It is clear that 66 once crossed the tracks on a now missing overpass. We walk up and down the fence looking for a place to cross the tracks. In the end we abandon the effort. We find nothing.

We retrace our path back half a mile where I scramble over a fence. Petra hands our equipment piece by piece over the same fence before crossing herself. Then for the second time today we drag ourselves and our carts up an embankment, this time 50 feet up to I-40 and walk the last mile into Ash Fork along the interstate.

But our day isn't over. We arrive in town after dark. It's cold. We reject the first hotel hoping for a better one on the other end of town. Google tells us there are two other motels. We trudge another mile only to find both not only closed but also far worse than anything we would consider staying in. We head back to the first place.

All during the walk back, Petra keeps saying, "They won't let us stay because we rejected them once. If you do that in Germany, they would never let you stay."

I answer, "They will be happy to take our $39. They would not let their pride get in the way of $39 income." I am right.

We walk into our room at 8:30. It's dark. We're tired and cranky and settle for, olives, a can of tuna, and some Ritz crackers from our backpacks. The restaurant is on the other side of town with the unacceptable motels. We were in no mood to return.

It was a beautiful day but just too long. Our official record shows we walked 29.6 miles (48 kilometers), the longest one-day walk of the pilgrimage.

Chevy Malibu

We walk back to the east end of Ash Fork in the morning and stop at the restaurant for a fine breakfast. As we eat Floyd strikes up a conversation with us. Floyd and his wife are about to celebrate their 50th wedding anniversary. He's driving his 1958 Chevy Malibu for the celebration. Today he is taking the already immaculate car up to Williams to give it a proper washing.

Petra has never ridden in a classic like this. I remember it nostalgically. Petra wants a ride. Floyd takes her out for a 15-minute spin. She comes back sporting a wide grin. Thanks, Floyd.

The Interstate

As we walk up to Williams we take I-40 because it's the only road up. Though most interstate highways across the country are off limits to walkers, bikers, tractors, and small motor scooters, some states, Arizona for one, let them all use the interstate where there are no alternatives. The shoulders are so wide that they are more comfortable and safer to walk than many other highways we walk as we cross the country.

Floyd beeps as he passes us an hour after we leave the restaurant.

About half way up the 1,750-foot climb (535 meters) to Williams we stop to rest. A state trooper pulls over and asks us if we need any help. We don't. Then he asks us where we are going.

"Jerusalem." I have come to like opening with that one-word answer for shock effect and to spike the conversation. It usually works well. Then we tell him the details. By now we have walked around 560 miles (900 kilometers). That alone impresses him. After again asking if we need anything, he wishes us well and goes on his way never asking for any ID.

In Williams we stop at the first motel we see and enjoy two days in an upgraded room with a Jacuzzi.

In our last four walking days before Flagstaff we walk 96 miles (155 kilometers)–far too much. 15 to 20 miles (24 to 32 kilometers) a day is reasonable and doable. But when we do more we have to take time off to rest like we did in both Seligman and Williams.

Marty brings new flags

The day after we arrive in Flagstaff, we go wait on a corner for my brother Marty. He is coming with his RV from home in Woodstock, Illinois. He says he's coming to buy us a coffee. He arrives with his 18-foot mobile home and takes us to have that coffee. But he stays. In the end he and his RV becomes headquarters and he accompanies us until we leave Albuquerque.

Even with the long days before Flagstaff, we are still too far from Albuquerque. We have to be there 13 March for an American Pilgrims of the Camino meeting. So as mobile headquarters, the RV gives us a place to sleep and cook and carries us 170 miles (275 kilometers) in the next three weeks. Along the way we visit the Meteor Crater, the Petrified Forest, and the Painted Desert. We would not have visited any of them without Marty and his mobile home.

Petra with her cart and Marty with his RV on the New Mexico Border.

We continue to push our carts even though we can leave them in the RV and walk without them. In their way they are our badge of the pilgrimage. We cannot leave them in the RV and walk without them.

Besides giving us some needed rides and a bed as we across Arizona, Marty is a valuable aid in another way. He is also our mailman. When he receives our mail in Woodstock, he scans what is important and puts it on a secure web page where we can read and act on it. Thanks, Marty.

A couple days after Flagstaff we meet our first walker, a Native American who walks a few miles every day. He carries a large walking stick like a pilgrim's staff. Can you imagine that only after 605 miles (980 kilometers) walking we meet our first walker and he is a Native American!

From Barstow, California to a little west of Albuquerque, we follow the Burlington Northern Santa Fe Railway (BNSF). For more than a month we wave at several trains a day. Many blow their horns and ring their bells to wave back. In time some blow before we wave. I suspect some engineers see us several times as we make our way across the deserts.

Another BNSF comes out of the desert to pass us and carry its goods east.

So many downtowns across America are like ghost towns. The stores have moved to the malls on the edge of town. We see so many empty stores in town centers as we walk across the country. Gallup and Grants are two examples though Gallup is only about a third empty. But Grants is almost completely empty in its central area. Someone told me it is because of the downturn in the Uranium market, the principal industry in Grants.

Gold along the road

America's roadsides are not very clean. Some are downright full of garbage. Generally I seldom pay much attention to the condition of ditches as I pass. But the roadsides in Arizona and western New Mexico beg to be seen. Besides, they are more visible when you are walking. Aluminum cans and beer bottles litter the roadside.

They start to have dollar signs attached to them, like the coins we have been finding along the way. Not only are they worth money as metal, they each have a 5-cent deposit on them, at least in Arizona. We see them as "gold" along the road. We see an opportunity. Some sows' ears are waiting to be turned into silk.

We contrive a plan to mine that gold sometime in the future after we are done walking. We take a pickup or our Honda Fit, go out on one of these roads, and park. Then one of us walks forward and the other backwards a half a mile picking up cans and bottles along the way and putting them into the bags. Then we cross the road and walk back to the car picking up as we go. We then pick up the bags and drive ahead a mile and do the same thing all over again.

We figure that with the number of cans we are seeing we can get good exercise and make a pretty good living working a few hours three or four days a week. There are plenty roads with cans and bottles to keep us busy.

We would have to watch for snakes and scorpions in the southwest in the summer. But we can avoid them by making this a late winter and spring job. That way grass or weeds that can hide the varmints and the cans would be dead.

But now that we have let the secret out, others can get in on the rush to the gold along the road and get it before us.... I guess that's OK. It will improve the looks of our roads if many of us get out and pick up the cans and bottles. You see people doing this near towns. But the cans are far from town too.

Wind

The wind has been blowing almost since we entered New Mexico. Today from Grants we have been squinting to keep the dust from our eyes. It blows against our right and often in our faces. Gusts are often over 50-mph (80-kph). But with the bright sun and temperature in the low 50s (10 C.) the walk is comfortable. The sun and extra work walking into the wind keep us warm.

Sky city

We blow into the Sky City Casino, on the Acoma Pueblo at the end of the day. Actually, we don't quite blow all the way into Sky City on our feet. Petra insists on stopping in a tiny village three miles short. Sixteen and a half miles (26.7 kilometers) is far enough for her in today's wind and dust. We call Marty to pick us up in the RV. While we wait, we enjoy a conversation with an artist in her shop. Like the Avi Casino in Nevada, the Sky City casino is in the right place at the right time.

We take a day off to prepare for our next week's walk to Albuquerque and to visit the Acoma Pueblo.

Acoma Pueblo is built on top of a vertical-walled, 370-foot (112-meter) sandstone mesa. People have lived there since 1150 A.D. Its web site says it's the oldest continuously inhabited community in North America and that the "mesa-top settlement is known worldwide for its unique art and rich culture."

According to their web page, Acoma Pueblo is a federally recognized Native American Tribe. Its land base covers 431,664 acres and 4,800 tribal members live in more than 250 dwellings, none of which have electricity, sewer, or water.

Acoma Pueblo Homes.

As we tour the city we also visit the huge San Esteban del Rey Mission, a Catholic mission constructed between 1629 and 1640 by the Acoma ancestors. The only access to the mesa top was by foot-hole paths until 1959. Many materials had to be carried from far away, like the mission's timbers which were carried on Acoma backs, from a mountain far to the north. A resident Franciscan Friar Juan Ramirez oversaw the construction. Their web site continues:

> "...the Acoma people themselves followed and implemented traditional building methods to ensure that this creation would withstand time and erosion caused by the natural elements. Clearly, the continued attachment of the Acomas to the structure and their dedication to its maintenance is an important part of the Acoma legacy. Others also recognize the significance of this massive structure and its contents for being, without doubt, the largest inventory of original material from its era in a still functioning building in the United States."

But all this was done under forced labor and forced conversions to Catholicism. And there were reprisals when the Native Americans rebelled.

I ask our guide, "With all the ill treatment you received from the Spanish, why did you rebuild the church after it was destroyed? After all, it was not for your religion."

"Because our ancestors worked on it. Because their blood and spirit is in the walls and roof. We did it to honor our ancestors."

Both the Mission and the Pueblo itself are Registered National Historical Landmarks.

The Haak'u Museum and Sky City Cultural Center preserves "this Native American culture, displaying Pueblo pottery and Native American artifacts and where you can experience this historic living culture first hand."

We really enjoy visiting this city on a rock. Read more about it on its web page at www.acomaskycity.org.

Ambassadors of dreams

We are following our dream to walk long, to walk across North America and on to Jerusalem. The walk and all the people we meet and places we see along the way are our destinations. We tell others about our dreams so many times. The interesting thing is that it often reminds the people of their dreams.

We can really never know what our encounters are doing or where they are leading us or those we are talking with but many quickly go very deep.

We would say we are following our dream to walk a long walk. And they would come back with, "You know, I always wanted to...."

We continually have chance encounters with people who teach us something or who need something we have to say. It is clearly not a one way street. We learn a lot being a catalyst. We realize that we truly have become ambassadors of dreams.

Once or twice a day we meet people like Joseph, a Pakistani in his 60s who is walking his bike on a Canadian bike path. When he hears our plans, he tells us that for some time he has wanted to walk in the hills and deserts of the Holy Land. "But I want to do it alone without my relatives." As we part his dream is again standing square in front of him, exciting him, enthusing him. And we walk away aroused and walking with renewed vigor because of the encounter.

Kathy, a store manager, wants to document the lives of elders on video. Later she sends emails telling us of her progress in making a similar project come to life.

Some people tell us of dreams fulfilled. Many have dreams not addressed for a long time. Others have not even conceived of their dreams. Our pilgrimage has become a means of inspiring others as well as of following our own dreams.

It is an honor to be given this task by the Universe, this task to be ambassadors of dreams, to get others to think about and feel what they really want to do in their heart of hearts. And every time we recognize it, we come away inspired.

Our walk has been always about a dream to walk a long walk, a walk of one to two years duration to see who we will become because of it. But it becomes clear as we walk it is not all for us. We walk for those we meet, too, and for those who ultimately read this book. We are all part of the One, we grow together.

We hope our story inspires you readers to remember your dreams, whatever they are, whether they demand you to walk, paint, visit a close or faraway place, write a book, make a movie, go to India by boat, or do something else. Now is the time. Don't wait too long. Your dream can fade leaving a big hole in your being if you don't act on it.

A meeting in the desert

We are walking fast to stay warm in the early March wind East of Grants and squinting against blowing dust and sand. We see a lone gas station along the road. It's one of those modern oases gas stations standing on the empty desert along a highway, in this case I-40 in the middle of New Mexico. We're walking the side road.

We decide to stop and rest. The wind pushes our carts around until we find a place on the leeward side of the building next to the air pump. I'm not ready to come back out and look for them in the ditch across the road.

Inside we set in a warm room at a plastic table on plastic chairs at a Subway sandwich bar. The wind is a distant memory. We take off our coats, scarves, and hats and make ourselves comfortable before ordering a coffee and eating a sandwich we bought in the morning at an earlier Subway.

Our rough appearance and entry gave us away as walkers. When Petra goes to the washroom, a guy comes over from the far corner and asks where we are walking. "To Jerusalem." By now we were familiar with the initial disbelief followed by awe when the truth settles in.

Then he says, "My wife wants to walk a long walk in Europe."

"How long?"

"Five hundred miles [810 kilometers]?"

"She wants to walk the Camino de Santiago?"

"Yes?"

"We have walked it a couple times."

"Is it safe?"

"Yes. It's very safe."

"Even for a woman alone?"

"Yes."

I get up and walk to the corner where his wife, Judy, sits and introduce myself. Petra returns and joins us.

Before any small talk, Ron, Judy's husband again asks, "Are you sure it is safe?" He wants assurance that his wife will be safe. I think he thinks his wife must be a bit off for wanting to walk *alone* in Spain when she is over 60.

Petra tells them how she walked alone from Germany across Switzerland, France, and Spain to Finisterra on the Atlantic in complete safety. She includes that she was not without fear, especially in the beginning. Then she adds, "If you decide to walk the Camino, the Universe will give you the support you need."

We say we are attending a gathering of the American Pilgrims of the Camino in Albuquerque in a week. Before we can tell her that it is a group of people who have walked and are about to walk the Camino Judy says, "I'm going to be there too."

Three pilgrims meet in the remote desert of New Mexico.

Goat heads

We continue forward. A little-used section of 66 heads away from the railroad and I-40 in several miles of straight but rough road across the desert. When I look back from the southeastern end, Mt. Taylor's snow-capped peak stands right beyond the end of the road. It looks like the builders got to the east end of this stretch, looked at the mountain, and decided to build directly toward it.

Petra walks an old section of Route 66 where a goat head gives my cart its first flat. Petra's cart's solid rubber wheels are immune.

The road is not friendly. It puts the first hole in one of my tires. In fifteen minutes Petra has it fixed using her Berlin bicycle-fixing experience.

Later the road takes us into the Rio Grande Valley into Los Lunas along the river south of Albuquerque. We see the first really green vegetation since California. Trees are in blossom. We don't see that again until we are in middle Kansas a month and a half from now. Petra says, "I know now why the Spanish settlers loved the Rio Grande. It is still a green oasis. It must have been even greener without all the modern upstream dams."

As we walk north into Albuquerque the traffic fills all four lanes of our route into town. It is the only through route. As we walk, four "goat heads" lodge in one tire and four in the other, all at the same time. "Goat heads" are a particularly hardy thorn ball looking like a goat head with horns and a Billy-goat beard. They are a well-known bane to bicycle tires here. We have four in each tire at once. Petra, my brother, and I set up a production line and have them repaired in a reasonable time. We were walking on the shoulder but with the goat heads we start walking on the edge of the pavement.

It doesn't take long for a squad car to pull up and usher us off the road. We protest but they insist. In the end we still walk the road but step off lightly when traffic demands the lane we are in.

A bicycle shop in Albuquerque fixes us up with extra thick inner tubes filled with some goop called "slime." We never have another flat on either wheel though we pull out many more goat heads and thorns as we walk both North America and Europe.

Our last Route 66 sign is on a street in downtown Albuquerque. As we leave 66, we head north for Santa Fe and Taos.

Pilgrims Meeting

But first we have a meeting of American Pilgrims in Albuquerque.

Our pilgrimage is not a heroic journey but (as life is) it is a humble one. It is not something to achieve but to partner with. It is humble because we say, "yes" to all our weaknesses and strengths.

Death and rebirth, a symbolic death and rebirth, are a goal and end of pilgrimage. When they are not, it is only a normal walk, not a pilgrimage, not a cathartic walk.

When we reached the end of our pilgrimage to Santiago, Spain in 2003 we died and were reborn. It was a true "reincarnation" in that all that was, was thoroughly washed and we made a new beginning. So through we have experienced a new beginning, old trash—and glittering gems—remain. Yet clearly, like a snake, we shed an old skin and begin anew with some markings of the old but with new skin and new freshness. We didn't remove all old restrictions and rigidity but we walk now with new outlooks and flexibilities.

These are a lot of intellectual words. In fact, when you get to your goal, you say, "I will never be the same again. I am a new person. It cannot and will not be life as it was. It will be something new."

These thoughts are in mind as we arrive at the American Pilgrims of the Camino gathering 13 March. This meeting is our only fixed-day destination on the pilgrimage. And we botch the timing. We would have been late had my brother not given us rides in Arizona and New Mexico that added up to 170 miles (275 kilometers) in his RV. Oh, we could have taken a bus.

As they define themselves on their web page, "The American Pilgrims on the Camino is a non-profit organization whose objective is to facilitate communication within the community of North American pilgrims, particularly those in the United States. American Pilgrims continually seeks meaningful ways to support the Camino de Santiago de Compostela." They are having a national gathering and we want to be part of it.

The year before at their meeting in Santa Barbara, California, we gave a slide show on our pilgrimage walk from our home in Germany over the Alps to Rome. It was an opportunity to introduce our book *Germany to Rome in 64 Days*.

We visit with many friends we met the year before and meet many new ones including Judy, Sue, and Gerry who become friends and also a part of our pilgrimage as we walk east to Jerusalem.

We visit with Judy, whom we met in the blowing desert last week. After enjoying two days of camaraderie with fellow walkers and some good talks, it is time to move forward again. As we leave Judy invites us to stay with her when we get to Santa Fe.

Of the several good meetings, the keynote was the best. Phil Cousineau led a seminar on pilgrimage basing it around his book, *The Art of Pilgrimage: The Seeker's Guide to Making Travel Sacred*, a book I have read a few times and found a good source of knowledge and insights on pilgrimage.

Since his is a book on pilgrimage and we are on a pilgrimage, I'll diverge a bit and finish this chapter with some notes on pilgrimage I gathered from this seminar. Most of what I report below is the result of chewing on the words, thoughts, and feelings of the talk. So where

I have changed Phil's message, I accept the responsibility. I either disagreed or just missed his point.

- When you return from a pilgrimage you are responsible to tell your story.

- The real pilgrimage is into the mind, the heart, and the soul more than along the road.

- Perhaps you will never return.

- When observing others look at how we are similar not how we are different.

- The word "travel" comes from the French "travail" meaning "work." Travel is not all fun.

- Pilgrimage is often triggered by a crisis and as such is a crossroads: "Life is passing me by."

- Ask yourself who inspired you to write? Who inspired you to walk your pilgrimage? Who gave you the inspiration to travel? Your answers can tell you a lot about why you are on, or about to be on, a pilgrimage.

- Live on the razor's edge. Your truth is often only there.

- Pilgrimage in the past was to touch the relics of some saint. It is still about touching, but now it's to get in touch with self.

- On on one of the first days of your pilgrimage, ask yourself:
    - Where am I going?
    - Where am I now?
    - Who is going with me?
    - What is my unfathomable longing?
    - What question am I taking with me?

- A strong and noisy threshold guardian stands at your door keeping you from leaving on your journey. Once you pass him (or her) you wonder why you waited so long to leave.

- Don't wait for someone to go with you. He or she may never join you and you could be waiting at your door forever. Rather strike out alone and learn about your own strengths and weaknesses. You will grow.

- On a pilgrimage you are most active and have the most doubts as you are two thirds done. A labyrinth also often gets close to its target two thirds of the way along its path but then swings far away from the goal before finally arriving. It accurately reflects reality.

- Walking is not *necessarily* a sacred happening.

- When you return ask yourself what was the gift? The 'gift moment?" The gift is the agent of change.

- Deep thoughts come when we move. Moving feet often mean moving soul.

- If you fall asleep at home sitting, get up; get out and walk.

- You often have to go out to find answers.

These words about pilgrimage are true also for most other endeavors of life because life itself is a pilgrimage and all sacred journeys in life are pilgrimages.

The Hacienda Antigua in northern Albuquerque where we stayed the first night after the pilgrims meeting.

Encounters on the road to Jerusalem

Spring on the high plains.

SPRING 2009

Heading Northeast

After a rousing weekend with the pilgrims, we head northeast toward Santa Fe walking older roads. Before leaving town we make the stop at a bicycle shop to strengthen my tires. Then we end the day at the Spanish-style Hacienda Antigua B&B before leaving the city.

Pueblos

As we push and pull our carts across the desert, we walk through Native American reservations. We make our way through the San Felipe and the Santo Domingo Pueblos.

Near San Felipe, a rough, old car full of boxes and junk stops. The driver leans out the window and asks, "Are you going to the next hippy camp?" He looks like he is ready for it. "Not today." We talk a bit and he moves on.

As we are about to enter San Felipe we are apprehensive about walking on Native American land though we have already done so in several places walking along Route 66 in western New Mexico. Admitting and facing our fear of walking on their land is an important moment.

We are moved by our treatment, touched by the openness of the Native Americans. Almost every car meeting or passing us stops to ask if we are alright, if we need anything.

One car stops and before anyone talks out stretch two hands with two cans, "Have some tea." There is no saying, "No." We take and enjoy them. Others offer more pop and water.

At one point we are getting ready to move after resting under a tree. A pickup stops. A young guy gets out and, moving toward the back of his truck, says, "I have something for you." He digs around in a bag and begins taking some things out and putting them into another bag.

"Here you need these more than I do. I am coming home from work and don't need them anymore. I want you to have them." He hands us a bag with some tacos, some canned bologna, bananas, applesauce, chips, and a couple other things.

"But we don't need this. We are not without food."

"No, I want you to have this."

We thank him and he drives off. There is no arguing with him. Besides, in order for people to be able to give, others must receive. Today we are on the receiving end though we don't think we need what we receive. Thanks.

Cochiti Lake

We arrive in the main square of Santo Domingo Pueblo around five and go to the town council hall to see where we can camp. We can't! No non-Native Americans are allowed to stay overnight in the Pueblo.

They offer to have an elder give us a ride out of town, explaining that the reason for the ouster is that they want to keep their culture pure. Herman, out elder, drives us ten miles (16 kilometers) north to a campground. We would enjoy talking with him longer but he is quickly gone.

Our camp gives us a wonderful view over the desert, Cochiti Lake, and its dam. We sleep well. With the detour north and west, we can't make our target, Santa Fe, the next day. We have to camp at a rest stop on I-25 eight miles (13 kilometers) short of the next campground.

With this extra stop, we do need the food that that Native American gave us yesterday. The Universe knows our needs and, through that Native American, gave us the food for this unplanned stop. Without it we would have to push an extra two hours forward tonight. Thanks to both the Native American and the Universe.

Santa Fe from our evening camping stop 19 miles from Judy's.

New Mexico Mountains

Santa Fe

The next day we walk into Santa Fe and call Judy, whom you now know from our windy meeting and the pilgrims gathering. She comes, packs our carts into her four-by-four, and drives us a couple miles to her home. Thanks, Judy. That maze of streets would take us a lot longer than it takes you.

We end up staying five days with Judy and her extended family. We stay in her guest house (casita) and use her car. How comfortable it feels lying in Judy's casita bed knowing we don't have to move for five or six days, the longest stop since the beginning of the walk. We let it percolate into us how tired we are and how much we have accomplished not only in miles, but also in stamina, emotionally, and spiritually.

We talk long of our Camino de Santiago experiences and Judy's hopes for her Camino. We show the whole family our Camino de Santiago slide show, *Hear the Call. Follow your Heart.* It recalls our experiences and exhorts the viewers to follow their dreams wherever they call them. In the end, Judy is more convinced than ever to walk.

Her husband is relieved that doesn't seem as dangerous as he thought it was. He seems resigned to her going.

Not long after we leave her, she begins her Camino in Spain. As we walk in Kansas, she is done and tells us how life expanding her experience was. We met in the desert, helped each other on our pilgrimages of life, and are now friends. A random encounter? Or a meeting set up by the Universe?

After the five days of renewal and regeneration in Santa Fe, we head for Taos. Remembering that the walk is the destination, we enjoy many new back yards and front yards as we make our way over the old mountain road to Taos. Along the way we encounter a mission, two bed & breakfasts, a snow storm, two artists, a private home, and a woman wanting us to deliver a message to the Holy Land.

Holy dirt

On the way we stop at a church in Chimayo in the footsteps of others who have made pilgrimages to this small church. Every year around 30.000 people take part in a Good Friday Chimayo Pilgrimage walk. Well over 100,000 visit the sanctuary each year, though not all come on foot.

Chimayo church.

They say miracles happen when people rub themselves with the holy soil in a hole in the small adobe church. Crutches hanging on the wall testify to the claim. Many take soil samples. The church replaces the dirt as it is depleted; several tons are put back into the hole every year. Petra takes some soil while I rub it on my arms. The

Spanish missionaries Christianized mud baths long-sacred to the Native Americans by building this church over them and then continuing the "pagan" tradition of the holy soil.

The church and its grounds have a pleasant and quiet atmosphere. It is good that we took the time to walk to Chimayo. Like our many stops every day, this is a pilgrimage destination in our bigger pilgrimage to Jerusalem and the even larger one through life.

At the Rancho Menzano B&B in Chimayo, Jody, the owner, greets us saying, "I saw you walking three hours ago and I knew you were coming." We had called ahead to reserve a room.

Jody lets us cook our own supper in her high-ceiling kitchen-dining-living room. We share the supper with her along with a lot of good conversation. Afterwards we sit around a large, outdoor fire she prepared for us.

Jody's breakfast is delightful, fresh fruit salad, juice, coffee, and a homemade breakfast burrito filled with potatoes, onions, a delicious salsa, and topped with two fried eggs from her own chickens. That huge plateful is followed by a just-out-of-the-oven pear pie. We both feel it is the best breakfast we had in the two years we were on the walk. We will go back to stay with Jody just to get that breakfast.

Jody is a self-made woman. She has had hard times because she is a single woman in a Spanish man's world. But she has overcome it; witness that she was elected (by those same men) Major Domo of the irrigation systems. She is the one who says who gets how much water when and who doesn't.

Before we leave, Jody calls ahead and sets us up for the next night in a B&B in Truchas. Thanks for everything Jody.

Snow storm

Between Chimayo and Truchas we climb 1,500 feet (550 meters) to 8,000+ feet (2,440 meters), most of it in a short distance. This is one of the steepest climbs of the pilgrimage. We make it, one step at a time.

In Truchas we meet a Spanish woman working in an artist's co-op shop. After we talk about our walk a while, she writes some words on a piece of paper and gives it to us saying, "Please, put this in the wall in Jerusalem." She is the first to ask us to take an item to

Jerusalem. Many ask us to remember them in our prayers when we arrive but few give us something physical to carry along.

The Farm House B&B in Truchas is really a farm house, a pleasant, big house. The snow that was threatening all day holds off until after dark. It develops into a late-winter blizzard that hits all of northeastern New Mexico and Colorado. Around 12 inches are on the ground when we get up. We stay a second day.

Petra wants to get out and make a clear path through the snow. I say, "It'll melt by tomorrow." She disagrees and goes looking for a shovel. (She loves to shovel. I am happy for that because then I don't have to do it.)

She comes back with a dust pan. "I can't find a shovel but this will do." Off she goes digging a two-dustpan-deep, two-dustpan-wide, fifty-foot (15-meter) path to the still unplowed street. She comes back exhilarated and tired. It is good she shovels it because when we leave the next day the snow is still 12 inches deep, and frozen besides. Without the path, it would not have been easy to drag our carts through the frozen, hard snow to the street.

The morning after the Truchas snow.

Our problem now is food. The only store in town is closed. Not to worry. Later in the morning Bill and Anna, artists living in Truchas, bring some foodstuff so we "would have something to eat". They talked with Jody and set up this B&B for us last night. At their invitation, we have a fine evening meal and conversation at their place that night. We eat and visit in their private gallery. We listen to Bill's musical bells made from welding gas bottles and look at some of Anna's paintings. I like the bells. If one of his bells is not mine someday, I might have to make one.

Over the mountains

The next day as we walk to Peñasco, Bill brings my forgotten sleeping mat from the Farm House B&B to me as we walk along the road. He says he is on his way to Taos anyway so it's no problem. Thanks for everything, Bill and Anna.

The hills and valleys along the way look like a nice place to settle sometime. Almost all the little villages have a store that is closed and no longer operating. I have no idea where people go to get their supplies-Santa Fe? Española? Taos?

It is not that easy to rest along the way to Peñasco. Snow is still on the ground. As we arrive in Peñasco, we actually see green grass through the melting snow.

At least there's a small store in Peñasco and a restaurant where we have a great beef stew, the best in a long time.

We stay in a private house in Peñasco. Newly-found friend Gerry from the pilgrims group in Albuquerque contacted Charlie, an artist, who allows us to stay in his place while he is away. The only down side is his friendly cat. We close her in a separate room so we can sleep alone. We feel sorry for her but we need to sleep too. Thanks Charlie and Gerry.

Taos

The next day we walk a long distance over the mountain and down into Taos.

The wind blows hard and cold as we provision ourselves and plan our next steps. We stay an extra day and make a cold walk twice from our motel to the town center a mile away.

We have two ways to get out of Taos and onto the plains. One takes us over a 9,100-foot (2,777-meter) pass and another over a 9,600-foot (2,972 meter) pass. The first is 24 miles (39 kilometers) and the other 31 miles (50 kilometers). Even the shorter is longer than we want to tackle in the cold weather. We try to find motels or B&Bs along the way but there are none in early April along the shorter route. One motel along the longer route doesn't shorten that long segment by much. This is our first major decision point since deciding to cross the Mojave Desert in a truck.

We debate this for some time. In the end we opt for the longer route to Red River via Questa with stops at a B&B just north of Taos and a motel in Questa.

The next day we walk north and west of Taos and stay in the fine Stewart House B&B where we immediately hit it off well with the owners, Sandy and Joe. We talk hours with them and their friends, Linda and Rodger, from Stevens Point, Wisconsin, where one of our friends, Karen, lives. The world continues to prove itself small.

Sandy thinks we are a little daffy for wanting to walk by way of Questa and Red River. "The bikers really don't like the road. Those who do ride it have bragging rights. There are so many steep ups and downs. It will be really hard to walk." That is one of the main reasons why we like to stay in bed and breakfasts: we get good information from locals who know the area were we are walking. [We have since driven over that road. She is correct. The ups and downs would have been brutal, though doable.]

She convinces us. The next morning we load our carts into Sandy's pickup and she takes us to the pass above Angle Fire and sets us free. She takes us far enough so that we can walk all the way to Eagle Nest.

We spent the better part of the day before yesterday trying to find a way to get to that pass to no avail. We changed to the Questa-Red-River route because we saw shorter inter-village distances. And now here is our helper, Sandy. ...What really happened is that the Universe wanted us to come to Sandy's place to have our wonderful conversations last night and this morning. Now it is ready to send us along the original route to Angle Fire and Eagle Nest. Thanks so much Sandy and Universe.

As we walk down the mountain, a county police car pulls next to us and the cop asks, "What do you have in those carriages?"

"Our baggage."

"You don't have babies in there?"

"No, it's our baggage."

"You are sure you have no babies? We got a call that someone was pushing carriages with babies down this narrow road in the snow." It is snowing lightly.

"You want to look. It's just our things. It's easier to push them than to carry them."

He doesn't look. We tell him about where we are going and WalkingEast. He wishes us well and continues down the road after telling us to be careful and safe on the narrow road.

Eagle Nest

We walk through a valley of grasses that stretches a few miles between mountains on our left and right and ten miles (16 kilometers) from Angle Fire in the south to Eagle Nest and beyond in the north. Snow falls in sporadic showers. The wind rages. Even with this winter-like weather, the valley enchants us. We feel we could live in the Eagle Nest area for a much longer time. It could become home someday. But we have to think about cold and snowy winters.

If we had followed our original plans to go the northern route through Questa, we would have completely bypassed the Eagle Nest RV camp where we stay. The camp is west of the road coming from Questa. We would have turned east there. But the universe sent us along the southern route to meet Bruce and Bridgett, the owners of the RV cabin where we stay. We cook our meal in their kitchen and talk long into the evening with them. We enjoy the food and the conversation.

The people we meet continue to be an important part of this walk. Even when we end up walking less than we want, we know these conversations are more important and powerful than walking a few more miles. They make us think and feel a lot. Thanks, Universe, for the opportunity to walk this pilgrimage.

Cimarron Canyon

Leaving Eagle Nest we walk with Bruce and Babette on their morning dog walk to the edge of town where they veer to the left as we follow the road. We really like the area. We walk up a couple hundred feet and look over Eagle Nest Lake and the rest of the treeless valley. Mt Wheeler, the highest point in New Mexico, stands snow-capped on the opposite side of the valley.

Up the road the narrow Cimarron Canyon offers us an enchanting walk the rest of the way to Ute Park. High walls close in on a partially frozen creek flowing over rocks through evergreens. The north-facing walls of the canyon are snow covered while the south-facing walls have only spotty snow. We stop often and linger long. The 11 miles (18 kilometers) we cover take seven hours! That's less than 2 miles (3 kilometers) an hour, quite a bit slower than our usual 2.5 to 3 miles (4 to 5 kilometers) per hour.

The moon at noon from the bottom of Cimarron Canyon.

Sitting next to a clear-water river is something we really have missed in the last three months walking. We enjoy the day.

1,000 mi. (1,620 km.) – April 2, 2009

After Ute Park, we are blown out of the mountains by 30-55 mph (50-90 kph) winds at our backs. We cross another border, a sign tells us we have left the mountains and are entering the high plains. And we can see it–the adobe houses of Santa Fe and Taos are gone, replaced by wooden houses and wide streets. Actually, the wooden houses start in Eagle Nest.

We have walked a thousand miles across deserts and mountains have been on the road for 87 days.

Held up by wind

We end up staying an extra day in Cimarron, held there by the wind. We take advantage of the delay by getting know some of the people in the shops.

We meet Valerie in her Gallery with a soda fountain and enjoy a few hours of conversation, coffee, and ice cream. And before we leave she gives us each a small medallion engraved with an angel. Thanks Valerie.

Cimarron has another Valerie. She works in the office of our motel. We talk with her long into the evening. When she hears about our dreams of walking and having little, she tells us of similar dreams of finding a way to free herself of not only a large inventory in her antique store but also of the burden of two large houses.

The next day the wind is still blowing but not as hard as yesterday. We started with no idea that wind can hold us back but it does, at least twice. When it is heavy and I am walking with it, it blows and pulls so hard on my cart that it feels like I am going down a steep hill. And when it blows at me, the *"hill"* is like a steep climb. Petra has the added disadvantage of a tall cart with wheels close together. The wind blows it over easily.

The Santa Fe Trail

As we leave Cimarron, New Mexico, we begin walking along the route of the Santa Fe Trail. It started in Santa Fe and went around the south end of the Sangre de Christo Mountains. We cut across the mountains to catch it here. We will follow the Santa Fe Trail generally all the way to its beginning in Franklin, Missouri. The trail, began in 1822, made its way some 900 miles (1,460 kilometers) across modern Kansas, Missouri, and New Mexico to Santa Fe (Map p. 330).

The trail was a trade route for carrying much needed manufactured goods to Santa Fe and furs and other goods back east. During the Mexican war of 1848, the US army used it to invade Mexico. Afterwards it continued to be a major trade route, a national highway to the new southwestern American territories. The railroad, built near the trail, provided a much more convenient, safer, and easier route to New Mexico. The trail lost its importance and died in 1880.

We can't walk on the actual trail. It's too fragile. Large parts of the original are gone and much is in private hands. Rather we walk along near its route on roads. Those walking the trail as it operated walked the same distance each day as we are walking, 12 to 15 miles (19.5 to 24 kilometers). They covered about the same distance in a month as we are taking.

Just south of Cimarron the Santa Fe Trail split. One route went northeast through very dry land. A longer route went north to La Junta, Colorado, and then back southeast along the Arkansas River to Cimarron, Kansas, where the two routes joined again. The shorter, "Cimarron Route," was faster but more arid and more prone to Native American attacks. Nonetheless a majority of the trail traffic followed the shorter route. The northern, "Mountain Route," though more hilly, had fewer hostile Native Americans and a lot more water and wood long the Arkansas River. We walk the Mountain Route because there are also more places to stay along the way.

The Santa Fe Trail on the High Plains of New Mexico.

Valerie from our motel gives us a ride 13 miles (21 kilometers) north of Cimarron to "Cold Beer." A sign on the only building in Colfax said, "Cold Beer." That's what the locals call the place. Thanks for the ride, Valerie, without it we wouldn't be able to make the Whittington Center today.

As we walked around Cimarron yesterday, we struck up a conversation with a Native American, Banjo. He was standing at his truck selling piñon nuts and his art work. As we walk northeast along this treeless, windy road today he stops to visit with us three times as the day goes on. He gives us piñon nuts and "arthritis-healing," copper bracelets. The third time he stops he says, "I'll be passing tomorrow heading for La Junta, Colorado, to do a rain dance to try to end this long dry spell we've been having. If I see you I'll stop and see if you want a ride." We never see Banjo again. But his Friday rain dance is effective because we sit all day Sunday, Easter, waiting in a motel for heavy rain to end. Thanks, Banjo.

We are walking north from Cimarron on a wide-open plain. There are no trees for miles. The only thing that impedes our movement, or that of anything else, is the ever-present, bobbed-wire fences on both sides of the road. We think they are to keep cattle in their fields. But there are no cattle most of the time. Or are they to keep animals off the road? All I really know is that they make it difficult to camp anywhere along the road in the west. They are always within 100 feet (33 meters) of the road—too close to camp.

Today we spot a distant herd of animals. They are running at an angle toward us and toward the road. As they get closer we can see they are deer. They keep running at top speed at the fence. Then they all leap over the fence in full stride just like a wave of water in a fast-flowing stream. They cross the road and spring over the second fence as easily as the first.

Half an hour later another herd approaches. These are pronghorn antelope. They also head full tilt for the fence. But when they get there they don't jump over. I can see the fence top. I can't see what happens but they are now running across the road. Then I see. They dip down and—*at full speed*—go *under* the fence. They can't have more than a foot (30 cm) clearance. Different animals, different techniques but the fence deters neither.

We stay tonight at the National Rifle Association's (NRA) Whittington Center, a shooting center south of Raton. The NRA has never enjoyed my support, and it still doesn't. But they have hotel facilities, and we need to use them–it is too far to walk all the way to Raton. The NRA people are friendly; we enjoy our stay.

We do have to thank someone unknown who left a third of a box of ice cream in the guest house refrigerator at the Whittington Center. It tastes good.

Raton Pass

In Raton we have a wonderful evening in the Heart's Desire B&B talking long and deeply with Barbara, the owner. She is an English teacher who dreams of going to Italy when she retires in a few years. She renews my interest in reading Chaucer's *Canterbury Tales*.

Petra begins walking I-25 up Raton Pass.

The next day we walk over the Raton Pass on I-25 into Colorado. The pass was once a treacherous stretch of the Santa Fe Trail. Many accidents happened on the steep, rugged trail. Someone even built a toll road to improve the situation (and to put a few dollars in his pocket).

I-25 is the only road over the pass. It is a long, steep climb. We are getting more used to high hills. I am getting to the point of when I look up at a big hill, I look down again at my feet. I take a step. I'm up that little hill. I take another step. I'm another step higher. I continue one step at a time. I can easily climb each a small hill defined by the step. In a while I am on top of the big hill. It isn't big; it's only one step at a time. It's a practice of being in the Now. I only walk one step at a time, not that whole hill I see in the beginning. So today I look up, look down, walk one step at a time, and soon I am at the top of Raton Pass with little real effort.

Sangre de Christo Mountains from Raton Pass along with Petra's cart.

At the top of the pass we stop to look at the beautiful snow-capped Sangre de Christo Mountains to the west. Petra snaps this picture of her cart and the mountains after seeing it from the ditch. It is now on the cover of this book.

A ride with Andy

After Trinidad, Colorado, we walk into a country so totally different from that of the previous three months: real fields and mid-western styled homes. The air even smells green and fresh in the mid-60s (19 C.). We walk six miles (10 kilometers) or so and it ends. The rocks return. After a few more miles we stick our thumbs out to request a ride across the upcoming 60-plus miles (86 kilometers) of parched land. We know of no place to stay in between so we ask for help.

No one is stopping. Then we see why. In the middle of the now rolling scrubby hills we come on a large prison. Signs always advise against picking up hitchhikers in such places. Even with no signs here, people must remember seeing them in other places. We walked on.

A few miles later Andy stops his pickup with his two dogs and trailer. Andy is in his early twenties and sure of everything–we can't be escaped prisoners–we "didn't have striped clothes or coveralls." And we are pushing strollers–no prisoner would be doing that. Besides he has a rifle in the back window, another on the seat beside himself, and a semi-automatic pistol in the glove compartment. He's prepared for anything.

He is going all the way to La Junta, our destination. We get in and he takes off. The land becomes dry. Little is growing. There are only a few places to camp–just as we anticipated. Little grass grows under the truck and its bouncing trailer either. We are doing 80 if anything. In 45 minutes or so we add 62 miles (102 kilometers) to the wheeled total of the pilgrimage. Thanks, Andy.

Down the Arkansas River

It's warm as we leave La Junta, Colorado. We are looking forward to walking a little used road around 23 miles (37 kilometers) to Las Animas.

The air smells after-rain-spring and the grass is beginning to turn green. A light wind blows. Few cars pass. Most that do are moving slowly, locals I supposed.

In a couple hours we are ready to sleep on a flat spot a little off the road. We pull out our mats, take off our shoes, and sleep twenty minutes. We are sure it's spring.

After a while we pass Bent's Old Fort. As the Santa Fe Trail began, Mr. Bent set up a trading post here in the middle of nowhere in southeastern Colorado along the Arkansas River. Today the fort is a low, rebuilt adobe structure half a mile (one kilometer) off the road. In its day it was very alone. We decide not to add a mile and a half (2 kilometers) to our already-long day and continue walking east.

A dog walks with us

We stop to eat under some trees but before we start eating a big white dog comes out of the forest and greets us with wagging tail.

We give him a pet and decide to put off our lunch lest we have to feed him too.

He follows us. After an hour we decide to eat anyway. We find a fallen tree to sit on and take out our sandwiches and olives. The dog isn't interested. He rests while we eat and then continues to follow as we leave.

Our first walking companion.

The only time he barks is when we pass a field of emus. A couple emus come over to check us out. They are too much for the dog so he gives them a couple barks.

The offending emu.

Five miles (8 kilometers) from where the dog joined us, he is still following us. We begin to fear he is lost and wouldn't be able to find his way home. I call the number on his collar and leave a message on the answering machine saying where the dog is. Funny thing is that once I call, the dog disappears. Is he unhappy about being told on?

As the day wears on, spring drains into fall. Even with my sweater, I zip up my jacket. And then I get my scarf from my backpack. By five it is a brooding November day with a cold northwest wind. It is no longer comfortable to walk.

Petra along a canal near Bent's Fort.

Cow dogs

Petra is walking a hundred yards (100 meters) ahead of me. We are less than two miles (three kilometers) from our destination. An old pickup pulls over in front of Petra. "Would you mind if I took you to a motel? I have been working out in this wind and I know how cold it is."

By the time I arrive, Petra says, "Yes."

I look in the cab. *Six* dogs sit on the passenger side. I have seen those 12 ears before. They passed us two or three times before during the day. *I suppose we can find a way to coexist for a short distance.*

We find a place to put our carts in the truck box between the other things and go around to get in the cab. "In the back." Rob says. The six dogs jump almost simultaneously behind the seat. They sit with their noses on the back of the seat. Impressive.

We squeeze ourselves in with odd tools and a lot of dog hairs. We were heading for a motel in town, but Rob takes us one on the north side of Las Animas, "It's a lot better than the ones in town."

After we get the carts off the truck, Rob asks if we would like to see the dogs closer.

"Yes."

He opens the door and says, "Into the back!" pointing to the truck box. They jump out in unison and, like a school of fish, wheel around and up into the back then turn around to look at us.

"We herd the cows together. …In the front!"

They again jump out in unison and spring into the cab. "We are family."

Thanks, Rob, for the ride on a cold, spring afternoon; and thanks especially for introducing us to your family.

The motel includes a good restaurant so we don't go out and eat. That is good because rain soon begins and doesn't stop until the next night. We stay the next day and spend our Easter Sunday looking out the window wondering if the downpours are going to stop sometime soon. Banjo's rain dances must have worked.

Dogs

Now that we told you about yesterday's seven dogs, let me introduce you to other dogs we met along the way. Though they are often called "Man's best friend," many people are concerned about them. People often ask, "How are the Dogs?" or "Have you had any problems with the dogs?" Our answer to the question before central France is an unequivocal, "No." After one incident in France (p. 238), we change the answer to, "Almost never."

Dogs are social animals. They protect their master's territory. Most of the time they bark at our passage. Some stay by their houses. Others run out to the road and stop at the border. A few come out into the road and check us out. Some look menacing. But they do nothing to us. When they get too close, I just face them and they usually stop. Few demand noise from me to stop them. Most stop on their own. Only the three dogs in France demand more forceful action.

The sign at left tells us there is an invisible fence holding back these dogs.

Some dogs have fences to stop them, others, fences to run through. And now there is a new fence, a buried electrical fence. We cannot see it. The fence encounter works like this: a dog starts running head-long at us; we put up our guard; the dog stops abruptly. The dog has a collar that gives him a shock when he is near a buried wire that sends a radio signal to the collar. A little sign somewhere in the yard (like in the picture) often tells us what we already surmise.

Leave those French dogs to their dark corner. We enjoy being greeted by the rest. A few even walk with us for a while.

Easter Monday

We leave Las Animas Easter Monday in cold, moisture-laded air. That afternoon we walk into Hasty, Colorado. We sit at a table under the roof in front of the general store drinking a coffee. The flag is flopping lazily in front of the wooden post office across the street. A dog moseys up looking for a handout. A couple joins us and talks for a while. They leave. The clerk comes out and sits with us. Hasty is anything but hasty. Life is slow and relaxed in Hasty.

In Lamar we stay in Jane's Third Street Nest B&B. Petra loves the large claw-foot tub. When we think there is no place to stay in Granada the next night, Jane lines us with Renée at a mobile home park. She has a mobile home to rent by the night.

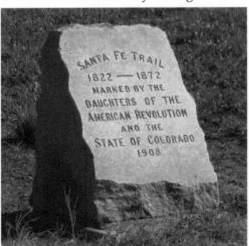

In 1908 the Daughters of the American Revolution set up stones like this all along the Santa Fe Trail from New Mexico to Missouri also.

The wind and the cop

As we walk toward Granada the next day the wind is brutal. It has already stalled us for two days earlier. It isn't bad enough to stop us but it's blowing heavily from the right, blasting us with every passing truck. The wind shadow of couple trucks actually blows Petra's cart over twice. It isn't pleasant walking.

Finally, Petra goes to the right side and begins walking with the traffic. Protesting, I give in and do the same. The shoulder is wide. We settle into our walk again, contented with not being pounded by every passing truck.

I am walking a hundred yards (95 meters) ahead. I look around and a cop is talking to Petra, reading her ID. Walking back I hear, "I came up behind you and you didn't even hear me. It's dangerous for you to walk on this side of the road. A car can come up a lot faster than I just did and hit you."

"But the wind makes it impossible...."

"It's dangerous for you to walk here."

He isn't listening to Petra. We are walking on the wrong side of the road against the law and that is that. "I am going to give you a warning and you have to return to the other side of the road."

Who is he anyway to decide for us what danger we can and cannot choose to endure? But the law likes to do that for us.

He takes my ID information too, writes out a warning ticket, and leaves us, saying we can get a fine if we are stopped again for walking on the wrong side. That is our only ticket on the walk.

We return to the left and put up with the wind and trucks. After walking a while more into the wind Petra takes off down a side road with a protecting line of trees, "I'm going here. I don't know where you are going." I follow. The path is longer but we arrive a little less buffeted.

We sleep well in our mobile home and we eat good food in a newly remodeled restaurant.

In the morning, Renée calls and lines us up with friend Rella Ann, who gives us a ride forward to make our walk shorter on a drizzly, windy morning. Rella Ann turns out to be a historian of Holly,

Colorado, the next town east. She shows us around town and around the former sugar factories. Holly is the home of the once well-known Holly Sugar, which merged with Imperial Sugar in 1988. Rella Ann recounts a lot of the town's history.

Syracuse

Rain is still threatening and we face 21 miles (34 kilometers) from Holly to Syracuse, Kansas. We accept Rella Ann's offer for a ride farther forward. Before we know it we are in a second-rate motel in Syracuse, Kansas (not Sicily). Not long after arriving, we know it would have been better to walk. The rain never materializes. It's only 10:30 and we have made our day's journey of 31 miles (50 kilometers) from Granada. We don't even think about continuing to the next town, 27 miles (44 kilometers) forward.

Walking into Syracuse center, we stop in Rebecca's coffee shop and stay a long time talking, drinking coffee, eating her cookies, and talking some more. The shop is a little, family-run place in the middle of town. We return three or four times in the two days we are in town and enjoy our talks each time.

On our first visit, Rebecca calls the local newspaper, a colorful reporter, complete with cowboy hat and mustache, the Colonel, comes over to the coffee house to interview us. It is the only interview that never appeared in print as far as I am able to determine.

Rain threatens again as we wake up the next morning. The weather forecast calls for heavy rains and the clouds confirm it as we get up. We move down the street from the motel to a furnished apartment with a kitchen where we can cook supper.

The second day we wander the town and take in the library and the museum. We talk long with Jonice, the woman caring for the museum, and learn a lot of the history of Syracuse and the Kansas plains. Here Petra sees for the first time the infamous piles of bones from countless buffalo killed only to rid the plains of food for the Native Americans. It's an awakening. Here also are the tools and utensils of the early European settlers.

At the library we use the internet and talk with the librarian about lining up libraries across the country to give slide shows about our pilgrimage once it is over and we have written this book.

In the evening a huge thunderstorm dumps on the town. Someone spots a tornado just south of town. But we would have been in Lakin by the time it had arrived had we walked. This Kansas weather is still a mystery to us. We have yet to realize that though it often looks like it is going to rain, it usually only rains in the late afternoon, late enough for us to easily arrive at a destination 20 miles (32 kilometers) from our starting point.

Petra's birthday

Rebecca buys our breakfast at her coffee shop as we leave the next day, Petra's birthday. We enjoy her spirit and conversation.

We celebrate Petra's birthday moving from Syracuse to Lakin. Google tells us Lakin has a motel and a B&B. Last night Petra called the Windy Heights B&B and was told they had no room. The motel doesn't sound inviting. So I call the B&B again as we begin to walk this morning. The B&B owner says, "I have no room right now but call back later, one of those booked may not be coming." Fair enough, we have lived with uncertainty many times before.

After walking a few miles, a car stops and asks if we need anything. That's nothing unusual. Cars often stop to ask that (a couple times a day anyway), "Do you want a ride." This woman has a big SUV with room for our carts. Not feeling like walking the whole 27 miles (44 kilometers) facing us, we accept and put the carts in the back. Lacy is a friend of Jonice, whom we talked with in the Syracuse Museum the afternoon before. They have been talking about us and Lacy decided to stop and see if we want something. After 12 miles (19 kilometers) and a lot of talk, we get out and walk the last ten miles (16 kilometers) to Lakin.

Standing in a park around the corner from the Windy Heights B&B we call again. "Yes, I have one room. Someone called and canceled."

We walk into a subdivision and up to Windy Heights, a spotless, brick and wood, middle-class home. Marian (I don't remember her real name) meets us at the door and shows us around. Our room is not the largest we have ever had; but the soft bed and the rest of the B&B is quite inviting.

The house is full because a high-school rodeo is in town this weekend and people from all over the state are taking up the beds in this tiny town. The motel is full too so it is good we found this room or we would be pitching the tent somewhere. More and more as we walk east we compete with local events for rooms: weekend games, weddings, and graduations in the spring.

Marian doesn't provide dinner so we have to go out somewhere. Chuck, Marian's husband volunteers to drive us to a nearby restaurant. We climb into his pickup crammed with garden tools. Chuck drops us at the local family restaurant and says he has to visit a friend but will pick us up on his way back. Inside we eat Petra's birthday dinner, a basic meal, but good.

Before we finish, Chuck returns and has coffee and desert with us. Tanner, the bus boy and Chuck's 23-year-old autistic friend, shoves the bill under Chuck's face and says, "You have to pay." I take it but Chuck protests and takes it back saying he was buying it for Petra's birthday. Thanks, Chuck.

Petra walks a desolate stretch of western Kansas west of Garden City.

Before Garden City a rivet holding the frame of Petra's cart together shears. The cart frame scissors down drastically to the right. We have to hitchhike. Thanks to the carts, a pickup driver and his wife, who think we were pushing babies, stop and give us a ride into town. The carts again help in an unintended way.

We are not expecting much as we enter Garden City, a medium-sized town in the western Kansas plains. We are tired and stay in one of the first motels we spot. After an uneventful night, we aren't ready to leave the town in the morning. We decide to head for a B&B we spotted on the Internet a couple days earlier.

But first we have to repair our first major breakdown. We find a hardware store, buy some bolts, nuts, and a wrench, and set up shop on the sidewalk. In fifteen minutes Petra reports the cart is standing better than ever.

A soda fountain stop

We walk toward the center of town where we suspect we'll find the B&B. We spot a small antique shop with a sign announcing "Coins." A guy wearing a kilt walks in.

"That surely must be an interesting place whether or not they can tell us where the B&B is." Petra agrees and we walk into the shop packed with small antiques and a case of coins. The kilted guy is talking with Tony, the shop owner. We all talk a while and we ask about the B&B. Turns out Tony is the brother-in-law of the B&B's owner. He encourages us to stay there before giving us a city map he drew. Then he sends us to the place next door to get the coffee we are also looking for. He warns us (tongue in cheek) about the owner, Bob, who, he says, "will talk your heads off."

Andy, Tom's customer in kilts, follows us into the restaurant and gives Bob some money to pay for whatever we want. Thanks, Andy.

Bob Petrus (Petra takes an immediate liking to him because he shares a similar name) has run this fifties-decorated soda fountain for better than ten years. At somewhere around 70, Bob has a thousand stories he tries to tell all at once. We listen and enjoy. We tell a bit of our journey too and as usual by now all are a bit in awe over it.

We have a sandwich. And Petra has her first ever milkshake and loves it. We both suck on it as we listen to more stories.

While Bob is entertaining us, Gary, a jeweler in his early 40s comes in quietly for coffee. He announces he is practice flying for the Air National Guard this afternoon. "Does anyone want to go with me?"

A consensus among those at the soda fountain says we should have the opportunity to see Garden City from the air. We are delighted.

When we finally tear ourselves away from Bob and his stories, we head for the Sunnyside B&B. Tony has called and announced our coming. Joanne shows us a couple rooms and we immediately choose the turret room. It looks out over the street corner and has a wonderful canopied bed. She offers it to us for a "discounted corporate rate." We accept. We like it enough that we almost immediately decide we are going to stay for more than one night.

Our Flight

Gary picks us up at the B&B early in the afternoon and takes us to the airport. We fly around the area in a one-engine plane for a little less than an hour as he adds flight time for his Guard duty. He even points out the house of Truman Capote's *In Cold Blood* in Holcomb. The flight is wonderful. Thanks, Gary. And thanks Universe for putting us in the soda fountain to say "Yes" to Gary.

We have a fine sleep that night followed by a great breakfast at the Sunnyland B&B. Later we stop at Gary's jewelry shop to get Petra's necklace cleaned. We ask if the seven or eight jewelry shops we see in town are not too much competition. He says no because they are known throughout the area and when someone wants jewelry they come to Garden City. Each shop has its own specialty. So the several shops actually help business.

Then we return to Bob's place for a malt and a shake and some more stories. In one he tells of an early job he had as a kid in a monkey suit. I tell him about Lyle, a long-winded story with an unexpected punch line. He says he has to take that one into his repertoire.

The special events of Garden City are not over. Joanne and Fred owners of the Sunnyland B&B set us up to stay at Joanne and Brian's home in Charleston tomorrow. The next motel or B&B is just too far to go in one day's walk.

As we leave this morning, trees are flowering and the leaves breaking out of their buds. Spring has come a second time for us this year. The first time was in Los Lunas, New Mexico, south of Albuquerque in early March. Today temperatures are in the high 70s (26-27C.) by mid-afternoon. It's April 22. Spring has indeed sprung.

We head east along the highway and I'm thinking about our interaction with the people we are meeting along the way. As we slow down these days and spend more time talking with people, we are finding our talk is not only of our walk and its joys and difficulties. But we are also talking about the wonderful people we are meeting along the way. We talk of following our dreams and they of following their dreams. Some days are quite dreamy.

Joanne and Brian

As evening approaches we walk off the main road, across a railroad, and look for Joanne and Brian's house. It is supposed to be close by. They are farmers. We call them and indeed it is close, we can see it at the end of a long driveway. We are staying with them tonight thanks to Fred last night. When the rain threatens, we get an unexpected surprise. They offer us a bed to sleep in. We were expecting to pitch our tent.

After dinner the rain clouds turn very dark. Brian checks out the storm on his cell-phone radar. This is new to us. We could use something like that. It's a nice tool for anyone out in the weather. We get one couple months later. Thanks Joanne and Brian for your hospitality and for the place to stay as well as dinner and breakfast.

In the morning Joanne gives us a five-mile (8-kilometer) ride so we can avoid a treacherous stretch of shoulderless highway. The ride lets us walk a country road along the railway away from the traffic.

In Kansas we spot the next grain silo along the railroad as we pass the one we have been watching the previous five miles (8 kilometers). Silo after silo, two hours apart, as we walk along the railway.

Kansas weather

The temperatures are moving up. Today they are in the 80's (high 20s C.) with fairly light winds most of the day. We are beginning to use our umbrellas to protect ourselves from the sun.

We have been noticing the past month or so that when small, puffy, white clouds begin to show up in the sky around 11 or 11:30, by one or two they almost cover the sky sheltering us from the fiercest sun of the day. When no rain comes, they dissipate by five or six. Problem is that with the really hot weather now, the sun is beginning to burn off these afternoon clouds before they can protect us much.

In Cimarron we stay in the Cimarron Crossing B&B hard on the highway. Though we sleep well, every time a truck passes it runs over some structure in the street that makes the house rattle. It's almost like both the street and the house are on a bridge and when a truck crosses a point, the resulting bump is carried into the house. It takes a while to get used to the disturbance.

Cimarron offers us our second ice cream soda fountain in a few days. We have a couple chocolate shakes for dinner. Some days nutrition takes a back seat.

We leave Cimarron at 7:10 this morning, our earliest departure to date. We're trying to outwit the weather and get in some miles before it gets too hot or windy. But the temperature quickly climbs to our hottest day and the wind blows harder and harder as the day goes on. It blasts from the south as we walk east. Every truck, and many pass, pounds on us with wind. I take my flags off the cart because they're being torn off. One blast knocks Petra's cart over. It's a busy and particularly hard day. Every step of 18.6 miles (30 kilometers) comes with no little effort.

Wagon tracks

As we take a break just west of Dodge City, we're treated to a view of several well-preserved wagon ruts of the Santa Fe Trail. It is not at all like the 2100-year-old, paved, Roman roads we saw in Italy. These tracks exist because thousands of wagons rolled over the prairie grasses for fifty years in the mid-1800s. No one planned them or paved them. The wagons just followed convenient paths and headed west. They didn't even follow each other in a line. Rather they spread out several wagons wide to distribute the wear on the fragile and sometimes muddy soil. If you have Google Earth™, you can see them. Or use the satellite setting of Google Maps™. Look for Dodge City and move a few miles west on US 50/400 to just west of Howell. They are clearly visible just north of the highway. The many right to left lines are the various paths of the trail.

Santa Fe Trail wagon ruts west of Dodge City, Kansas. The dark meandering feature is a much later canal. (Source Google Earth)

Just before Dodge City we are welcomed by the silhouettes of ten cowboys riding their horses along a large stone wall announcing the city.

The cowboy capital

Marshall Dillon, Katy, and Festus are nowhere to be found as we arrive in Dodge City. Petra tells me *Gunsmoke* played long in Germany as *Rauchende Colt* (*Smoky Colt*). Imagine Festus speaking German.

We find Kurt and Enid's Boot Hill B&B and check in. When they hear we have been walking in the wind and heat all day, they upgrade our room to one with a huge whirlpool tub. Petra is in it almost as soon as we are alone in the room. I am not too far behind her. Then we talk long into the night with the owners.

We take off the next day and visit Boot Hill Museum and its famous cemetery across from our Boot Hill B&B. Even though the B&B is built over part of the cemetery, no spirit woke us as we slept either night there.

To get a feel for this "Cowboy Capitol" of the world we also walk from store to store in the remade period stores of Main Street. I can hear the thud-chink, thud-chink, thud-clink of the men's boots and spurs on the wooden sidewalk and the swish of the billowing dresses of the women. The only life beyond those memories now is that of a few curious tourists and the actor-historian-storekeepers behind the counters.

Petra poses with the welcoming cowboys on the way out of town.

Storms

Storms continue to follow us through Kansas. In the morning as we prepare to leave Dodge City two large thunderstorms are already in the neighborhood. We don't want to walk in thunderstorms, rain, yes, but not thunderstorms. I watch the TV radar for half an hour and realize the storms are traveling parallel to and a few miles on either side of the road we will walk. From my little knowledge of weather, I know that that makes the road a safe place. The two storms are sucking in all the energy of the area. As long as they move parallel to the road, it will never rain on the road.

Today's destination is 38 miles (61 kilometers) in front of us, much too far to walk. Before we leave we call Joanne. We stayed on her farm a few days ago. At that time she offered to give us a ride if we needed it in the next few days. She calls her sister Rebecca and then calls us back saying Rebecca will give us a ride later in the morning, on her way home from church.

On the road, it's dark on both sides but blue sky peeks between fluffy white clouds above us. Lightning flashes often but thunder only occasionally rumbles on one or the other side in the distance.

The calm air smells of rain. Besides the sound of the tires of the passing cars, the only other sounds we hear are each other's voices and the plunk, plunk, plunk of our feet on the pavement. We remain dry all day.

We walk over 11 miles (18 kilometers) on the arrow-straight road before Rebecca pulls up. The storms are still flashing on both sides. We put our carts in her SUV and drive forward 17 miles (27.5 kilometers) to a crossroad with a gas station. We get out and walk the last ten miles (16.2 kilometers) to Kingsley. Thanks Rebecca.

Midway, USA

Though the rain never touches us, the streets are wet as we walk into Kinsley.

We walk down several streets before we find Susan and John's Tucked Inn B&B on the far side of town. As many B&Bs, the Tucked Inn is a couple rooms in Susan and John's home.

A sign at the entrance to Kinsley gives it the name "Midway, USA" saying it's 1,561 miles (2,530 kilometers) to both San Francisco and New York.

John is on a carnival museum board here. They say that the traveling carnival got its start in Kinsley. According to their internet site, at various times from 1907 until the 1980s, Kinsley has been home to six carnival companies. That rich carnival history inspired the establishment of the National Foundation for Carnival Heritage in 1991. In 1998, the Carnival Heritage Center opened in downtown Kinsley.

John takes us on a private showing of the Heritage Center later in the evening. We enjoy marry-go-round horses, animals, signs, tickets, news articles, and other carnival paraphernalia. This must give

Kinsley two names: not only "Midway, USA," but also "Midway of the Midway in the USA."

After a several thunderstorms in the night, the sky looks wrung out in the morning. John gives us a ride 15 miles (25 kilometers) to Garfield so we can comfortably walk to Fort Larned. Otherwise we'll skip it because our motel for the night in the town of Larned is just a bit too far to include the fort if we walk the whole way. We walk almost directly into a 20-mph (32-kph) wind across the flat Kansas plain. By now it is getting old hat and we just bear with it.

Today's Ft. Larned is a reconstruction of a fort that protected the Santa Fe Trail. I'm glad we visit it even though it's a lot more spit-shined and pretty than I think it ever was in its working days.

The law again

As we walk, the road has almost no shoulders. We push our carts with one wheel in the right-of-way getting off when we have to. But there is only grass and weeds left of the pavement so we walk on the busy road more than we'd like. Petra is complaining and I am cringing with each passing car. "Why don't they think that a walker needs some room on the side?"

A county squad car pulls up in front of us blocking our way. The cop gets out, comes forward, and asks, "Don't you know it's illegal to walk on the right-of-way of a highway?"

"But we have to. There is nowhere else to walk. There's no shoulder." Petra answers.

"But it's illegal. You can't walk here."

"What are we supposed to do?"

"I don't know. But you cannot walk here."

After four or five exchanges that are getting nowhere, the cop says, "I can give you a ride to town if you like. That would get you to town and off this road," implying that jail could be the destination.

Time to cool this down a bit. I intervene, "Ok, we will get off the road when someone is coming."

"And what do you have in those carts?"

"Baggage." Then we tell him about our pilgrimage. Petra and he back off their face-off.

The cop finally lets us go warning us not to be in the right-of-way when a car is coming. We agree and try our best to comply, not an easy task with nothing but high grass and weeds to the left.

The very next day, another cop pulls up and asks, "What do you have in there?" pointing to our carts.

Once again, "Our baggage."

"What are you doing out here?"

We tell him our story talking for ten or fifteen minutes. Then I ask, "Why did you really stop us?"

"We got a call that someone was out here walking in the right-of-way with babies."

"Who called you?"

"A woman who works for the Kansas welfare department."

*Did we look that dangerous that she couldn't stop herself? Why did she call the cops? Isn't it **her** job to protect the children of Kansas? Those "babies" might have been hit or died of heat exhaustion in the time it took that cop to get to us.* I decide not to hit the cop with these questions and observations, but I feel the woman isn't doing her job very well.

He wished us well as he left.

Quarter of the way

Sitting in Great Bend later I make some interesting and surprisingly accurate calculations (really guesses). I figure we are about a quarter of the distance to Jerusalem. Given that I can multiply how far we have come by four and come out with the following chart that compares the estimates with the actual distances we covered. They are surprisingly close.

	To Grand Junction	Estimate to Jerusalem	Actual to Jerusalem
Walking	1,300/2,100*	5,200/8,425	5,318/8,620
Riding	600/970		
Total	1,900/3,070	7,600/12,600	7,679/12,925
	*miles/kilometers		

As of today we are moving along at 15.4 miles (24.9 kilometers) per day counting only the days we are walking.

Curiosity offers a stay

As we prepare for the day after Great Bend we face a too-long 34 miles (55 kilometers) to Lyons. We call the Herzog House B&B in Ellinwood but they have no rooms. We'll have to hitchhike again at the end of the day. Then the phone rings. It's 10:30 PM. It's Greg from the Herzog House B&B saying they have a place for us after all if we are still looking for a room in Ellinwood. The Universe comes through again.

This morning we easily walk 12 miles (19 kilometers) to Ellinwood along pleasant back roads away from the narrow shoulder-less roads of the past few days. As we walk into Ellinwood I am struck by how immaculate it is. Every yard is bright green and trimmed like it is part of a golf course, just mowed this morning. The town is a bit too orderly for me. It even smells like mowed grass. I think they must have a roving committee making sure all lawns keep within city standards. Otherwise, surely one or two lawns in six blocks would be untrimmed. All are trimmed.

We find the Herzog House B&B in a section not quite so squeaky clean. It's closed. We leave our carts and walk into town, two blocks of old stores. Peggy Sue runs one, an antique shop with all the things one expects in an antique shop. It's a nice store. We talk with Peggy Sue about Ellinwood and her store. We tell her, "Walking like we are doing, we have little room for the kind of things you have here, but we do need new cups. The plastic ones we have are not working for us anymore." We find a couple cups that suit us. Peggy Sue gives them to us. Petra uses hers more than a year before she breaks it. I'm still using mine more than two and a half years later. Thanks, Peggy Sue.

We discover that Ellinwood also has several underground tunnels below the street-level stores. Most were closed long ago but a few remain to be toured. Later in the day, a local, a bit of a showman, gives us a tour of an early version, underground mall. We get to sit in an underground barber chair and cowboy bathtub to say nothing of visiting the cowboy brothel.

Before the tour we return to Greg and Tasha Herzog's B&B and get acquainted with them and their daughter, Ashley, as well as our home for the evening. It turns out that after we called the first time last night, they went online and looked at WalkingEast.com and decided to make up a room for us. The room was available all along but they felt too busy with their other work to do the B&B thing too. In the end they were curious. They decided they wanted to meet us so they went the extra mile. We are happy they did. After breakfast Greg gives us a large home-made summer sausage. We eat it piece by piece for more than a week. Thanks so much, Greg and Tasha, for your hospitality.

The next day is May Day. We face a long 22 miles (35.6 kilometers). We walk a gravel road a mile north of the highway and enjoy a day almost totally free of traffic. The wind blows hard from the side and front. But we make it, once again one step at a time. We are tired at the end of the day. The distance we walk stretches out to 25 (40.5 kilometers) by the time we get done searching for a motel in the evening. But the predicted 50% rain never happens–we got the 50% non-rain. Thank you, Universe.

My niece Renée lives in Lyons. We call her at work and ask her to pick us up and take us a mile or so back to a passed motel when others prove full. We're too tired to walk. The next morning Renée takes us to the next town where we have a fine breakfast, something not available in Lyons according to her. It was fun visiting with you, Renée.

Hedrick's Exotic Farm

Today we're leaving the Santa Fe Trail. It continues east. We're headed south to visit my sisters. We'll join it a gain around Hillsboro.

Rain catches up with us half way to Nickerson. A young couple in a pickup stops and offers us a ride. We accept. They, too, think we have kids in the carts. The Universe has given us something to help us get a ride when we need it. Thanks for the ride even though it was in a way under false pretext.

They drop us at Hedrick's Exotic Farm B&B in Nickerson. Molly offers us an upgraded room. We reside above the kangaroos. We can walk out of our room and look down on them from hall windows.

Hedrick's is, indeed, an exotic animal farm. Besides the kangaroos, emus, yaks, giraffes, pigs, eland elks, buffalos, ostriches, camels, and many other off-the-wall critters greet visitors. We wander around checking them all out. I feed a giraffe with a stick of food in my mouth. Petra pets the soft noses of a pack of camels.

The next morning, we bottle feed white buffalo, zebra, and eland babies. And then we get on a camel and take a ride. With all our wanderings around the world, it's the first time either of us has been on a camel. The animals are used for petting zoos across the country. When we are in the area again, we'll stop at this place run by a dedicated and enthusiastic woman. Thanks for the fun and information, Molly.

Petra pets camel noses at Hedrick's Exotic Farm.

Edie

In Hutchinson my sister Edie hosts a wonderful dinner party for us. Relatives, in-laws, and friends welcome us to central Kansas. We enjoy our time with them. It is good to see Edie again after more than eight years. Thanks so much Edie for the wonderful time.

Marcia

The next day as we are walking into Hesston in a light drizzle a woman in a van stops and asks if we want a ride. We decline saying we are walking by choice and anyway we are only going a short distance to my sister's here in town. "Where are you walking?"

"From California to Jerusalem." She leaves after a few more questions.

But a couple blocks later, another woman and a guy with a camera come down the street toward us. They are press, called by the first woman. They interviewed us on the corner in the rain. Our picture complete with colorful, wet umbrellas was a fine companion to the interesting article they wrote about us.

We stay that evening with my sister Marcia and her husband Dan in Hesston. Here also I have a lot of family history to catch up on. She has four kids and more grand kids. We don't get together often any more. Like many other families, once the parents die, the siblings often float apart these days. Besides, because Marcia is 15 years younger than I, we never got to know each other much even as kids. I was off to college before she was three. So it was like meeting her again for the first time and getting to know her all over.

I know there must be someone else who doesn't drink coffee. But I have never met anyone until Marcia. Someone gave her a Starbucks card and she happily gives it to us. Thanks, Marcia. We are truly happy you do not drink coffee—though we think you do not know what you are missing. We intend to have some nice coffee with the card.

Even with Dan's ride several miles out of Hesston the next morning, the 18 miles (29 kilometers) to Hillsboro over hilly, gravel roads makes for a long day. Twice, flooded streams block the roads forcing us once to backtrack a mile and another time to walk with a lot of effort through fields dragging our carts around the water.

Eleven miles with a dog

As we walk, a dog comes out of his driveway and follows us down these country roads for 11 miles (18 kilometers). He is having a grand time running up the road chasing birds out of the grass and running back to us. He must have covered 22 miles (36 kilometers) as we cover those 11. At one place we detour through a field to bypass that flood in the road. He follows. Petra remembers so many pheasants in Kansas. They fly out everywhere. This dog flushes at least a couple dozen.

Near the end of the day we walk a busy highway. Our dog knows nothing about fast vehicles. More than one truck hits his breaks to miss the dog. Now we are afraid for him. But we can do little for him other than leave his fate up to the Universe.

While we check into a motel that night on the edge of Hillsboro, he lies down next to our carts and waits for us to return. When we take our baggage in, he is still there. We pat him on the head and thank him for walking with us. In the morning he is gone. He must have wanted a good excuse to run in the wilderness with someone. I am sure he found his way back home. He was marking his path every few hundred feet all afternoon.

Another interview

In the morning we stop at a coffee house in Hillsboro for a mid-morning brew and talk a while with the people. Before you know it they have us in the Hillsboro Free Press office for an interview. It turns out to be one of the best interviews during the pilgrimage. Don Ratzlaff's article is accurate and captures the meaning and spirit of our walk well. In one place he quotes me:

> "I don't like 'peace walks,' but in fact this is really a peace walk because we are, by experience, saying, 'this is a peaceful place. There are problems and there are bad things, but this is, by far, a peaceful place.'

> "A lot of times in the media you read about the bad guy," he added. "And everybody asks us, 'Isn't it dangerous out there?' But I remind them that the bad guy is only one out of 100,000. There are 99,999 who are fantastic people."

We walk a little out of our way this afternoon to the Outdoors B&B in Marion. Linda has a house with three rooms dedicated to the B&B. Since no one else is here tonight, Linda gives us the run of the house after talking about her art work and showing us her flying squirrels in her own house up the hill.

What do you see? This woodcarving is in a window of the Outdoors B&B in Marion, Kansas. I am intrigued by what I see. Look at it a while…. Do you see an old Chinaman reading a book or an eagle sitting on something? Or? Linda, the artist, never saw the Chinaman.

We realize how quickly we ran in and out of Marcia's two nights ago and since we have a house for a night, we invite her over for dinner and some more talk. After all, she is only around 30 miles (48 kilometers) away.

Kansas depends on water. We are never far from a sprinkler system like this as we walk across the state.

Yvonne

When we stayed at the Windy Hills B&B in Lakin, Kansas, four weeks ago, we met Yvonne and her husband and children at the breakfast table. We talked a quarter of an hour about our walk and their rodeo trips around the state. Before we parted Yvonne said, "You have to stop at our place when you get to eastern Kansas. I will make you the biggest and tastiest steaks you have ever tasted."

We accepted her invitation and then went our separate ways, they to a high school rodeo in town and we to the next town east, Garden City.

Today we are walking toward rural Ramona and Yvonne's home. We talk long with Linda at the Outdoors B&B this morning. She gives us a ride part of the way. After we then walk only seven miles (11 kilometers), we call Yvonne for a ride the rest of the way to her place. In the evening we have that steak. It is surely one of the best I have ever had.

But much more than the steak, we enjoy our time with Yvonne and Tracy and their teenage children, Kate and Tanner, as well as visiting with Tracy's father. We take horse rides and tour their ranch operation (hundreds of feeder cattle) before the steak.

They are going away for the weekend to high school rodeo but they ask us to stay and rest until they return Sunday. We accept and enjoy a restful interlude in their new home.

They are interested in Italy. When they return Sunday, we show them our slide show on our walk from Germany over the Alps and down the Via Francigena to Rome three years earlier. Then we have another delicious meal.

The next morning we leave with a bag of cookies, several bags of beef jerky, and a pile of good will. Yvonne walks with us the first mile. When Petra realizes her sunglasses are missing, she calls Yvonne who brings them to us at our hotel in Herington in the evening.

We eat the cookies rather quickly but that delicious jerky lasts us for several weeks.

We thank Yvonne for such a great and loving weekend. Like so many others, Yvonne spoke with us for so short of a time before opening up her heart and inviting us into her life and home.

The morning after Herington the wind is blowing hard at our side again and rain clouds are building up. Greg, who gave us the summer sausage at the Herzog House in Ellinwood, passes by in his tire-delivery truck 13 days after we stayed in his B&B. He toots and gives us a wave.

After a couple hours, we rush into a barn and wait out a thunderstorm. Drizzle and black clouds linger as we get back on the road. We give in and hitchhike into Council Grove.

Last chance stop

When the Santa Fe Trail was in full operation, Council Grove was a busy place. The Last Chance Store, built in 1857, was, indeed, the last chance for those headed for Santa Fe by way of the Cimarron Cutoff to stock up on supplies. This included wood. Like now, few trees grew west of here. They still say in western Kansas that "Three trees make a forest." People needed wood for firewood and to repair broken equipment.

In keeping with our thoughts about history where we are walking, Council Grove is an important place.

> In 1541 Coronado from New Spain crossed the river where Council Grove is today.
>
> In 1825 under a tree here (the Council Oak), The U.S. government and Osage Native Americans signed a treaty that gave the government the right of way for a public highway through here, Santa Fe Trail.
>
> Council Grove then became the main central rendezvous for those traveling the trail.
>
> From 1825 to 1847 the crotch of a tree was the official regional post office. Travelers took the letters going in their direction.
>
> In 1873 the Kansa (Kaw) Native Americans, who had been moved around several times earlier by the government, were removed from their reservation near here to

Oklahoma Territory, thus opening the land around Council Grove for white settlement.

The second day in Council Grove we choose to wait out threatening storms at our hotel.

The Kansa Native Americans have established a large historic park seven miles (11 kilometers) east of Council Grove. With the weather not cooperating today, we take the owners of a restaurant up on their offer give us a ride out to the Kansa park. We walk around the large park and then walk back to town.

The Kansa are the people of the "south wind." We have been feeling a little too much of their south wind in Kansas. In fact, the wind is almost always out of the south.

By late afternoon the rain has not materialized. But the TV radar shows rain at the other end of our planned walk; so the decision to stay is good.

Now our plans are to go south and stay south of the Santa Fe Trail for good. But all plans are subject to change.

Flint Hills

The next day the weather forecast is again for storms. We ignore it and head south along KS 177 over rolling hills covered with grass and grazing cattle. The hills have too much limestone and flint to be cultivated. The top soil is less than a foot (30 centimeters) deep before the rocks take over. The Flint Hills look much as they did when the white men came two hundred years ago.

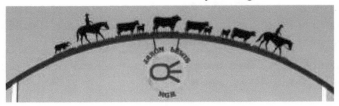

A gate decoration at a ranch in the Flint Hills.

The animals we see as we cross the country react to us in various ways. Horses and cattle interact similarly with us. Often they first stand in their field and just look at us. Then they walk in our direction; some run. Once they are at the fence we can often reach over and pet them. Then a curious thing happens, especially when we don't go over and pet them. They ran away at full speed and after a hundred yards (90 meters) or so they wheel around as a group and stand and look at us. Then they run and wheel again and again till they are far away. Horses like to make their way back toward the barn as they run.

We speculate on this running and the only plausible reason we can come up with is that they are seeing us with our carts as one being, a cart-man, something strange they have never seen before. They have a mixture of curiosity and fear forcing them to check us out but also to run away. No farmer we met gave us a better explanation.

Donkeys never fall into this running mode. They are neither bothered by us nor overly interested in us, though some do come over to get their heads scratched.

Temperatures along the road are in the low 70s (23 C.) and the wind is gentle today. Despite the weather forecast, there's no sign of yesterday's rain. Clouds shade us from the sun throughout the morning. Only one car or truck passes every 1 minute and 20 seconds–20 in 30 minutes. It sure would be nice if all our walking days were so comfortable.

Gift of a massage

Tonight, we get a room in the Prairie Fire Inn in Strong City and head into town for something to eat. We walk up and down the street checking out several places. We really want to sit outside and have a beer and something easy to eat. The Longhorn Bar and Café, has what looks like a patio out back. A couple is sitting at a table on a cement slab. We go in and ask about it. "Sure, you can eat there. Go on out that door." We have a few beers and some food and talk long with several from the area. As we're about to leave the owner, Larry, picks up the tab. Then he gives us a unique ride in the pitch dark several blocks to our motel on his golf cart which has no lights — our adventure for the day. Thanks for everything, Larry.

The next day brings the wind back at more than 40 mph (64 kph) from the south. Every truck we would meet would toss us around. 70% humidity and 86 degree (30 C.) heat added to the wind translates to unstable air. We decide to stay, to take another weather day.

Instead, we walk a few miles south to Cottonwood Falls. The falls are smallish at 5-foot (1.8-meter). In fact the "falls" are actually a dam for a long-gone mill. We have lunch and tour the central courthouse. As with so many other towns in the area, history plays a major part in what tourists learn about during their visits. Agriculture plays a quiet second.

Yesterday we met Linda from San Francisco in a small museum along the way from Council Grove. She pays for a massage for Petra at our motel. She says anyone walking as long as we have been walking needs a massage. Petra agrees. As we leave the next morning, I learn that a massage is waiting for me too. I miss it.

As the afternoon draws on evening, storms let loose on Strong City pouring on us and blowing away things north of us. It's black up there. It's good we stayed. We could have been in this weather had we been walking.

Temptation

On the way to Emporia the next day Petra asks, "What kind of temptation would be strong enough to make you seriously consider ending this walk?"

Spontaneously, I say, "If someone were to offer us a permanent place to live along the Camino de Santiago in Spain, a place where we could meet and perhaps house pilgrims passing us along the path, and funds to support the house, I think, that would be a temptation that would make me seriously consider ending the walk. If we could not put off accepting the offer and had to make a decision within a few days or weeks, the choice would be difficult."

We have no realistic answer. The question and lack of an answer shows the seriousness and value of this walk. I like the question. We continue considering possible answers. In the evening I post the question in our WalkingEast journal.

A couple days later, friend Rich E. leaves a note on our journal posting about temptation: "Have you ever been engrossed in a dream, and then, suddenly awake and wonder, 'How would my dream have turned out if ....'" If we succumb to a temptation to stop before this pilgrimage is done, we'll never know what it might have been. It better be a powerful payback to take us stray from this walk because I want to know who I am, who we are, after we have done this. That can only happen if we keep to the path and finish it.

The cycle of life

As we walk old US 50 on the way to Emporia, we are reminded of the cycle of life. We approach a buzzard standing next to a form on the road. He flies away. The form is a dead opossum. As we are nearly over her, we see movement. Six babies are trying to suckle her. The largest steps off the mother and stretches up, huge mouth open, and hisses loudly at us. Then he rejoins the others trying to get milk from their mother's dead body.

I drag her body into the grass beside the road. It is already stiff. She has been dead for some time. Surely no more milk is coming for the kids. Except for the largest kid who has a slight chance of surviving, the others will soon join their mother. The bird is back standing near the body as soon as we leave. The life of these opossums will soon be transformed into the life of that bird and his companions. There is nothing to do. The cycle of life shows itself so clearly. I still see that huge open mouth boldly warning us off, that mouth likely closed forever as I sit in a motel only a few hours later.

Many animals are dead along the road across America. We see five or six carcasses almost every mile (1.6 kilometers) we walk east of the Rockies. No animal species is spared this heavy end: dogs, cats, deer, antelopes, turtles, raccoons, snakes, opossums, frogs, toads, snails and birds of all kinds are only the more common dead on America's highways. There is less road kill in Europe, unless someone was picking them up sooner. Or more likely, less wildlife is left.

1,500 mi. (2,430 km.) – May 17, 2009

Later in the day as we rest in a cemetery just before Lebo, we call our friend Judy from Santa Fe. She is already done walking the Camino de Santiago. She left for Spain after we visited only two months ago and here we are only in mid-Kansas. We could have walked the Camino almost twice in that time.

After a tiring 21-mile (34-kilometer) walk from Emporia to Lebo we find only a tired-out, 1-star motel run by a Sri Lankan who tells us on the phone a restaurant is open next to his motel. It isn't when we arrive. But since we have no other choice besides hitching forward, it is our home for the night. The place has seen its better days but it does have a kitchen. Petra cooks up lentils and cuscus and the owner (to sooth his karma for saying restaurant was open?) gives us some chicken wings from his own kitchen. We eat well.

The restaurant isn't open in the morning either. We settle for blueberry and banana nut muffins from a gas station smelling of old cooking oil. Some days breakfast is not all you wish for.

Today's walk is relaxing. Forests line the road most of the day. When the trees are not there, ripening wheat ripples in the light wind. And for a change the temperature doesn't get above 75 (24 C.).

Less than luxury

After such a walk, we enter Eisenhower State Park. As pilgrims, sometimes we are treated to luxury and sometimes to much less. Judy's in New Mexico and Yvonne's a few days ago were the former. Truxton, Lebo, and now today Eisenhower are surely the latter. We arrive at the gate and ask for a primitive campsite. We walk three quarters of a mile and find a group of neatly laid out campsites. After putting up our tent we realize the toilets are locked and there's no water. And this cost us $8.50?

Ok, if we would be little more ambitious after our 18 miles (29 kilometers) to walk another mile (20 minutes) into the park (realizing we have to walk it out again tomorrow morning), facilities are there. We're too tired to walk farther. We live with what we have but still walk a mile to the camp host's spot for water.

In the morning we visit a little information area at the gate before we leave. They have a few snakes in an aquarium display. Petra has a snake crawl on her and likes the polished feel. One slithers on me too but I'm not as excited as Petra is.

I leave our tent pegs at the camp site as we leave and have to double back (another mile!) for them. But a ranger at the gate gives us a beautiful alternative road to walk. We see no cars for five miles (8 kilometers). The roads, so small they are almost paths, are tree-lined and cool. Thank you, sir.

We stop in Lyndon for a delicious, huge hamburger. Owner Wild Bill wants to give us a couple of his Easy Rock Café hats for the walk.

We decline, "No thanks, we have our old reliable straw hats and we have no room for new ones. Storage is limited when you carry or push everything."

Where next?

As we arrive in Ottawa the next day, we finish walking 100 miles (162 kilometers) in five days. Though we are tired, we are not overly so. Much of this joyful walk has been over little used back roads and in good weather. We find a room in a comfortable motel and settle in intending from the beginning to take an extra day to rest, though we know it will not be all rest.

In the evening we begin to tackle our route east of here. We do this almost every evening. But this time it is a bit more complicated than usual because we have to make sure we have motels or B&Bs in at least four towns. We want to connect up with the Katy Trail in Clinton, Missouri. The question is what path do we take to get there. The direct route east doesn't pan out. The towns with motels are too far apart. So we try another and another route. One looks promising. Then we discover the second day's stop isn't a valid place to stay. Google, our main source for lodging information these days, says there is a place. When we call, the motel is in another town. That happens. The internet is not infallible.

The straight way is not always the best way so we change directions and look for a more northerly route. That should work since there has to be places to stay in the southern Kansas City area. And even though it will take us longer to get to the Katy Trail, we will be back with the Santa Fe Trail again for a while.

We aren't done with route planning until the middle of the second day. Petra does the washing while we are planning in the morning. We're tired and testy from all the planning. Later we go shopping for more summery clothes, shorts and light shirts. And I buy my third pair of shoes. I'm still not satisfied with the ones I have had so far; I try different brand again. With limited storage room we buy things as we need them.

Two days ago as we walked along a little-used country road another dog followed us for a few miles. As we walked with the dog, an older man stopped in his pickup. He was concerned about the dog in the road. We told him he was not ours and where he came from. We also told him we were walking across the country and eventually to Jerusalem. Now two days later and several miles away I stand in a checkout line in Wal-Mart in Ottawa and the guy in front of me, seeing my backpack, asks if I was walking. "I just saw a couple walking south of here. They were walking to Jerusalem."

"Were they walking with a dog in the road?"

"Yes."

"And you stopped in your pickup?"

"Yes."

"That was us."

Stan

The next morning we head north toward Baldwin City. Though a thunderstorm seems to be heading our way from the southwest most of the day, it never gets to us. It's a good day for walking though it's a bit hotter than ideal. As we walk into town late in the afternoon, we stop in Stan's antique shop to ask where the Three Sisters B&B is. Stan offers us a coffee and invites us to pizza later in the evening. And when Petra mentions that it could be time to replace her doll-stroller, backpack carrier, he lines up someone with a real stroller she wants to pass on. In the end it's too big. Besides, Petra is still too attached to hers to let it go.

Stan walks with us to the edge of town the next morning and we continue east. He gives us a vile filled with Holy Land soil and asks us to bring it back to the Holy Land for him. We do just that. Nineteen months later we let the soil fly into the air over Jerusalem.

We stop at a park along the road and find some four-leaf clovers. When we start walking again, Petra looks for them and finds more along the road. It is a lucky day.

A major junction

Near Gardner it's time for our afternoon rest. It's hot. A new park offers a tree with a shaded, low wall around it to lie on. There are no other trees with resting places. After resting, we read the historical markers. In the early- and mid-1800s this place was a noisy hub of transportation. People and horses and wagons were jockeying for position here and getting ready to move. The noise must have been a wild cacophony in the bedlam. The smells would have reminded you of your father's barn. Many of these people were on their own pilgrimage like we are. But they were on one-way pilgrimages to somewhere in the great unknown West to make new lives. Three major trails split here: the Santa Fe, the California, and the Oregon Trails. Little, save these new placards, is left to tell us how important this place was. There are no tracks, no buildings, no monuments. They have long since been obliterated, covered by modern construction and roads.

Two bottles of ice

Once we get moving again, Mike Gardner says hello from his driveway and offers us the shade of his driveway tree to rest. We take him up on the offer. Then he sticks some coins into his old Coke vending machine and retrieves two wonderfully cold cans of Diet Coke for us in exchange for telling him a bit of our tale. He also gives us two frozen bottles of water to cool us as we continue our walk. Thanks, Mike. I think Petra holds that ice cube to her neck until it's all water.

In Olathe I write in my journal that we have been walking 139 days and that these days the pilgrimage "is trying us day after day. Why are we here? It's too windy. It's cold. It's hot. It's humid. There's no wind. But then also, it's a beautiful day with puffy clouds, a light wind, and in the low 70's. It's like life everywhere else but a bit more intense when you are out in it day after day like the farmers, the construction workers, and so many others."

We plot out our route along the Santa Fe Trail to its beginning near Boonville where we'll catch the Katy trail. The scenario tonight puts us in Boonville in 10 walking days. We project the next five days to be 10 to 12 miles (16 to 19 kilometers) each, a luxury after a batch of near- and over-20-mile (32-kilometer) days. We're trying shorter days to address the heat and humidity. It's nice not being forced by geography to walk long distances. We can even stop at places in between to get coffee or ice cream, or both!

Border changes

As we arrive in Missouri we notice an immediate change. Missouri is not Kansas. This border crossing really brings us into another world.

Missouri has many less sidewalks and the ones that are here are more buckled than the ones in Kansas. We have to walk beside busy 4-lane streets in town. Yards are more ragged and thinner. As we walk across Missouri we see many infrastructure problems, like bridges with crumbled concrete, rusted girders, and large potholes.

Kansas City Royals

Looking for our bed for our first night in Missouri, we head for a hotel we found on Google last night. When we find it, it's a Holiday Inn right across from the Kansas City Royals baseball park. My knee-jerk reaction is, "That one's going to be expensive. I think there's another place a bit down the road."

We walk against the throngs heading into tonight's game. Over the hill is a lower profile place. Inside they tell us they have nothing left save a $109 suite. We decline deciding that the Holiday Inn can't be any higher and if we are going to spend that much, we'll do it in style in the Ballpark Holiday Inn.

We walk back with the crowds and enter the Holiday Inn. We get a nice upper-floor room away from the ball park and spend only $58.27—so much for pre-conceived impressions. In the evening we have a great time at the bar watching the ball game, joking with the bar tender, and having a few brews. They say the teams stay here in the same hotel. We don't see them the next morning.

A time of honor

As we visit Independence, Missouri, Petra posts the following on our WalkingEast journal calling it "Time to Honor":

> We have been more than 140 days on the road. I just looked at all our pictures and the trail we have walked. It is time to honor ourselves and the Universe and say thank you to our bodies with all the muscles and cells that have made it possible to reach Missouri. We say thank you too seldom. After all our pilgrimage experience we should know better.
>
> What is the best way to honor all the miles we have walked, all the growing, all the experience that we gained, all the people that we meet, all the help that we got, all the birds that we heard, all the dogs that welcomed us, all the

wind that blew through us and cleansed us, all the love we have felt every day we walked? Do we sit a while and let the tears of joy and thanksgiving run? Do we sit and rest a while as the next stage looks at us?

I think we are arriving at a new stage. What this will be I don't know yet. It would be great to be going slow and with the flow without setting an aim to reach, just walking without much planning and preparing for where to get food and where to stay. Here in the US it is almost impossible to find a small store with some fruits and daily needs like bread and cheese along the path (or even downtown!). I am just now dreaming of Europe and the small shops and bakeries. It sounds like I am almost ready for Europe but there is a bit to walk here yet. We just got to know Kansas and now we have to get used to Missouri and how the world works here.

I am a little bit afraid about the summer heat and mosquitoes, that they might become so many that it becomes difficult to rest with our mats. Walking in winter and spring is so much easier. When the pilgrimage distance becomes as long as this one, you can't choose your season anymore. We have to learn to walk with the seasons as they come and adapt to the changes.

In Independence, we stay three days to rest. We visit the National Cathedral of the Community of Christ Church, an offspring of the Mormon Church. The stainless-steel building spirals 300 feet into the air dominating the Independence skyline. We go in. As we finish an inspiring tour, they ask us to light the candle for their afternoon Peace prayer. You see, we, as pilgrims walking to Jerusalem, are celebrities for the afternoon. We met several wonderful people. We receive many blessings along this pilgrimage. This afternoon surely has its share. Thanks to all at the Community of Christ, Gert, Donald, Ms. Loving, and several others.

Another day we visit the National Frontier Trails Museum honoring the three trails that left Independence in the early 1800s, the Santa Fe, the Oregon, and the California Trails. The emphasis is on the latter two. We enjoy revisiting many things we saw while walking the Santa Fe Trail from the west over the past month and a half.

Lost camera?

As we get ready to leave Independence, I discover I don't have my camera. "Where is my camera? Did I leave it in the hotel where we were yesterday?"

Petra answers, "No, you had it at the museum after that. But do you remember that hook almost behind the toilet in the bathroom? Could you have left it there?"

"Could be. It wouldn't have been the first time." I thought as I hung it there, 'I better not forget it.'"

We start walking toward the museum and call as soon as they are open. The camera is still on the hook. We slow a bit relieved of the urgency of our morning walk. Petra says, "You need to have a check list whenever you go someplace anymore." OK, but then she left the massage oil somewhere in the last couple days. Does that mean we both need to do the check-list thing?

Walking earlier

A couple days later we're in Oak Grove sitting for a second day in a KOA Kampground soaking up shade as the sun bakes the world into a 90-digree (32 C.) heat bath with high humidity. It's June first. We face 22 miles (36 kilometers) tomorrow. Now that the heat has set in with force, we have to find that new way of walking to avoid the mid- and late-day heat. We have to begin starting out early in the morning and resting during mid-day heat. Our plan is to get up early and be ready to walk around six am. Changes. This walk continues to demand changes.

Being next to a 24-hour truck stop allows us to have breakfast at five and move early. As we leave in the heavy, early morning air, we swear we smell jasmine, the delicious, sweet odor of jasmine. It's like we are back in India. The fragrance is coming from the flowers beside the road. But they don't look like jasmine. Later we find out they are honeysuckles. We are in a honeysuckle Eldorado with so much vibrant, virgin green. We are in a new and different world.

A foot- (30-centimeter-) wide snapping turtle shows up on the edge of the road about to walk into the right-of-way. It's the first turtle we've seen on the walk. I try to be a nice guy and nudge him back toward the ditch. My reward is a lightning-fast snap toward my shoe. But I am still young enough to move my foot out of its way. From here forward we see many turtles but far too many are dead on the road.

As we pass big water puddles and ponds along the road, croaking frogs go silent. They don't stop when cars pass. They are used to the cars but not people. Things have changed in the past 100 years.

The battle of Waterloo

A couple nights ago I spotted Napoleon, Waterloo, and Wellington on the map. Today we are walking through them. Waterloo is little more than a cross roads. The other two are small towns. The Wikipedia entry for Napoleon, Missouri, says, "There are stories that circulate claiming the names of the towns of Wellington, Waterloo & Napoleon relate to the battle of Waterloo, although there doesn't seem to be any record substantiating this." Record or no, who would believe anything else?

As the day progresses, rain clouds move in. We stop in a park under a shelter and stay more than an hour while it pours. When we return to the road, rain soon threatens again. "The clouds are going away from us." I tell Petra. She disagrees. She is correct. In a half an hour we are in one of biggest downpours since we started. Our umbrellas only shelter us a little. It's getting too dangerous to be on the now-dark road. Besides, the spray from the cars in such a downpour is heavy. We call Marcia at the Ryland House B&B in Lexington just a couple miles ahead and beg a pick up. We take shelter to little avail under some trees. Someone comes out of the nearby house and says, "You know, you are standing on private property?" "We do." And we continue doing so until Marcia picks us up fifteen minutes later.

Lexington

Lexington is a beautiful city once the rain stops. It is bedecked in June's most virgin greens and late spring flowers. It is steeped in confederate history, a town most worthy of a day's stop to see it in a little depth. So we stop for six days and take an early summer break. Besides, I got a fever from the storm and need to heal.

Lexington is proud of its part in the Civil War. Its court house has a cannon ball in one of its pillars. The south won the battle here just before the official beginning of the Civil War.

Marcia at the Ryland House B&B treats us to some meals and introduces us to her mother and a friend before leaving for Chicago on some business. Before she leaves, we pay her for four more days and she gives us the run of the house. Thanks for the trust and everything else, Marcia.

John, Marcia's friend, looks in on us periodically to see if we need anything. One evening he takes us out for a wonderful Mexican dinner. Thanks, John.

Lexington has a coffee house and book store where many meet and talk. We meet Alma in the coffee house. Alma lived in the Santa Fe part of her life. We muse on the differences between the two places. She says, "There are many differences but my favorite concerns my doctor's questions during an exam in each place. There my doctor asked, 'Do you practice safe sex?' Here he just assumed that, with my 60 years and weight, I didn't have sex. He was chagrined when I told him it was a false assumption."

One evening Alma takes us to a Cherokee Christian information meeting where we learn a lot about the Cherokee culture. She also gives us some good nuts and dried fruit for a trail mix as she drives us to Marshall when we leave.

We arrive in Arrow Rock along with threatening clouds. After checking other B&Bs, we arrive at the Arrow Rock Inn B&B. As we stand outside the door the clouds let loose with a huge downpour.

We take that as a sign to stay for the evening in Linda's century-old house. We have a large, upstairs bedroom with windows on three sides for cross-ventilation.

It is Sunday and all the restaurants are closed in the evening. Linda takes up the slack and prepares us a fine dinner. As we talk about our planned route to the Katy Trail the next day, Linda suggests we walk to Blackwater and then on to Pilot Grove in order to make our day's walk somewhat shorter and on less traveled roads. It turns out to be a comfortable alternative on a hot, humid day. Information like that makes staying in B&Bs a valuable asset. Thanks, Linda.

In Blackwater we are the only guests in the remodeled air-conditioned hotel. We use that air. Blueberry pancakes make our breakfast memorable.

The Katy Trail

In the 1890s the Missouri-Kansas-Texas Railway, Katy for short, was built west from St. Louis along the Missouri River. It was during a time when few roads existed and those that did were impassible for much of the year.

The Katy flourished in the beginning. But first the auto took away the passengers and then the trucks the freight. In 1986 it ceased operation. In time the Missouri Department of natural Resources gained procession and with significant donations from the private sector the Katy Trail opened in September 1996. Running from Clinton to St. Charles and 225 miles (365 kilometers) long, the Katy Trail is the longest rails-to-trails park in the US. Most of its route follows the banks of the Missouri River (See map on p. 330).

When we first learned about Katy before leaving California we were excited about such a long trail through nature with numerous campgrounds. Our initial timing put us on the Katy in May or June, a time when we expected the weather to be ideal for camping. Little did we know how hot spring can be in Missouri.

On 11 June we walk over some serious Missouri hills on a hot, muggy day on our way to Pilot Grove, mile marker 203 on the Katy Trail. We arrive at our first serious non-auto pathway in the 1,756 miles (2,845 kilometers) we have already walked. The sun shines brightly as we step onto the brilliant white, six-foot-wide, gravel pathway stretching out to a tunnel of trees several hundred feet to our left. It rounds a long, lazy curve to the right. The wind blows and birds chirp as we take a seat next to a covered billboard describing this section of the Katy.

The Katy Trail follows the route of the Missouri-Kansas-Texas Railway.

Pilot Grove B&B

We call the Pilot Grove B&B again to tell them we have arrived. Delores picks us up. They are remodeling the B&B in town so she offers us a room in their home.

Petra pushes her cart up to the Pilot Grove stop on the Katy Trail. We have been anticipating this for a long time.

Dolores fixes a great dinner during which husband Virgil, a farmer, says, "No work with the soy beans tonight. I'm ready to hear some serious stories." And that is just how it happens. We have joyous conversation late into the evening, our introduction to the Katy.

A Katy train from a poster at the Pilot Grove stop. The Good old days?

Santa Fe Trail beginning

The next day we walk to Boonville where we can see the Missouri flowing by our hotel. The following day takes us to New Franklin, the end of the Santa Fe Trail. We say good-bye to it and head for a nearby campground. The pleasant though hot stay on the campground is spoiled somewhat by kids partying into the late hours. At one in the morning, Petra gets out of the tent and goes over and tells them, "Ok, you have had your fun but now it is time to end it. Quite time was supposed to be at ten and it's already one."

Someone's peaceful resting place along the Missouri.

"This is a campground. If you want quite you should stay home. No one comes here just to sleep."

"The party is over." Petra repeats.

Half an hour later she is back in their face. "Now it's time to end the party." It works though it takes another quarter hour for them to really quiet down.

Mosquitoes

A few days later we stop at Robert and Maggie's, a store with food among other things, in Wilton. We talk long and then Robert, a Native American, gives Petra a free chiropractic treatment. Afterwards, we join them for lunch. Of the pesky mosquitoes, Robert says, "I don't like to kill anything but I have no qualms over mosquitoes. I figure I'm being good to them moving them quickly on to their next life." Then he adds, "There were a lot more mosquitoes last week but the birds have eaten most of them."

We would enjoy taking Robert and Maggie up on their offer for a place to stay for the evening but we already reserved a place in the next town.

Frankie and floods

Frankie, a blue-eyed cat named after Frank Sinatra, presides over the Globe Hotel in Hartsburg just before Jefferson City. Jeanette, the owner, tries her hardest to keep him outside away from the guests. But every other time someone comes in the door Frankie makes his way in also. It is almost like a dance as he goes past me and I pick him up and deposit him outside again several times.

The Globe Hotel.

Floods in general and specifically the flood of 1993 come up in almost every conversation with people along the Missouri. Jeanette's Globe Hotel suffered along with so many other places. Water reached the second floor. She lived in the second floor for a year afterwards while the first floor dried out and they repaired it. After replacing all the first-floor dry wall and floor, she reopened a year later and is still running strong. She is 70 and runs the place alone. We enjoy our visit and the fine supper she makes for us when the local restaurants are closed. Thanks, Jeanette.

We visit Jeanette after the walk as we drove over our walking path in fall of 2011. As she moved things back down from the second story to the first after a 2011 flood threat, a heavy bookshelf chased her down the stairs and broke her leg. She greeted us from a wheelchair but her spirit is still lively. We enjoyed visiting a second time.

It is mid-day. The temperature is over 95 (35 C.). Ninety-five also accurately describes the humidity. Mosquitoes attack out of the slow wind blowing with us down the path. All is normal for the Katy Trail in Missouri.

Vicki and her bee

When we ate breakfast back in Blackwater, Missouri, nine days ago, we met Vicki. She invited us to stop as we pass her place near Tibbetts. We detour half a mile up a hill off the path to visit her. She prepares a fine lunch we eat under a tree in the cool shade. A breeze, unknown down on the wind-protected Katy, makes our stay under the tree doubly comfortable.

She has a barn that she is thinking of converting into a hostel for those walking and cycling along the Katy Trail. It is a good idea though she is only a few miles from the only other hostel along the trail, the one in Tibbetts.

As I eat the meal, a sword of pain shoots through my foot. A bee stung me in the foot. Or I stepped on her and drove her stinger into my foot. Whatever happened, my thoughts race beck to when I was ten, 57 years earlier when I was similarly stung by a bumblebee, my last bee sting. That time I broke out in horrible hives that lasted for days.

This is not the place to repeat that early experience. I do my best to stay calm; everyone applies their favorite remedy and a couple extra to my foot. We rub raw onion on the sting then sassafras leaves. Vicki heard once a burning cigarette would congeal the poison. I apply a red-hot cigarette ash to my foot. Someone remembers vinegar helps. We put some on the foot. I sit with my foot on an ice pack for a while only to have that interrupted for a couple other remedies.

In the confusion the good lunch fades into the background. But I sit back with the ice on my foot, eat some more, and sleep a bit.

It's three as we get moving again. We decide to walk a few more miles to the Tibbetts hostel instead of staying at Vicki's. It is still early and we have to walk 15 miles (24 kilometers) beyond Tibbetts the next day. That would be closer to 20 (32 kilometers) if we stay with Vicki tonight. We are not prepared for a long, hot, humid walk along the Katy.

As we leave Vicki, the sting is not bothering me much. One or all the remedies together did the job and by the next morning my foot is working well with only a slight feel of the sting. Two days later there's no trace of the bite—and no hives.

Petra says no

Did I say the Katy is hot and humid? It's also mosquotes and no wind. No, it's not "no wind"; it's 2.5 miles-per-hour (4 kph) wind at our backs so the result is no wind as we walk forward at 2.5 mph. But the Katy is also beautiful. Trees, fields, cliffs, and the Missouri River line the path. Everything is green: green trees, green grass, green weeds, and green moss. The sky is often deep blue with puffy clouds—when it isn't raining.

One day is particularly uncomfortable with the heat index hanging around 110 (43 C.) most of the day. Today's trail end offers a nice campground, just what we envisioned along the Katy. But as we draw near it I protest saying, "I want air conditioning tonight. I am not ready to sweat in a tent all night."

We call a B&B. The owner picks us up at the trail for a fee. We are happy to pay it. But when we get to the B&B he drives by saying, "I have to get some beer. I haven't been there yet today." So we ride along with him another ten minutes so he can get his beer. As he gets out of the car to go to the bar, he points to the bank and says, "There's the ATM." We don't need an ATM. We have money. We need a room.

When we return to the B&B, he shows us three mediocre rooms in his old remodeled house announcing they are $80 each. "Let's go down and I'll show you the toilet and tell you the rules."

In the kitchen Petra announces, "We're leaving. You are much too expensive. We have walked many miles and have stayed in many Bed and Breakfasts. Your price if far too much for what you are offering."

Both he and I are startled, but for different reasons. I don't think he expected such a strong rejection. And I, I have no idea where we are going to stay tonight. I pay him for the ride and we leave.

Outside I immediately ask, "And where are we going?"

"Remember the place with a cabin I called the other day?"

"Yes?"

"It's just around the corner. I saw it when we drove by."

She is right. Less than a hundred yards (90 meters) away is Steamboat Junction Campground. And right in front is our cabin. And it costs less than the third-rate B&B we just were in. Downstairs is a kitchen and upstairs a bedroom with windows on all four walls. It isn't big. But it is cozy. The Mitsubishi wall air conditioners silently cool the space. Petra says that night converted her to Mitsubishi air conditioning. We rest well.

The heat, humidity, and mosquitoes continue to bully us as we walk the route of the Lewis and Clark expedition two centuries earlier. Many historical markers tell their journey along the Missouri. They battled the same elements as they paddled their canoes against the current. They smeared cattle dung on themselves to ward off the mosquitoes. At least we have Off.

Old Treloar store fronts along the Katy Trail.

Petra along the Katy Trail.

SUMMER 2009

Continuing to swelter

We have had an awful lot of summer already. It's June 21 as we stop in Herman. We're suffering here from heat, humidity, and mosquitoes. 110-degrees (44 C.) and above heat index is already too much. I don't want to think about what we have to look forward to in the coming months.

Time to stop?

When we stop in Herman, we notice the B&B needs repairs and painting. On our second day we ask the owner, "Would you consider us helping you fix up your place in exchange for room and board?" That would keep us off the road and out of the heat for a while.

"No. I don't have money to buy paint let alone pay you room and board to work for me."

It's the first day of summer and we're ready to quit or stop for a while. We even check the Amtrak schedule for trains to Woodstock, Illinois, our home base, to sit tight for the summer. In the end we decide rather than stop we will just get an earlier start and walk shorter distances.

We are in the middle of Missouri's wine country. Germans were enticed in the 1800s to an area alleged to be much like the Rhine River and ripe for vineyards. Many came and today there is even a Rhineland, Missouri, to say nothing of Herman, surely of German origin.

We visit a local winery the first afternoon. After trying several wines and telling the hostess about our walk and this book we are planning to write, I promise I will include her in it. As we leave she says, "Remember, my name is Denise. That's D-E-N-I-S-E." So here you are, Denise. Thanks for the conversation. We enjoyed your winery.

Gerry walks with us

At Marthasville we are joined by Gerry, a friend we met in Albuquerque at the American Pilgrims of the Camino meeting. She is planning to walk the Camino de Santiago and wants to walk with us for the experience with her full pack in the heat. She could have hardly picked a hotter day. It is another Katy 110-degree (43-C.) heat-index day where my shirt and arms are totally wet within an hour of getting on the path.

We walk slowly. The wind refuses to give any relief. And the mosquitoes are ever present. At noon we stop at the only place with shade that day and slept half an hour in the grass. When we begin again, Gerry keeps walking. She is 64 and never has walked any long distance before in good weather let alone this heat. When we arrive in Augusta we are once again rung out and ready for an evening in another air-conditioned B&B. I am impressed with Gerry's performance.

Terri and Nick

At the end of the next day Terri and Nick of Kirkwood pick us up in Weldon Springs and take us almost 20 miles (32 kilometers) to their home in Kirkwood to host us for the evening. We met them earlier at the Globe Hotel in Hartsburg where they invited us to stay with them. They show us the town, treat us to ice cream, and wait for us while we get a new phone after we wash our old one with our clothes. In the morning they bring us back to the trail with new mosquito dope and our new phone complete with weather radar. Thanks, Terri and Nick.

Ma and Pa

The next day we walk into St. Charles, the end of the Katy near the Mississippi River. But before Missouri is over I must tell you about "Ma and Pa" of the Lococo II B&B at the end of the trail. They drive the "Kids" (as they called us) around town that night and for a round-about ride to Brussels Ferry the next day (read: he was lost!). We enjoyed staying and talking with them. Thanks Ma and Pa.

The weather and mosquitoes make this Missouri section of our pilgrimage difficult physically. But the people we meet make it a joy. These are a memorable 15 days (13 walking) and 130 miles (211 kilometers). That's a nice round average of 10 miles (16.2 kilometers) per day on walking days. The summer demands these shorter days. The overall average in North America is now 14.7 miles (23.8 kilometers) per day.

What's our day like?

Though we meet and talk with many people and so many things vary from day to day, our daily activities have a familiar routine. I'll try to present that framework, that skeleton in this section.

Our day starts when we get up between six and seven. In summer when the days are hot and humid we try, though we didn't always succeed, to get up at five or earlier. That way we can walk earlier and then rest in the hottest part of the day before walking the last miles when it is a bit cooler again.

Next we clean up and pack and have breakfast. Breakfast is provided in many motels and all B&Bs. When it is not one of those plastic motel breakfasts so often of low nutritional value, we eat before we leave. But the farther east we walk in North America, the more we opt for stopping at a restaurant for breakfast after we leave the motel.

The clean-up, pack, and breakfast activities take around two hours as we walk through North America. Little in the routine changes. We often note the time and try to shorten it, but two hours is what it takes. By the time we are almost done walking in Genoa, Italy, the time is down to an hour and a half with even a little less a few times.

We have a well-established routine for our day on the road. We walk around 2.5 miles per hour (4 kph) on good days. The model walking day looks something like this: After walking the first two hours (five miles - 8 kilometers) we find a comfortable place to rest. In the cold times it's in the sun. When it's hot, it's under some tree. We put down our mats and take off our shoes and socks (even if it's cold) so our feet can dry out. Then we lie down and sleep for 20 minutes to half an hour. When we get up we walk another two hours, sleep, and this time eat whatever it was we are carrying for lunch. Sometimes we stop at a restaurant instead for some small food. Then we walk another two hours. That makes 15 miles (24 kilometers), a little more than an average day's distance. If we walk farther, we repeat the walk-rest cycle.

So that's the ideal walk-rest cycle. It doesn't always work that way. When it is raining, resting is difficult to impossible. Sometimes we just don't find good stopping places. Sometimes we just skip one or more rest stops. But when we do that, we feel it. We get tired a lot sooner in the afternoon.

We give unmeasured room for people contact. We just fit them in where they come and adjust the rest of the time as well as we can.

With the rest times, around seven hours passes with these three five-mile segments. If we start walking at ten, we are pushing five to six. When conditions are ideal, we are in our destination town, city, or campground around that time. Often it is earlier or later depending on the distance we were covering that day.

Now comes the part of the day I never have been able to completely come to peace with—looking for a place to stay at night. When there is only one motel, it is Nirvana; we have no choice. Otherwise, we often check out two or three places before finding the one we are ready to live in for the night. We get so we can tell fairly quickly whether we want to stay, often as we walk through the entrance door (See p. 178 for a look at what we see as an ideal hotel room).

When someone invites us to stay with them as happens many times, we are spared this search as well as the search for a restaurant.

After settling ourselves in the hotel room and cleaning up a bit, we go out into the world again to eat. When you eat night after night in restaurants, sometimes it is a wonderful experience; sometimes it gets a bit boring, sometimes you don't even want to go out again to eat. As we reach the end of the pilgrimage, we long for our own kitchen to cook a fast soup and sit down and enjoy it. Our kitchen is clearly one thing we miss a lot on the road.

Sometimes we go to a store to restock food or other items before returning to the hotel.

Back in the hotel our day is not always done. Sometimes we wash clothes (either by hand or with washing machine, something usually in American motels but missing in Europe).

Next, we scout out where to stop the next night or nights and what roads or paths to walk the next days. We try to do this for three to five nights at a time. This search is usually Internet work so when the place we are staying has no Wi-Fi or computer, we look for a place with one or the other before returning to the hotel or B&B. That scouting includes finding potential hotels and calling them to see whether they have a room. Sometimes they don't even exist: the Internet says they exist but they don't. This scouting can take one to two hours some nights. Though it is not always so, I usually manage the paths and roads to walk and Petra the hotels or B&Bs.

Finally and most importantly, we like to give each other foot and leg massages in the evening before we go to bed. The massages are so helpful for relaxing and getting our tired feet and legs ready for a night's sleep.

By the time we go to bed at ten or eleven we are tired. Six thirty comes quite early the next day.

Illinois

The morning is sunny and the temperature is still in the low 80s (25-27 C.) as " Pa" from the Lococo II B&B drops us "Kids" at the Brussels Ferry across from Grafton, Illinois. We are almost back in my home state, Illinois, albeit a good distance from home in Woodstock way up north.

We take a calm ride across the Illinois River on the ferry and walk a few miles into Grafton, a typical river town with stores and boat harbors strung along the Illinois and Mississippi Rivers. The two rivers join here so the harbors in the northern part of town are on the Illinois and those in the south are on the Mississippi.

Gerry's Elsah

The trees and grass of Grafton are green and the roads and sidewalks a bit unkempt. We stop at a bar/restaurant along the river and have more than one cold ice tea. The heat is so intense that Petra has heat blisters on her road-side leg.

The Illinois, Missouri, and Mississippi rivers come together here.

We are going to our friend Gerry's in Elsah, Gerry who walked with us a few days back. We are not too sure where she lives. So we call her for directions and she offers to pick us up. We protest but she insists.

She takes us a few miles south along the Mississippi. The road winds along the river under high cliffs with trees decked in their spring, virgin green. The water is deep blue and thin clouds float in a no-less blue sky. It would be nice walking but we'll take the ride for a change.

We turn in at a break in the cliffs and drive back into the village of Elsah crowded into a couple small valleys. Gerry takes us up one valley to her home and our home for the next ten days. Forested hills climb up both behind the house and across the street. The sun comes in through some of the trees.

After a couple days, Gerry leaves to visit relatives. We rent her house for the next eight days. It's quiet, a nice place to rest from the last couple weeks' heat in Missouri. The weather even cooperates, cooling off enough to take the fire from the sun for a while.

Tackling the never-ending planning task, we work on our route north. Details show somewhere around 30 days to Woodstock. In the end that is a bit ambitious—it actually takes us 40 days. Our planned (and actual) path takes us pretty much along the general path we originally visualized in California–north on the Great River Road along the Mississippi as far as Moline and then east along the Hennepin and I&M Canal Trails and up the Fox River Valley.

We take the time for longer-term planning as we sit here. We are currently considering going into Wisconsin from Woodstock, crossing Lake Michigan to Muskegon from Milwaukee, and then heading straight east across southern Ontario to the east coast. This new idea leaves out Ohio and some eastern states, but we expect to be cooler. It's our answer to the heat and humidity we have been enduring.

We don't sit totally still here in Elsah. We walk up to the bluff at Principia College just to the south. We look out over the trees and the confluence of the Mississippi, Missouri, and Illinois Rivers far below. The two largest rivers in the U.S. become one here and the Illinois adds its burden to the mixture.

The Mississippi near Elsah.

One day Petra rides a bike as I walk the four miles (6.5 kilometers) to Grafton along that beautiful road on the Mississippi cliffside. I apply for a new passport at the post office. It was almost ten years ago that I last renewed it a few months before I retired in September 2000.

On the fourth of July we have a potluck lunch with the people in Elsah and in the evening we sit on the Mississippi and watch fireworks to the north in Grafton, to the south in Alton, and across the River in two or three other communities.

We finally head north along the Illinois after a needed ten-day rest. The first night we camp on a hill in the almost empty campground at Pere Marquette State Park. An empty campground is an enjoyable place to stay.

A ride across a bridge

The next day we head out over flat, flood-plain farmland. As we rest under a tree a farmer, Gary, stops in his pickup to talk. When we tell him we are going to Hardin he says, "You can't walk across the bridge over the Illinois River. It's too narrow. You'll have to call the police or someone to give you a ride."

We still have quite a way to go so we acknowledge his warning and continue walking. A couple miles down the road Gary stops again to repeat his warning and says we can ride with him if we want to. He can come when we get near. I say, "Do you want to take us now? Then you don't have to wait for us to get there in a couple hours."

He is surprised, thinking, as others do, that we only walk and don't take rides. We load our carts into his pickup and take off. Along the way he shows us some points of interest including a fifteen-foot high sign at a car repair shop. There's a car on top. He says that during the flood of '93 only the car was out of the water.

When we get to the Illinois River crossing, the center-raising draw bridge is indeed narrow. We probably could have walked across but we would have held up traffic at times. Before Gary leaves, he and his wife take us to afternoon lunch at a friendly local place. Thanks, Gary and Joyce for the ride and the lunch.

The Illinois River at Hardin, Illinois.

The next day we walk early over the narrow, hilly land that separates the Illinois and Mississippi Rivers. After two weeks on the flat Katy Trail and then the ten-day rest at Gerry's, I have forgotten about hills. But we have some biggies today as we walk the peninsular Calhoun County. My legs are getting used to it all over again. In some places the road goes straight up and down hills with no attempt at leveling them much.

Larry's riverfront

We arrive at the Larry's riverside farm. He is the husband of a friend of Gerry's in Elsah. We spend the afternoon and evening talking with Larry and enjoying a good meal. We also walk through the grasses and plants in his bottom land along the Mississippi and out onto sand bars in the river.

But now we have to consider our options. Our walking is seldom straight forward. Earlier we intended to stay overnight with Larry. But now we realize that we can skip two idle days if Larry takes us north in the evening. Those idle days would be days waiting for opening lodging ahead. It feels good to move. We have just had ten days resting at Gerry's. So we thank Larry for his offer to stay and ask instead for a short ride.

In the end we stay at the Heartland Lodge near Nebo. It is a fine place for hunters and a beautiful place to stay, but it is far out in an ambiguous place south of Nebo. Last night Google told me it was where it wasn't. It does that sometimes.

First flight

Little towns sometimes only have a little history to latch onto. Nebo has its little piece of history. Cal Rodgers landed in Nebo in 1911 during the first flight across the US. A sign told us his flight took 49 days following the railroad. He landed 69 times (sometimes crash landed) and had a special train accompany him with mechanics, spare parts, and his wife.

When we arrive in Pittsfield with its five or six motels and hotels we find almost all rooms taken up for weddings, reunions, and a street fair. In the end we finally find a good room. A maple tree even stands outside the back window. It's time to begin to think about reserving ahead on weekends during the summer vacation time. We haven't done that yet this spring.

Walking north and west

Our route in southern Illinois is no longer east. It is basically north. WalkingEast is a misnomer here. In fact, today we are walking west on our walk east. We are heading back toward the Mississippi. We're trying to keep our days below 12 to 15 miles (19 to 24 kilometers). It's too hot to do otherwise.

Even with the effort, some days are longer. The very next day we walk 16+ miles (26+ kilometers) to Barry. When we arrive we find no place to eat. Everything is closed on an early Sunday afternoon. Good enough. When we get our motel room in the Ice House Inn, Petra cooks up a fine pasta and chardonnay dinner followed by ice cream from the Shell station across the street. Gas stations these days fill up more than cars.

The Ice House Inn is a remodeled ice house first built in 1843, a hundred years before I was born. In those days they cut ice from rivers in the winter and stored it in ice houses to use in the following summer. Since then this place has had several uses including a sheriff's office once. Many rooms have no windows, since in its original configuration windows would have presented a definite negative effect on the stored ice. We had a room *with* a window, two in fact. A bedroom without a window is not nice.

The next day we stay at the Kinderhook Lodge B&B mainly because we are not ready to make a long trek into Hannibal today. Some women are quilting. Petra talks with Rosemary and she takes some time from her quilting group to fix Petra's shirt. Petra is hoping the shirt lasts to Jerusalem. At least it may last through the summer now. Thanks, Rosemary.

At Kinderhook we watch a dozen or so deer grazing in a corn field. The owner, a farmer, says that around here farmers plan on losing about one tenth of their corn crop to the deer.

Mark Twain

The next day in Hannibal, we are immersed in Mark Twain. He's everywhere. Once again, a town uses its history to help finance its present.

We take a river boat excursion, just an hour ride down river and back. Talking with the captain, we muse that no more passenger boats ply the Mississippi taking people from town to town these days. He said, "The people don't want to take the time any more. Town-to-town boats haven't been around for several years now." People want to quickly see many places instead of enjoying a few leisurely.

2,000 mi. (3,240 km.) – July 16, 2009

In the next week we walk forward through Quincy, Illinois, Canton, Missouri, Warsaw, Illinois, Nauvoo, Illinois, Dallas, Illinois, and into Burlington, Iowa. We are making our way up the Mississippi. It is a marvelous walk through river-bottom land. Vast corn and beans fields spread out far to our left and right all day long one day, tree-lined state roads along the river enchant us next, and then more fields. The 70s (23-26 C.) blow in our faces pushed by a light wind. Our umbrellas protect us from the sharp rays of the sun.

Marty's back

My brother, Marty, drives down to meet us in Hannibal but his RV dies on the way. He arrives a couple days later in Quincy after replacing the fuel pump. He walks with us a bit but mostly we hang out together at night as we sleep in his RV a few nights.

Sunday morning we cross the Mississippi from Canton, Missouri, on a ferry. Marty, who takes up conversations with everyone, says to the guy working on the ferry, "This is my brother and his wife. They are walking across the country."

He answers, "They don't have anything better to do?" Then he tosses a cable to the side and goes back to his cabin. He must have had a long night last night.

A dragon fly poses along the road.

Marty and Petra on the Canton Ferry.

On the way to Burlington, Iowa, we have our first serious rain in a long time. It arrives as we enter Lomax, Illinois. We take poor shelter under a tree before continuing into town. Marty is scouting forward and finds The Pink Bar and Grill. We come in after him and have some of the top pancakes we eat on our pilgrimage. We spend a couple hours waiting for the rain to end as we talk with the owner about the world, running a bar, and our walk. In the end we ride the rest of the way with Marty. Rain lasts late into the evening. We'll stay in a B&B tonight and Marty in his RV.

An Illinois turtle stops to greet us as we walk by on a hot gravel road.

Marty heads home in the morning with a leak in the RV roof. We stay another day. As I rest in the afternoon I remember our time in India five years ago. I remember a picture that captures it so well—Petra sitting in a window, a crow in a tree, subdued light, a doll elephant hanging in the window. And then I remember the warm temperatures, the breezes, the noise of crows and horns, the smell of the exhaust, the people, and the joy. India is a destination after Jerusalem. But I digress. We still have a few miles to walk to Jerusalem.

Storm over our tent

We walk into the Keithsburg, Illinois, campground early, after 12.5 miles (20.3 kilometers) on a hot July day. The next stop is 16 miles (26 kilometers) farther. We are in no mood to walk 16 miles in the heat.

Many campers have the better spots along the Mississippi. We scratch to find a spot for the tent for tonight. We finally stake our claim on one. After we set the tent up, we head into the town to find a place to eat.

We choose a bar with a kitchen and sit a long time first eating and then just watching the people and the weather on TV. It's the weather that keeps us. The day is custom made for a classic mid-western thunderstorm: hot and humid with winds out of the southwest. On the radar, a bright, red line of storms stretches across eastern Iowa heading southeast toward us.

We have a beer and watch. The line comes closer. It gets dark outside. The line is now at the Mississippi at Davenport, Iowa, 45 miles (73 kilometers) north. It's time to go.

We head back to get our things in order. It's just after nine Saturday night. Parties are going strong with a lot of people noise. We prepare the carts for the rain, closing them up tight.

We get into the tent and zip it up as tight and wait.

In less than five minutes the leading winds hit the campground. Our tent flaps and holds tight. The rain comes, heavy, pouring rain. The wind blows. Lightning flashes. Thunder shatters the air. The tent shakes violently. I hold its support rods. We shake together. We are dry. The storm rampages.

In half an hour it is over. The campground is quiet except for a few raindrops still hitting the tent. We, Petra, the tent, and I, have sustained our first major storm well. Thank you, tent.

Night in the Slammer

A couple days before we arrive in Aledo, Illinois, Petra does her normal Google search for hotels for the next few nights. She finds one that looks promising and calls to see whether they have a room. They do. Then she announces "We are going to stay in the Slammer B&B in a couple days."

"The slammer? Do you know what that means?"

"No. What does it mean?" Petra's English vocabulary amazes me sometimes. She knows so many words. But "slammer" is not one yet.

"It's a slang word for 'jail.' We are going to stay in jail!"

Two nights later we stand in front of the Slammer Restaurant and The Great Escape B&B. A former sheriff of the late 50s, Dick, bought the jail after the county built a new one. Not wanting to have the building destroyed just because it was old, he converted it into a B&B and restaurant.

We befriend Dick and his wife, Jenny, at dinner. After eating and talking about the Slammer, they take us to another of his projects, an old train depot also destined to be destroyed when the railroad no longer needed it. He converted it into a meeting hall for the town complete with a considerable variety of railway memorabilia. A caboose and the drive wheels from a steam engine he's rebuilding stand outside the depot.

We finish the evening with a chocolate swirl ice cream cone from McDonalds since the regular ice cream shop is closed. This is Petra's first McDonalds ice cream. We drive around town until we are done with our cones, also a first for Petra ("We would never drive around and eat like that in Germany."). Petra likes the chocolate-vanilla swirl enough that we look for it in several McDonalds after that but never find it again.

The next day a cop stops near us as we rest in a country park around lunchtime. He comes over and before he has a chance to say anything, Petra says, "There are no babies.... We get this question all the time." We tell him our story and about the Slammer where we were last night. He knows Dick.

The cop says that one time a sheriff picked up someone in southern Illinois who was going to cross the state. They gave him a ride to the next county line. In the meantime they called that county and had a squad car waiting to pick the guy up. They repeated the call county after county all the way up the state giving the guy a ride until they let him out at the state line.

By the time we part, we have no fear of being given a ride to the county line, three miles (5 kilometers) away. He knows our plans and wishes us well.

Great River Road end

It's a week since Burlington and we are in East Moline for a rest day after six walking days. The whole Great River Road National By-way walk from Elsah to Moline took 20 days (18 walking days) and 300 miles (485 kilometers) – all save 37 mi (60 kilometers) on our feet. The walking days averaged 14.6 miles (23.7 kilometers) per day, much better that the 10 miles (16.2 kilometers) for the Katy Trail.

This national by-way and the smaller country roads along the Mississippi offered so much to see and digest. And the people continue to be the most inspiring.

We end another phase of the walk and tomorrow begin a new one, the Hennepin and I&M Canals across Illinois.

Hennepin Canal

The Hennepin Canal was once a hope and dream for a commercial connection between the Illinois and Mississippi Rivers. It never worked commercially. Built in the 1890s, its locks were smaller than those in the Illinois and Mississippi even then. So no one could use it with a fully outfitted barge from the bigger rivers, a classic case in poor planning. In 1929, its record year, only 30,161 tons (27,360 metric tons) were carried on the canal. That was only about 1/600th of its estimated capacity. Recreational boats used it till the middle of the 20th century when the locks were replaced with cement walls to maintain water level creating a long, narrow lake connected with several waterfalls.

Scenarios for New York

We have been thinking about the end of the American walk in New York in a few months. Facing a boat ride to Europe in winter has become heavy as we make our way east. Tears flow as Petra voices that perhaps we have to take an alternative to that slow container ship to Portugal.

We could take a much longer time to go to Portugal. We could fly to India to rest a couple months. This would be a fine ending for our trans-continental pilgrimage here and a good way to begin the second half in Europe next year. Besides, Petra can already smell that sweet incense and taste *masala dossa*, to say nothing of an Indian chai made by a road-side vendor.

Our time in India would be as much part of the pilgrimage to Jerusalem as our steps across this great land and all the rest starting in Lisbon. We are only taking a round-about way to get to Lisbon. Everything along the way is pilgrimage.

All this living in the future instead of the Now. We digress. Let's get back to Now.

We're not walking alone

Walking along the Hennepin Canal, we stay three days in Annawan. Petra calls ahead the second day to check out room availability a couple days ahead. The guy at the motel informs her that a walker, Jim, stayed at the motel the night before. He said Jim came from somewhere out east.

We're sitting in lawn chairs in front of the motel the third day in Annawan as a bearded smaller guy gets out of a car, picks up his backpack, and comes toward the motel.

"Hi, Jim. How is walking?"

He is surprised by Petra's question. "Just fine. Who are you?"

"We're also walking across the country. Have a chair and tell us about your walk."

Ok. But first I want to see your feet."

We show each other our feet. His have some nasty blisters. Ours have none.

"How do you keep from getting blisters?"

"We treat them well and give them a rest every two hours. We take off our shoes and socks and let our feet dry out while we sleep half an hour. Do you rest?"

"Not often."

"When was your last rest day?"

"Twenty one days ago."

"Twenty one days! Wow! We try to take off at least one day every seven. And when we are tired we take off more."

Jim is walking across the country in stages. Last year he walked three months from the East Coast to Ohio. This year he is tackling the second quarter. And as we finish this book in late 2011, he recently finished his walk at the mouth of the Columbia River in Oregon.

We have dinner together and exchange tales and information about what is ahead for each other as we move forward.

Petra and fellow walker Jim Bragg.

We tell him about our encounters with the police and he tells us about one of his:

> I wasn't very presentable that day. I had been walking long. After asking my name and where I was going he said, "Why don't you get in and I will give you a ride."
>
> "No thanks, I want to walk."
>
> "You don't understand, I am not asking you if you want a ride, I am telling you to get into the car. I am giving you a ride to the county line."

As we part the next morning we tell Jim to take better care of his feet. He and we know he isn't trying to set any speed record. We keep in contact and in the next days he takes off several days for his feet.

A raccoon

Though we see several dead raccoons along the road, we only see one alive. The next morning as we walk the Canal, we spot a raccoon lying beside the path. I walk by thinking he is dead. But then I feel he isn't. I walk back. We look closely. He raises his head, looks at us with sleepy eyes, and lies back down to resume his nap. He has no fear of us. He doesn't care about us.

We do see two other raccoons but they are in a painting in our motel room one night in Michigan. A Native American child stands in a path with two young raccoons beside her. They remind us of their sleepy, Illinois brother.

The Hennepin Canal proves to be a quiet and enjoyable walk. We laze along and are a little sad when we are done with it after only four walking days.

Petra needs shoes

In Bureau Junction Petra realizes she has misjudged how long her current shoes are going to last. We have around 125 miles (200 kilometers) to Woodstock where the next pair is sitting at my brother, Marty's. Her current pair was getting less and less comfortable as she walked last week. Finally we call Marty and ask him to bring them to us as we pass through Utica.

Several faces of the Hennepin Canal.

Pushing his luck

Petra is walking a hundred yards ahead as we approach Peru, Illinois, late in the afternoon. It is late on a hot day and we are tired.

As Petra nears a junkyard, the Auto Salvage Co., an older man comes out and walks over to meet her. "Where are you going?"

"We're walking across the US and then to Jerusalem."

"Then you must need a drink of cold water. Do you want to come in and have one?"

By then I have caught up and we walk into his already-closed office. He gives us some water and we talk about our walk. Then he asks, "Where are you staying tonight?"

"In one of the motels as you enter town."

"They are not nice; go up to I-80 and stay there. They're a lot better."

"But that's two miles out of our way and by the time we go up there tonight and return to the I&M Canal tomorrow, we will have walked a couple extra hours. We're too tired to go there tonight."

"I can give you a ride up there if you want."

"We would appreciate that."

He goes out in his yard of hundreds of stacked junk cars and rounds up his pickup. We put our carts in the back and head out.

As we drive north he reveals that he is 80 and that he dreams of visiting Europe and traveling around to several countries. "But I have to work ten more years first."

"Maybe you should do it now."

When we get to the motel, he helps us get out carts off the truck and then says, "Let's go inside and get you signed in."

"We can do that. Thanks for your help."

"No, I am going to pay for your room tonight."

We sign in and he pays with a hundred-dollar bill. He gives Petra the change and says, "Have a good dinner on me tonight."

We thank him and Petra adds, "I think you should seriously think of taking that trip to Europe now and not wait for another ten years."

Coffee and an eagle

Expecting another hot and humid day, we leave our motel early. We skip another plastic, motel breakfast in favor of finding something along the way.

We soon pass several stores and spot a Starbuck's Coffee. A strong coffee always is always good for me in the morning.

A guy in his thirties holds the door for us as we enter. But his eyes are on our flag, not on us. "You are from California?" He asks as he follows us through the door.

"We are." And we explain our pilgrimage, that we are following our dream of walking to Jerusalem from our front door.

As we talk, Ralph, as he introduced himself, brings us coffee and a roll. He continues, "Your trip is amazing. We really miss California. We're from there and would like to go back some time."

"Why don't you?"

"All the usual reasons. We have two children. The job market is tight. It's a big commitment. But it would sure be nice."

"But why don't you go?"

"I guess we are afraid to take that step?"

"How old are your kids?"

"Nine and eleven."

"That's young enough so they are not too connected with the other kids in school. It's a good time to do it. Sometimes you have to step off the cliff and believe that the Universe will provide what you need."

I pause and add, "Think of the eagle. Every time he steps off his nest to fly, he has to fall a couple seconds before he gains his flight speed. He has to believe it will happen. We have to learn to do that too." I do not know where that came from, only from the Universe. It was never in my mind before.

He sits thinking. We finish our coffee talking about other things. But as he leaves carrying coffees to his colleagues at work, he says, "Thanks for making me think. Thanks for pushing me a little." Later He sends us an email to tell us he and his family are preparing for their return to California.

I&M Canal

We walk down through Peru to the Illinois and Michigan (I&M) Canal and begin walking east towards Utica and Ottawa.

Utica

Utica and Ottawa, like Garden City, Kansas, are filled with encounters and a few eddies to boot. Our odyssey here starts with my brother, Marty, dropping off the new shoes in Utica, the town before Ottawa. With new shoes, Petra is walking smoothly again. It is surprising how when shoes break down, they do so quickly.

After Marty leaves around two, we decide to stay in Utica for the night. The hotel we check out is not our place. No one answers the door or the phone at the B&B we visit next.

We walk a few doors down the street and stop in the Peru Foothills Co-op to see whether they have a suggestion for lodging. Gerald, the owner, offers us cookies and good conversation. We talk long with him and his friend, Dr. John Firehawk, a Native American homeopathic doctor. In the end Dr. Firehawk gives Petra healing flower extract and we all say a prayer together for our journey.

Our driver, Dr. Firehawk, Petra, and Gerald in the Foothills Co-op.

Marcia's B&B

Gerald calls several places as the afternoon passes and we talk. Finally after a few tries, he connects with Marcia's B&B east of Ottawa. She has a room. A guy, part of our conversation group that afternoon, drives us to Marcia's, 14.5 miles (23.5 kilometers) ahead.

We have a restful evening talking with Marcia and a good night's sleep. The next morning fellow guests at Marcia's B&B give us a ride back to Utica so we can continue our walk where we stopped the afternoon before.

Walking in the rain

As we begin walking, rain begins falling. We have a short 10.5 miles (17 kilometers). The rain persists, sometimes coming down heavily. Our umbrellas keep our tops dry but by the time we get to Ottawa, our feet are burning. Our wet shoes are beginning to blister our feet.

We have an early dinner and stop at a bar for a wine before calling Marcia to pick us up to stay at her B&B again. She is in town. We are not ready to walk another hour and a half to her place.

Alfie

The next day Alfie, a local freelance reporter whom we met in the bar the night before, comes out to the B&B to interview us. He also invites Ottawa's mayor to join us. We stand together with the mayor and Marcia for a picture that finds its way into the ultimate flowing, flowery India-style article. We enjoy the interview and the write-up.

The interview lasts long and prevents us from making our planned destination once we get started. Instead we walk only 5.5 miles (8.9 kilometers) to a B&B in Wedron. The next potential stop is too far down the road.

Swimming

Before we leave in the morning Marcia invites us to swim in a near-by swimming hole if we stop early, so we call her and spend the afternoon floating in a gravel pit lake in Sheridan. It's a lazy, crazy, hazy day in summer. We enjoy it.

As we leave the lake, Petra says she doesn't want to stay in the new B&B. She doesn't feel good in it. She goes back to Marcia's B&B and stays for the night while I stay in Wedron. This is the first night of our walk that we sleep in separate locations.

The next day I start walking alone. After an hour or so Marcia drops Petra off along the road to join me. We walk to a campground north of Sheridan in a log cabin on the RV campground. But we see Marcia once again. Petra left a blouse at the B&B and Marcia brings it to her along with some pie for all of us.

We are indeed in an eddy here: Utica, Ottawa, Utica, Ottawa, Wedron, Sheridan, Ottawa, Sheridan, and then Marcia returns again. Thanks to everyone who made this an enjoyable three days.

Petra's hat disappears

Someone lifts Petra's blue hat during our time here. She discovers it as we are leaving. Thinking it might have blown off the cart yesterday, we search the road back a couple miles and the mile into the campground and can't find it. It's gone. Who would want a hat filled with sweat from walking six months

across the U.S.? We come back later with the car when we are staying a couple weeks in Woodstock and search farther. It's gone. She loved that blue cowboy hat. A friend gave it to her as a gift and she wore it constantly.

Walk with our feet?

A few miles down the road a young teenage girl came toward us, "Did you see a woman walking her dog?"

"No. Is she lost?"

"No, she's out walking the dog. She's my mom. What are you doing?"

"We're walking from California to Jerusalem."

"Do you walk with your feet?"

"Yes, we have walked here from California."

"I didn't know you could do that."

"You can and we have."

We leave her with an expanded world and new possibilities.

89 and 17 kids

Later the same day we walk past a Road-Closed sign deciding to see whether we can get through with our carts. In a mile and a half we come on a tree-trimming crew and get by easily. We strike up a conversation with a woman who has stopped to talk with one of the crew. She invites us to stop at her mom's place a couple miles down the road. We stop and visit and have iced tea with her 89-year-old mother who had 17 kids, many who are in the room with us. She is spry and alert, but dying of cancer.

Mike on the Fox River Trail near Aurora, Illinois.

We are in my home area now. In the next few days we make our way north along the Fox River. We walk through Aurora, where I lived in the late 80s and early '90s.

While staying in Aurora overnight, we go to the Roundhouse Restaurant, a converted Burlington Northern Railway round house. The waitress asks what brings us to Aurora and what are we doing, we say we have walked from California and are walking to Jerusalem.

She comes back from getting our drinks and asks, "This 'walking,' is it a different kind of driving?" We couldn't believe our ears, but that is exactly what she said. She had no idea of walking so far.

Petra with the foxes on the Fox River Bridge in St. Charles, Illinois.

As we enter suburban Chicago, the number of walkers increases.

In St. Charles an enthusiastic Gujarati Indian motel clerk hooks Petra up with another German woman who is in town working for an American company. She comes over and we all talk about our walk and the woman's experiences in the American work place and her problems with getting even a cell phone without a Social Security number.

The next day we stop in Elgin for a couple nights with friends Don and Louise Cerny. Thanks for everything. We enjoyed our time with you.

Woodstock

We arrive in Woodstock 16 August. My brother Marty, another brother Cork and his wife Diane, my Aunt Annie, along with cousins and nieces and nephews live in Woodstock. We borrow Marty's car to move around with and we stay with Cork and Diane. We visit many including Aunt Annie, the surviving member of my mother's generation. She still works as a seamstress for many in town. Thanks everyone, for everything, especially the encouragement.

We enjoy 17 relaxing days off. One night several classmates from high school get together and have a dinner for us to celebrate our arrival on foot. We get to know each other again after as many as 49 years. Classmate Wally and his wife Fran have us over for the dinner one night. Thanks, everyone.

Petra needs a hat so it is mine as we leave Woodstock.

Fall on the Erie Canal.

FALL 2009

Wisconsin

We are back on the road September 2nd, the beginning of meteorological fall. We came north to get out of the heat of Missouri but now heat is no longer a factor. We worry more about snow than heat in the coming months.

Bull Valley bull

Our final encounter with the law comes just a few miles from Woodstock as we get back on the road. The up-scale and snooty village of Bull Valley has a well-known police force with a reputation of having little to do besides harass people passing through their community. There is a story that they once gave a guy a ticket for going one mile an hour over the speed limit. He protested. The judge sided with him and reprimanded the police for being too vigorous in enforcing the speed limits.

I tell Petra as we enter the village that a cop will stop us. Sure enough, within a mile one pulls up and asks for our IDs. He actually calls them in. No other cop has done that, even the guy who gave us a warning ticket in Colorado.

"What do you have in those carts? Someone called in and said two suspicious people are on the road pushing carts."

"It's our baggage."

He asks to see inside. We show him. He is satisfied, gives us back our IDs, and lets us go.

With this last cop, we leave all law-enforcement officers behind. No more stopped us for the rest of the pilgrimage.

Aunt Annie and Marty join us for late afternoon dinner in McHenry. After all, our motel is only a bit over ten miles from where we started. They can do that in half an hour by car.

When we leave the motel in Richmond, Illinois, two days later, the owner gives us some money and tells us, "When you get to Jerusalem, put this in a poor box or in the Wall."

Tom walks with us

As we head toward Milwaukee, friend Tom Trausch, an artist and the host of the classmate party while we were in Woodstock, walks six miles (10 kilometers) with us on the third day. It is a joyful break to meet and walk with a friend a few hours on the path. We have an open invitation on WalkingEast for anyone to walk with us at any time but few have done so.

Petra walking a bicycle path in Wisconsin.

A visit with Jim

While in Franklin, Wisconsin, I send an email to our fellow walker, Jim Brag (p. 134), to update him and see where he is. We get an email right back. He is done walking for this year and is just up the road at one of his children's home. Do we want to come up and join them for a meal and get-together? We do. He comes and picks us up and we celebrate his family gathering and how far we have all walked already.

Soon we are in Milwaukee getting on a ferry to cross Lake Michigan. It takes us a couple smooth hours to Muskegon, Michigan.

Michigan

We take another break as we arrive in Michigan. Friend Mike Beres takes us several miles north to his home on Gun Lake south of Ludington. We spend a pleasant couple days lazing around with him and his wife Karen. They return us to Muskegon where we take up the walk again. Thanks Mike and Karen.

2,500 mi. (4,050 km.) – September 2, 2009

We walk three bike paths and many small back country roads across Michigan. We seldom contend with heavy traffic. It rains a few days, but we enjoy mostly pleasant fall weather.

Fall hay in Michigan.

Our story precedes us

Several newspapers interview us in Michigan, one by phone. In Six Lakes in the middle of the state, a published interview arrives before we do. We're walking down a brushy road looking for a place to rest around noon. Finally, there's a campground. We walk in and ask if we can rest under one of their trees for half an hour.

"Are you the ones walking to Jerusalem?"

"Yes, how did you know?"

"You're in the paper."

We were interviewed in Howard City a couple days earlier. The church group having a picnic here today invites us to join them. We eat well, tell them our story, talk about their stories, and then take that rest under the tree. Thanks, people. We enjoyed our time with you.

Later in the day someone yells out as we pass, "Are you the walkers?"

Blueberry pancakes

In Merrill we go into a restaurant for pancakes. It is so smoky that we retreat to the sidewalk. But what pancakes! They were well worth sitting on the hard bench to eat them. They're up there with the best blueberry pancakes on our two-year pilgrimage.

A Michigan deer.

Who's awesome?

When we tell people we meet about our ongoing pilgrimage across the country, they often respond with "Awesome," "Great," "Amazing," "Remarkable," or some similar superlative. But many we meet deserve those words much more than we who are only walking 14+ miles (23+ kilometers) a day.

For example, take Angie's story. We walk into the Pleasant Soul Café in the small town of Attica, Michigan. Two years ago Angie, a single mother of 9- and 10-year-old children (or was it 10 and 11?), started this up-scale coffee and sandwich shop in a rather small town, not in a populous suburb. Few thought her efforts were wise. But it was her dream. She set her dream in motion without knowing whether it could work. She now opens at five every morning and works all day and all year with little time off. She has time with her kids but a lot less than she would like. She is proud of the business she has established, the faithful customers she has, and the work she has done to make the business a going enterprise. She bubbles over with enthusiasm under that load. And beside all that, the food is great.

Now here is someone you can call "Awesome," "Amazing," and "Remarkable." And we have met many more like Angie. The country is full of Angies doing their day-in and day-out work. They are living their dream enthusiastically. Just because we have chosen to walk every day for a couple years doesn't put us in a special class. Look around. You'll find many Angies. Are you one of them?

Angie, Laura, and Petra at the Pleasant Soul café.

When we get to Port Huron, Michigan, we have a repair job. The support brace on of Petra's cart breaks coming into town. A clerk in a hardware store helps us select a hose and hose clamps to repair it.

We sit in the Edison Hotel in Port Huron, Michigan, for a couple days wondering how to cross the bridge into Canada. The word is we cannot walk it. I am also nervous about crossing borders.

Canada

Finally we begin to walk over the bridge. An official stops us at the tollgate. "What do you want here?" "To Walk across." "You can't." But he takes us to the office and calls a Michigan Department of Transportation pickup to give us a ride to the Canadian side. Our driver is excited about our story and Canadian customs quickly pass us into their country.

The bridge from Port Huron, Michigan into Sarnia, Ontario (on right).

The tourist bureau at the end of the bridge fills us in with a sleeping place; our internet and phone research found nothing for 25 miles (41 kilometers). With the new place we have an easy 15 miles (25 kilometers) to begin our walk straight east across southern Ontario. We are set to go international. We're planning on visiting Ontario's versions of London, Paris, and Woodstock.

Six-dollar beer!

Leaving the tourist bureau we enter the city of Sarnia. It's different from the U.S. The streets are smaller and there are a lot more small stores. And the beer is $6 a glass! That day the Canadian dollar was actually worth a little more than the American dollar. As long as I can remember, it has been between $0.65 and $0.70 American for a Canadian dollar. Petra buys fresh baked bread, olives, and Italian sausage from a little, European-style, neighborhood store, something we seldom see in the U.S.

When we try to call the U.S. that night we discover our unlimited minutes Verizon cell phone is only "unlimited" in the U.S. We have to use our 800-number international calling card for reasonable-rate calls as long as we are in Canada.

We stay near Wyoming, Ontario, the second night. Sue, the owner of the remodeled Maefield Horse Farm Lodge makes us a fine dinner since we have no car to go out to eat. The bedroom is done in light wood, one of the more pleasant places we stay on our walk. Our stay with Sue is a wonderful introduction to Canadian B&Bs. Thanks for everything, Sue, including the lunch package the next day.

The wind is back

It rains all night in Wyoming. As we leave in the morning, the rain has stopped but the cold wind blows 45 mph (75 kph) against our backs. We are wrapped up with our scarfs and sweaters. We don't have to push the carts; we hold them back. We are the ones being pushed. We have our share of cold wind, drizzle, and some heavy rain as we walk western Ontario. In Canada we walk mostly back roads in the west and bike trails in the east.

The night after Wyoming we enjoy another good evening with supper and good conversation, this time in the House of Angles B&B in Watford, Ontario. Marilyn and Leroy open their B&B for us because we are walking. The B&B has been closed for some time because of illness. The next morning, they say they think they are now ready to open to others. Thanks Marilyn and Leroy. I'm glad we influenced you to consider reopening. You have a nice place.

What a change the next night! We stay in an upscale hotel with an invisible staff. We pay the bartender in the attached bar-restaurant and see no one otherwise associated with the hotel. It is a good night though a bit on the monastery side.

What's the day like?

You have been reading so far in this book about the places we are staying with little about is happening in between the stops. After all, this is a pilgrimage *walk*. There must be something to say about the hours we walk every day. Well there is but in western Canada where it's flat, the walk changes little from day to day. We walk country roads past corn and bean fields and cattle. Sometimes there are horses. The grains are mostly mature but little is harvested. There's been too much rain. It's too wet to harvest. They have to wait till later in the fall to harvest after everything dries out more. Our back and front yards change many times a day, but the same things are in them—grain, farms, cattle, and flat country fields and roads.

In London we stay in the Guest House on the Mound, a converted hill-top convent that serves as a long-term stop for family members of people in the nearby hospital. We rest an extra day and enjoy cooking our own soup in a somewhat institutional kitchen.

Happy Thanksgiving

October 12, Columbus Day in the U.S., is Canadian Thanksgiving Day. The harvests come in earlier in Canada so an earlier Thanksgiving is appropriate. The holiday makes little difference in our lives; we walk as always.

How fast is too fast?

How fast do we want to do this pilgrimage? Back in Paso Robles we decided to walk. That gives us a chance to see many things close up and still make progress forward.

Cyclists we met often ask why we don't cycle. We can cover a lot more territory in less time. But cycling is clearly too fast. We would miss so much at their speed. And we can never turn around and cycle forward while looking backward. At least *we* can't; we aren't acrobatics. On a cycle you can't stop on a dime and look at something. A cycle brings with it inertia: when you are moving at a certain speed, inertia alone is enough to keep you from stopping when you would stop walking. To see that something you pass, you have to stop and go back to look at it.

We have opted for walking's slower speed. The walk is the destination. When you are already at the destination, there's no need to hurry to get somewhere you are not. Our environment changes at least every hour. Every hour we have a new back yard to look at and enjoy. So much passes us every day.

How can we ever begin to really look at it all even walking? One morning in southern Ontario we are walking with a soybean field in our "yard" to the left. I watch as the rows pass one, two, three, four.... They pass quickly one after another. I notice some weeds between the plants. *What are they? What do the individual plants look like? What insects and spiders are crawling on the plants? What is the soil like? Are rabbits chewing on the plants?* I don't have time to explore all that. We have a town we want to get to this afternoon. We can't stop to look at such detail to say nothing of whatever is going on to the right and in front and behind us. And we are on our feet, not on a bicycle, let alone a motorcycle or a car. Is walking still too fast? It is this morning.

So is the destination still the walk? That field? Or is it the town we are going to that evening? To be correct, it's both. Like in life, something has to be sacrificed as we go down the road. We cannot do everything. This afternoon I have to be satisfied with recognizing the detail I am not seeing. Other times we stop and look, sacrificing the next destination for a while. We arrive, just later than planned.

Martha

We spend an evening at Martha's Simple Pleasures B&B in the country outside Thamesford. Martha lives alone with three nearby sons who run the large farm around her. Originally from the Netherlands, instead of driving us to a restaurant, Martha invites us to a wonderful dinner. We have a great time sharing stories. After her husband died, Martha opened the B&B, a long-time dream. Two of her sons stop in to visit while we are there.

Martha's breakfast the next day has a wonderful Dutch touch. As we are ready to leave, Martha will not take payment for the dinner, for the breakfast, or for our night's lodging for that matter. And she becomes one of our most loyal followers, checking out WalkingEast.com, our web journal, almost daily and emailing encouragement often. Thanks so much for everything Martha.

Interview on the road

Martha gives us a lunch package as we leave in the morning. She calls the newspaper after we leave. In mid-morning reporters from the Woodstock (Ontario) Sentinel Review interview us as we walk along a rolling back road to Woodstock. The article's web version includes a video of us; the only video of us on the whole pilgrimage. See the Press Articles on page 343 for their web page address.

Winter already?

As we leave Woodstock, Ontario, 14 October, we get our first taste of winter—*snow*. I know, it's only a few, fluffy flakes flying in the wind but it *is* snow and it *is* accompanied by a heavy, 40-degree (5-C.) wind blowing 25 mph (40 kph) directly in our faces. Not since the early spring has the wind blown so uncomfortably.

In Paris, we stay in a good B&B run by an Englishman. Now we begin to walk Ontario's bicycle trails. There were marked bike trails earlier, but they were just on normal car roads. Now we have dedicated bike paths and former railroad rights-of-way, some beautifully tree-lined protecting us from the sun when it is hot. A fine path wanders around Brantford though it adds a few miles to what our walk would be on the roads through town.

Big is in the small

One day we stay in the Bear's Inn in Ohsweken on the Six Nations of the Grand Indian Reservation. There we meet a shaman from the Netherlands here to visit with tribal elders. We drink coffee. We talk about our pilgrimage and how sometimes we forget why we are on the walk. Today Petra sees no importance in a walk that involves nothing world changing. The shaman says, "The big things happen because of the small things. Meeting people and talking and sharing life and passion and love stories, all these are small things but we never know what kind of seed we are sewing. The world changes with the small things."

Delightful energy

Our friend Sue Kenney picks us up in Hamilton. We met her at the Pilgrims gathering in Albuquerque in March (p. 49). Sue is a pilgrimage lecturer, teacher, author, and guide with a book on the Camino de Santiago.

Sue takes us to her sister's in Grimsby where we stay for the night with her and her sister's three almost-13-year-old triplet daughters, Jacqueline, Leslie, and Rebecca. The energy level is amazing. We have a wonderful time.

The next morning Sue returns us to near where she picked us up the day before and we walk back to Grimsby without carts. We follow the Waterfront Trail along Lake Ontario for a couple miles. Then the trail puts us next to a noisy freeway in the middle of a lot of home construction and dust. We tire of it quickly, leave the trail, and go inland to follow a much more comfortable county road. Not all walking trails along the way are the best places to walk.

We spend another high-energy evening with the triplets, Sue, and her sister Pat. Thanks so much, ladies, for a most pleasant stop on our way to Jerusalem.

Leslie, Rebecca, Jacquelyn, Sue, and Petra, a great quintet.

Lost on a country road the next afternoon, we meet Ted driving his tractor as he crosses an intersection in front of us. He sets us straight. Later he calls and invites us to evening dinner. We choose to not accept his invitation. We haven't found a place to stay yet and it is already after six. Sometimes, like in "normal" life, you have to say, "No," even when you would much rather say, "Yes." It could have been an interesting visit with Ted and his family.

3,000 mi. (4,860 km.) – October 21, 2009

Before entering Jordan, Ontario, we face the most dangerous half mile (one kilometer) of our walk, anywhere. We walk the tightest shoulder of the walk in North America. A guard rail holds us close to a narrow road filled with cars and trucks. Several times we choose to step over the railing rather than stand next to the road. We get through in one piece but our stress level is high when we finish.

What's a hamburger?

After finding a B&B in Jordan we set out to find dinner. Our choices are few. We end up in a bar with sandwiches. The place is pricier than normal. I chose a hamburger. As I begin to eat the "hamburger," it tastes more like meatloaf than hamburger. I call the waitress' attention to it. "Yes, we have special ingredients in it. That is our trademark sandwich."

"But it isn't hamburger. The menu says 'Hamburger.' This is meatloaf with bread and all those other things in it."

"It's our hamburger." Nothing more. No apologies, No offer to substitute it with something else if I don't like it. You order it. You eat. You pay for it.

In the U. S. when you order a hamburger, you get a hamburger — with no additives. You order a meatloaf sandwich when you want a meatloaf sandwich. Back at our B&B our host says that most restaurants in the area have their own special mixtures they put in their "hamburgers" and they are proud of them.

Canadian restaurants as a rule are quite different from their U. S. counterparts. Besides not offering to substitute something else if you get what you're not expecting, they seldom show interest when you are not satisfied. Their portions also are often smaller, sometimes much smaller, than U. S. portions; and they cost more.

We stay three days at the Old Port B&B in Port Dalhousie to regroup and sit out rain. The owner's homemade granola is just about the best granola we eat in North America.

A bridge rises to let a boat through on the Welland Canal, the shipping connection between Lakes Erie, and Ontario.

The Red Coat Inn in Queenston offers us dinner in addition to the normal B&B breakfast. We enjoy our stay. Queenston's claim to fame is that British, Canadians, and Mohawks held off an American invasion force here during the War of 1812.

The Falls

The American (closer) and Canadian Niagara Falls.

The next day we walk the last 13 miles (21 kilometers) to Niagara Falls ("The Falls" to those around here) through bright autumn reds, oranges, and yellows in brilliant sun.

The day can't be more beautiful. In Niagara Falls, Ontario, we visit all the views of the falls and are duly impressed as everyone always is by the size of the falls and the volume of water falling over them. I can't really describe them. Petra says, "Try."

So here goes. Huge amounts of water pour over Niagara Falls' rock walls. Here are some numbers with comparisons:

- 20% of world's fresh water is in the great lakes and most of it flows over the Niagara Falls.
- The American falls are in the U.S. and a rather straight wall visible best from the Canadian side. They are:
  - 176 feet (54 meters) high – almost 60 yards on an American football field or the width of a soccer field.
  - 1,060 feet (335 meters) long – one fifth of a mile (1/3 kilometer), the distance thunder, or any other sound for that matter, travels in a second.
  - 150,000 gallons (570,000 liters) of water flows over them every second – how do you compare this to something commonly known to people?

The American Falls.

The brink of the Canadian Falls.

- The Canadian Falls, also known as the Horseshoe Falls because of their crescent shape, are 2/3rds in Canada and 1/3rd in the U.S. They are also best viewed from Niagara Falls, Canada. They are:
  - o 167 feet (51 meters) high – 55 yards on an American football field and a little less than the width of a soccer field.
  - o 2,600 feet (790 meters) long – almost half a mile (0.79 kilometer) long.
  - o 600,000 gallons (2,270,000 liters) of water flows over them every second.

So they are big. And the water keeps rolling over in a constant jet-engine roar and rain-drenching spray minute after minute, hour after hour, week after week, year after year, century after century.

Petra, I don't know that the numbers help. Everyone still has to visit Niagara Falls to even begin to experience and feel them.

Back in the States

We walk over the bridge into Niagara Falls, New York, and pass through customs in minutes. The officer asks us what we have in our carts and passes us almost before we can say, "Our everyday things."

We take a few pictures but don't tarry long in the city. We head for the post office to pick up Petra's shoes.

No shoes

Petra is supposed to have a pair of shoes waiting for her in the post office in Niagara Falls. The Internet shoe outlet normally ships them free by UPS. That doesn't work with the post office; it has to arrive via normal mail (USPS). Petra asks the outlet to send it USPS, and pays extra for it. When we arrive to pick up the shoes, they are not at the post office. After several calls, she learns that they sent the shoes by UPS anyway and the post office refused them. The shoes went back to the outlet. Petra tells the Internet store about our walk and why we can't wait a long time for the shoes. The outlet air freights them overnight. Petra has them at our motel at nine thirty the next morning. Thanks for covering your mistake so well.

Two gifts

November is beginning to show its dreary self. Heavy rains meet us as we head out of Niagara Falls this morning. We only get to the edge of town before stopping at a Holiday Inn. When Mandy and Christine, the managers, hear our story, they offer us a reduced rate. When we leave the next morning they charge us nothing. As we walk forward, they call the Lockport Holiday Inn in the next town and set us up for an invitation from Gloria, the manager there, for another free night. Two free nights in a row! That's a fine welcome back to the States. Thanks, ladies.

The Erie Canal

Sunshine and bright yellows, reds, and oranges accompany us along the smooth Erie Canal tow path. But the fall colors are near to their end. Each rain strips more leaves from the trees.

The first boat we see on the Erie Canal. Petra protects herself from the constant drizzle as we walk along the canal tow path.

Railway Museum

Rain and wind hold us an extra day in Medina a few days later. We take the opportunity to visit a huge model railroad layout at the Medina Railway Museum. We were also interviewed by the Batavia (New York) News. We also enjoy some wonderful Italian food at a local restaurant and fine conversations with Pat and Bob who run the Garden View B&B where we stay.

The Erie Canal is an early commercial highway from the east to the Great Lakes. It's still used by recreational and a few commercial boats. Villages and towns sit picturesquely along its banks. By the end of our first week, only a few lonesome bright yellow maples are left with leaves. Trees and houses reflect in the often mirror smooth water of the canal.

The DeWitt Clinton, a tiny part of a huge model railroad layout in Medina, New York.

We walk eastward along the tow path, the path the donkeys and horses used to pull the barges up and down the canal. In Rochester, we make a long detour as the canal crosses the Genesee River. There is no aqueduct. The engineers designed the crossing allowing the canal water level to fluctuate with the river's level. The locks on each side take up the differences.

Erik and Susanne

Just east of Rochester we spend two evenings with my nephew, Erik and his wife Susanne in Penfield. It is good to get to know Erik again after not seeing him for many years.

Dinner in Palmyra

As we enter the Canal Town B&B in Palmyra, Barbara, the owner, asks us, "We would like to invite you to dinner with us tonight. Would you consider it?" "We would." We have a wonderful dinner including many samplings of husband Bob's collection of local wines. Thanks, Barbara and Bob.

Scrunching east

The next morning we walk across the bridge to the gravel tow path. Scrunch, scrunch, scrunch, scrunch, scrunch, scrunch, step after step we begin anew our walk, one step at a time. Scrunch, scrunch, scrunch, scrunch, scrunch, scrunch, the now-bare trees play with the warming sun. A little less shade would be more comfortable. Scrunch, scrunch, scrunch, scrunch, scrunch, scrunch, trees and houses on the far side of the canal mirror upside-down in the deep blue water. Scrunch, scrunch, scrunch, scrunch, scrunch, scrunch, ten minutes pass, fifteen, and then an hour. Scrunch, scrunch, scrunch, scrunch, scrunch, scrunch, birds twitter, a flock of crows caw, a hawk screeches high above. Scrunch, scrunch, scrunch, scrunch, scrunch, scrunch, another hour passes and we find a place to lie in the grass under a tree to sleep fifteen minutes. Scrunch, scrunch, scrunch, scrunch, scrunch, scrunch, we are back on the path. Scrunch, scrunch, scrunch, scrunch, scrunch, scrunch, a pontoon boat with a box house for a cabin put-puts by. Scrunch, scrunch, scrunch, scrunch, scrunch, scrunch, red, yellow, blue, purple, and orange flowers line our path. Though fall is hard on us, the plants are still preparing to make seed for the next season. Scrunch, scrunch, scrunch, scrunch, scrunch, scrunch, we walk forward in 30-inch (75-centimer) steps until they add up to 15 miles (24 kilometers) and we are another day closer to Jerusalem.

In Clyde we knock on the door of the 42-room, Erie Mansion Bed and Breakfast. Owner Mark, bedecked in long, heavy overcoat and a broad-brimmed leather hat, opens our conversation with, "You won't find your run-of-the-mill B&B sissy foo foo here." We don't.

After a quarter of an hour of chit-chat he takes us on a tour of the house. A Harley Chopper and huge leather couches sit in the TV room. Other motorcycles and an antique high-wheel bicycle grace the tall, dark halls. The Honeymoon Suite includes a canopied, double-king-sized bed. Our original bedroom is decorated with "tasteful erotic art," as his web site says. But the room he upgrades us to, the Erie ("Eerie" perhaps is better) Room, is the best of all. Alligator skulls and skins sit on shelves and hang on the walls. The skulls of a lion and a couple dozen other animals adorn shelves and chests throughout the three-room suite. A 24-foot snake skin stretches around one wall above three windows.

Erie Mansion

The Erie Manson in Clyde, New York.

As Mark shows us around, he points out a well-supplied liquor cabinet in a billiards room and tells us he can neither sell nor offer us a drink at the B&B. It is against his license but "If you happen to try something from a bottle and I don't see you, there's not much I can do about it." After he checks us in, he takes us to a local bar for a beer in his personal yard-high beer glasses.

Among his previous activities, Mark ran a limousine service in New York City. Pictures of many rich and famous hang in the upstairs halls. But after running the business for several years, it was time for something new. The Erie Mansion is the answer to his dreams.

We sleep in a huge, four-post bed with the skulls. We really enjoy our stay and have a peaceful sleep. The ghost, who they say haunts the stairs where he hung himself years ago, never appears.

Petra and Mark with Mark's unusual beer glasses.

Canal law

Walking along the canal one day, we pass a mural on a building wall with pictures of canal traffic and "Canal Law #169: Speed and meeting of boats and preference in Passing." It said:

> "No float shall move in any canal faster than at the rate of four miles an hour [6.5 kph] without the permission in writing from superintendent of public works: except that upon any of the enlarged canals, a boat may move at a rate of speed not exceeding six miles an hour [9.7 kph], to be fixed by the superintendent of public works.
>
> The master of a float meeting another float, shall turn to the right, so as to be wholly on the right side of the center of the canal.
>
> When a boat used chiefly for the conveyance of persons overtakes any other float not used chiefly for that purpose, the master of the latter shall give up to the former every practicable facility for passing and if necessary shall stop until the former has fully passed.
>
> Every master or boatman violating any provision at this section shall for each offence forfeit to the state the sum of ten dollars."

Bill and Jeanette

A couple days later we meet Bill and Tom Williams, locals out for a bicycle ride to the next town for a lunch. Bill ("Willy Willy" as his brother calls him) invites us to stay with him and his wife for the evening.

Bill and Tom Williams with us along the canal.

They go off to their lunch as we continue walking east. When they catch up with us later in the afternoon Bill loads us into Tom's van and takes us to his home in Cicero, ten miles (16 kilometers) north of the canal.

During our conversations at dinner, Bill and Jeanette mention they'd like to visit Europe but don't like to fly. We suggest a container ship. "You can go to Hamburg or Valencia from New York in nine days or so for a lot less than on a cruise ship. Just type 'freighter travel' into Google." We tell them about our container ship voyage from Italy to India five years earlier. They are avid boaters who even have boated the entire Erie Canal. Our conversation leaves them with the glassy eyes of kids on Christmas Eve waiting for Santa as they think about taking a freighter to Europe. Thanks Bill and Jeanette.

Boxing Hall of Fame

In Canastota, New York, the Boxing Hall of Fame is across from the motel. It is not on our list of stops. We don't even know it exists. The Days Inn manager where we stay not only picks up the tab for the motel stay but also gives us tickets to the Hall of Fame telling us it is worth a visit. After a couple hours we agree. We even touch the ring from Madison Square Garden where Ali and Frazer fought in March, 1971. The visit brings back memories from deep within of the early

'50s and the Gillette Cavalcade of Sports. I remember the jingle with the bell that played between each round as my father religiously watched each Wednesday evening. "…you'll look sharp (ding), you'll feel sharp (ding), you'll be sharp (ding) with the quickest, slickest shave of all."

In Verona at the Inn at the Touchstone, our latest brush with a casino, we play $10.50 for over three hours on the penny slot machines. It's a bit like 25 mindless solitaire games on the computer, not exactly intellectual, but needed at times to let the mind spin free.

Snow?

As the days go by I worry more and more about snow. After all, it is mid-November and this is upstate New York. People along the way are saying that this November's weather is unusual, that it should be raining, cold, or snowing by this time of the year with temps in the 40s instead of 50s. The year before it started snowing in October and that snow didn't leave till the end of the winter. I don't look forward to walking along icy, snowy roads. The thought doesn't bother Petra, "We can wait for a few days if we have to just like we have waited for other weather, like in Truchas and Cimarron." In the end, snow is never an issue.

One day we walk up from the canal bottom land and cross over the hills to cut off a big loop in the canal route. It is great seeing a long distance again. Except for a short route near Clyde a week ago we have walked low ground and flat land since Illinois in mid-July. Today we are on hilltops. We can again see several miles both north and south.

A fatal breakdown?

Petra's doll-buggy, gift-of-the-desert, baggage cart breaks both supporting frame bars and collapses as we approach the Hazelnut Farm B&B in Fort Plain. Parts have been breaking again and again since Kansas. We have repaired it many times. Now it is broken in two. This is the end for me. "It is really done. It's time to leave it, to get something else."

"No, I have had it all this time. I'm not going to abandon it. I am going to fix it. Do you give up a partner just because he gets very ill or breaks both legs? I can't just leave it."

The "fatal break" that wasn't.

"Aagh!" is all I can manage to that logic.

Owner Art at the Hazelnut Farm B&B is also a farmer and tinkerer. When we show him our problem, he goes to his tool shed and cuts the heads off a couple bolts. We use them as interior dowels in the collapsed frame and secure them with hose clamps. A stretched bungee cord finishes the job, pulling the wheels together and raising the cart. That done, Art and Susan loan us their truck to drive into town for supper. Thanks.

The Hudson River

At Albany we turn south and go down the Hudson River on the final leg of the walk across America. We are walking in 2009, the 400th anniversary of Henry Hudson's exploration of the river.

Thanksgiving

We celebrated Thanksgiving more than a month ago in Canada. Now on our American Thanksgiving we find ourselves in Hudson, New York, in a B&B with little food in our bags and no restaurant open this evening. We ask and walk around looking but find none open. In the end we have pretzels and a couple beers instead of turkey for our 2009 Thanksgiving dinner. But that doesn't stop us from thanking everyone who has been part of our odyssey and quest the previous ten months. Thanks everyone. Thanks, Universe.

Petra's cart looks a bit like new on the road a week later.

As we walk through Saugerties we are only nine miles (15 kilometers) from (Rock Concert) Woodstock, New York. We don't even consider walking nine miles off the path.

My left foot has been bothering me a bit too much. I think the last shoes did some damage. But now to make it worse, I step into a hole on the way back from a trip to the side of the road and really stretch it badly. I am in a lot of pain. Several ice packs, a massage, and a new set of inserts later and it feels on the mend. But that foot bothers me for at least the next nine months. It develops a large "thwap" as I walk. Petra can tell whenever I am coming.

The road to Poughkeepsie is a copper, zinc, and nickel mine. In a few miles we find $1.18 in coins along the road (33 cents, 3 nickels, 2 dimes, and 2 quarters). We pick up two cents at a time again and again. Since we arrived in New York State we are finding a lot more coins along the road. We found few in the Midwest and Canada. So far we have found $57.32 along the road since starting (that includes 30.75 we found in a slot machine and 12 golf balls @$1 each). We only have to add $1.05 to that to equal the cost of the hotel the night we were across from the KC Athletics stadium in Kansas City,

Missouri. I don't know why Americans discard money like that. We found only one 2-cent coin in all of Europe.

Poughkeepsie Bridge

The newly converted railway bridge, a footpath over the Hudson at Poughkeepsie.

We enter Poughkeepsie crossing a new walkway bridge over the Hudson River. Hundreds are strolling across on the sunny November afternoon. A group salvaged a railway bridge and changed it into a walkway to the tune of $38 million! As we sit in our hotel room we can see it making the wide crossing. The Mid-Hudson Bridge just south of here was the only car bridge between Albany and New York City when it was first built in the mid-30s.

In Poughkeepsie we are within commuter-train distance of The City. We can take the worker train to The City at any time now. Up-state New Yorkers and the rest of the world call it "New York City." But now that we are getting so close, it is just "The City," like it is "The Falls" in the Niagara Falls area but "Niagara Falls" everywhere else in the world.

The City is indeed closer than we think.

–Kill

Several names end in "-kill" in this area. There are Fishkill, Peekskill, Spackenkill, Catskill, and many others. My curiosity gets the best of me. Google tells me it comes from the early Dutch. It means "creek" in Dutch. So the Catskill Mountains are the "Cats Creek" Mountains

In Beacon we are Ed Benevente's guests. He is a local artist transplanted from LA. We meet him in a store as we are looking for a motel. Thanks, Ed, for good conversation and the place to sleep in a town without motels.

3,500 mi. (5,670 km.) – December 3, 2009

It feels strange being in the immediate suburbs of a huge city and also being in the mountains along this huge river, the Hudson. It is good to see and feel that.

After Peekskill we walk high up a mountain valley to get around a car-only parkway crossing a bay on the Hudson. In the end we walk across the dam capturing the water for New York City. My feet scream at me as we near the end of a day with so much climbing up and down. The pulled ligaments in my foot contribute as much as the hills to the soreness.

Mariandale Retreat Center

We spend the night in the Mariandale Retreat Center in Ossining where we are invited to take part in a retreat that night and the next day. The retreat, on transitions, comes at an opportune time since we are about to change from American to European walking. We sit out rain as we renew ourselves internally.

Transitions are about the immediate boundaries of the Now. They are about our fears of losing what we have and apprehensions about what will replace them in the future. We have to learn to live in the Now and to accept that we will receive what we need when we need it. Transition times are the intense times when we are about to, or in the process of, stepping into the great unknown before us.

We are clearly at that point. We have walked across America and are about to cross the Atlantic and begin a new kind of walking. What will the winter be? What will the path be? How will the people be? We will get what we need to know about the walk when we need it.

Hastings-on-the-Hudson

The next day we see patches of snow as we walk to Hastings-on-the-Hudson along the old aqueduct that one time carried water to The City.

It's around five and we're wondering when we are going to eat tonight, now or after we get to the hotel somewhere in front of us. Just then a woman, Betsy, stops and asks, "Would you like some beef stew? I made some extra." We would. Then we ask where the hotel is. It's farther than we think. "Maybe you would like to come to my home and stay with us for the night and then we can eat together." We accept gratefully and have a wonderful time talking the evening away. Thanks for everything, Betsy.

Cannibals

Before I continue the narrative into New York, I want to recount this lesson I learned many years ago. I was wandering in East Africa. One day in Fort Portal, Uganda, a shop owner asked me, "Where are you going next?"

"To Kisoro."

"You can't go there. They are all cannibals down there." He spoke with no little fear in his eyes.

A couple days later I was in Kisoro being asked, "Where did you come from?"

"Fort Portal."

"And you are all right? They are all cannibals up there." He answered with the same fear in his eyes.

The two Western Ugandan towns were only about 200 miles (325 kilometers) apart. Yet the people knew each other so little and feared each other so much that they considered each other to be cannibals.

That has always stuck with me. I call it the "cannibal syndrome" and apply it to situations when someone knows little about someone else and thus fears the other unreasonably. It is unreasonable and almost always unwarranted and untrue. Yet we all suffer from it from time to time.

The cannibal syndrome strikes me as we enter first New York state and then as we enter The City. My life-long internal picture of New

York State was that of a stogy place, a place I would have no interest in visiting, much less living in. The people fared no better. And my stereotype of the city north of Central Park was that of a warren of gangs and crime, no place to tarry in, let alone stay in for any length of time, especially overnight.

You have already read about our passage along the Erie Canal and the Hudson River. I have said more than once it is among the better places along our pilgrimage, a place where we could even live for a time. Strike one for the Cannibal Syndrome.

As we left the Erie Canal heading south on the Hudson River, Petra casually says, "Maybe we can stay on Manhattan a day or so before going on to Anna's in Brooklyn."

I shudder. So many old stereotypes race through my mind. So many movies over my lifespan told me it is not the place to stay. I'm looking forward to rushing through and quickly crossing the Brooklyn Bridge—into a place I also hold reserves on staying.

"No way!" I answer reflexively. Staying in Manhattan is not at in my wildest dreams a possibility.

I'm feeling and thinking the same things so many asked us along the way: "How can you walk in big cities like Albuquerque? Murders happen there." "How can you walk along the roads, you are going to be hit?" "Aren't you afraid people are going to rob you along the road?" We have long since answered these and many more negative questions reminding others of the universal goodness of the people we meet. Yet here I am still carrying an infantile phobia for New York City.

We meet several nice people who live and have lived in the Bronx, Harlem, Brooklyn, and Manhattan as we approached to the city. Yet I still have some fear as we start walking down Broadway into city. The first night we stay in a hostel in Harlem—yes, that feared Harlem. You know what? Everyone is great. And the streets are clean and lively. Strike two for the Cannibal Syndrome.

Then the next day we walk through Central Park, that "den of druggies and petty thieves." Not so, it is clean and pleasant. We meet people who spend chunks of every day of their life in Central Park and love it. I love it too by the time we get to the south end. Strike three.

And if you need another strike, we continue down Broadway all the way to the Brooklyn Bridge through the city's vibrant heart. It's a joy to experience the city's vitality and life. No less than all across the rest of the country, the people are wonderful in the entire city. Yet another strike.

What a concrete lesson telling me not to beprejudge. The pilgrimage lays the Cannibal Syndrome in its grave once and for all for me. (I hope.) Think of it, it makes so little sense to judge anyone or any place before giving that person or place a chance to represent himself, herself, or itself.

Entering the City

We leave Hastings and have a wonderful walk down Broadway through Yonkers and the Bronx. It's an amazing walk through the city, totally contrary to my cannibal-syndrome pre-judgments. By the day's end we walk into to L Hostel in Harlem on upper Manhattan. The people in L Hostel welcome us warmly as they hear about our walk. The manager, who is from Jerusalem, gives us an upgrade when he hears we are walking there. "If you are walking so far, you need some extra rest." The place is really clean and inexpensive by New York City standards. If I come back to the city without a place to stay, I'll stay at L Hostel. They even find us an Ethiopian restaurant just six blocks away.

The next morning, we walk down 7th avenue into Central Park, take a circuitous tour of the park, walk down through the theater district on the Avenue of the Americas, and rejoin Broadway for our final cruise through Manhattan. We see the many faces of Broadway those two days. So many faces. So many different people. So many different neighborhoods. It is an overload even for me and I have been here before. Petra keeps saying, "So many people." And we have been in India where there so many more people.

People are pushing around so many delivery carts. We and our carts disappear into the crowd of carts unnoticed. We are just two more delivery people pushing our goods down the street.

We have made it to Central Park in The City.

Anna

We leave Manhattan via the Brooklyn Bridge, an adventure in its own right. A spider web of steel cables surrounds us as we walk a center catwalk sidewalk. The Statue of Liberty and Governor's Island along with the Verrazano Bridge are clearly among the many sights to the south. A ship pulled by two tugs and in tow by another passes under the bridge. The horns and tires and engines of hundreds of cars and trucks split the air.

Soon Anna is welcoming us into her home in Brooklyn. We stay with her for the week we are in The City. Thanks, Anna.

We have only a few short miles to walk to the Atlantic to complete the American half of this pilgrimage. We'll wait for the off-and-on rain to stop. Meanwhile we spend a couple days doing a lot talking and Internet surfing for our next steps.

We revisit thoughts that first surfaced in western Illinois. We talk about taking a break and flying to India to rest a couple months. We even buy a Lonely Planet India book and look at possible itineraries.

In the end, we settle on Lisbon and continuing the walk now. Wanting to go to Germany for Petra's Mother's 80th birthday played in the timing and decision also. That's in late February. If we go to India, it will be for more than a month and a half.

Final nine miles

On Saturday, December 12, our sixth wedding anniversary, we finish our pilgrimage in America as we walk nine miles from Anna's to the Atlantic at Coney Island. In pilgrim tradition, Petra burns a pair of pants and some socks she wore out on the almost 11-month walk. As we return to Anna's, we get off the subway at the Atlantic-Pacific Station, ending our trip from the Pacific to the Atlantic.

We have finished the first half of this pilgrimage. We walked 3,585 miles (5,808 kilometers) in 252 days. Adding in rides and rest days, we have covered 4,510 miles (7,307 kilometers) in 342 days. That's an average 14.2 miles (23 kilometers) per day walking.

We have arrived at the Atlantic at Coney Island on 12 December 2009.

The ideal inn

Before moving on to Europe, we think about our daily searches for a place to stay at night. By the time we arrive at in New York City after eleven months walking, we have spent over 150 nights in motels. That makes us minor experts on motels. But we still get burned. Everything here is based in our experiences. This "list" developed over time. Almost everything listed here is here because it has burned us at least once somewhere along the line. This is the product of experience.

Here's how the far-from-scientific operation played out each night. The choices and inspections are often by feel and error prone. But it is helpful and fun to have a list to remind us what to look for.

Our search begins a few days early as we scan the Internet for motels near our proposed destinations. On a holiday or weekend after our first few months, we often reserve a room though we don't like doing so. Reserving frequently results in a less-than-satisfactory room when we arrive. So we try entering a town with no reservation whenever there is a reasonable chance of finding an open room.

Choosing between hotels in a particular town begins outside. Does it look tidy? Once in: Can we smell cigarette smoke or mildew? Have they cleaned the carpet? Are the persons behind the counter friendly? Courteous? Too busy? Will they let us look at the room first?

When the place passes these tests, we get down to choosing a suitable room. We have to see the room they are offering us not a sample room. "They all are the same" doesn't cut butter. *There is no such thing.* Every room is unique. If we cannot see the room, we leave unless there's nothing else nearby.

At the room: What is the initial smell (Smoke or mildew? Leave.)? How big is it? Is it big enough for us and our carts? Do the windows open (No? Leave)? How is the bathroom? Do the sink drain and faucets work? Is the sink good for washing clothes when we have to? (No. Is there a washer in the motel?)? Does the toilet work? How does the bed feel? Is it big enough? Does the phone work and allow us to call from the motel? Is there a view from the window of something other than a parking lot, wall, or highway? Is there a bright light outside that will shine in during the night when we leave the window open? If so, can we block it? Is there air conditioning, kitchen, highway, or cooler noise that will hinder good sleep? Do kitchen smells or other unpleasant odors come in the window? Does the hotel have Wi-Fi? Does it work in the room or do we have to sit in the lobby? How is the carpet? Are there enough lights? Do they work? Are light bulbs missing? Can the motel correct what is unsatisfactory? How do I feel standing quietly in the room?

When we can answer these questions and the ones about the motel itself to our satisfaction without too many compromises, we can say, "Yes" to the room. Otherwise, we ask to see another room or head for the next motel. We seldom check more than two or three rooms in the same hotel.

Of course, another motel around the corner can be calling our name to check it out also before accepting a room from either. When there is only one motel, we have to take what's offered. Usually that is fine. But sometimes it's marginal as it was in Truxton (p. 32).

All this searching and choosing often takes a lot of my already depleted energy at the end of the day. I seldom enjoy it. Some days I would rather just keep walking than go through this ritual.

So what is our ideal motel room? The room is on the top floor, has two firm queen beds or a king bed. The bathroom is fully functional with bathtub/shower curtain that does not stick to us when we take our shower. The faucets and showerhead are free of calcium. It has hangers we can remove from the closet and hang in the room to dry clothes. The functioning telephone allows us to call outside with our 800-number calling card. Two comfortable chairs stand at a table. The lights allow us to see and to read a book at night while sitting in the chairs. There's a high enough table and another chair where we can use the computer with functional Wi-Fi or Ethernet supplied by the hotel. A ceiling fan is so much better than air conditioning. When there is the latter, I want the fan too. We must always be able to open the windows for comfortable sleeping, even in the winter (we'll shut off the heat). And outside those windows there should be no bright lights, highways, kitchen smells, idling trucks, air conditioning units, garbage bins, or fire-engine stations.

In the end feel determines whether we stay in a particular room. We have stayed in many rooms with far less than these ideals and a few with most of them. When a place feels good, we stay. When it doesn't feel good, we leave, even when it *should* be OK because it has all the *right* things listed above.

One last dynamic plays into the choice: the friction between the "best" place and "a place to sleep." Petra looks for the "best" place, a place she can call home for a month or more. I tend to the other end, ready to settle for "a place to sleep" tonight and leave tomorrow. When the friction between us gets high, we often settle for something less than Petra would prefer or something that has taken longer than I would take to find. Often both are true.

Then we go to Europe. Everything changes. Beds are smaller. Rooms are colder and wetter. Smells are heavier. France's beds and rooms are tiny. And no hotel, pension, or B&B has a washing machine.

Nothing is perfect, but we do pay for a room when we stay in one. In a way every night we decide, like buying a house, which one do we want to take as our home for the evening? My standards are often lower than Petra's, especially when I am tired.

Thanks for the gifts

As we walk, we try to keep track of the gifts we receive. Those gifts that in some way can be assigned a value (like a ride, food, or a night's stay) I assign one. We add up all these gifts and are quite astounded and humbled by the total we came up with. You who have supported us in America have done so to the tune of around 20% of our total expenditures for our pilgrimage across America. We are very thankful for your help.

We also receive help from several in Europe but I fail to keep accurate track of exactly what that is. I can only say here, thank you to all of you who have helped make this pilgrimage so great.

For the gifts without monetary value, we thank you also. To name a few, thanks go out: to the weather spirits who gave us mainly wonderful weather; to the dogs who walked with us and those who barked and wagged their greetings; for the good thoughts and words you sent us; for your prayers; to the winds that carried us on; to the sun that warmed us in the winter even though you scorched us in the summer; to the cumulus clouds that showed up just before noon in the summer to shade us; to the horses and cows that ran over to check us out and greet us; to the mosquitoes that didn't bite us; to the heat of Missouri that not only drove us north so we could decide to walk across southern Canada but also gave us free sauna baths; to the thousands who gave us their smiles and inquisitive questions; to the wide shoulders for walking along roads; to the birds who sang to us so often; to the summer shade trees; to the Universe for assigning this wonderful Pilgrimage to us; to our legs and knees and feet for carrying us all these miles; to each other for enduring and celebrating and dancing through life together; to all the ancestors who prepared our path and walked their paths before us; and to life and health.

The statue of Liberty, France's gift to the U.S. on it's 100th birthday.

A rainy, walled Portuguese road.

WINTER 2010

Camino Portugués

After our rest in Brooklyn we fly 15 December to Lisbon, Portugal, the closest destination in Europe from New York.

We arrive in Lisbon on the 16th after a long and tiring flight with a six-hour layover in Brussels. Both planes are packed. A week of walking would have been easier. Petra catches a cold on the first flight, her first of the year. We arrive exactly 11 months after beginning our pilgrimage.

From here we intend to walk the Camino Portugués, the path from Lisbon to Santiago de Compostela in northwestern Spain.

Lisbon

Riding into Lisbon on the bus from the airport we know we are in a different place than New York. Trees are green. Grass is green. Palm trees are green. Everything is green. And in the city the buildings are monumental and colorful. Streetcars still run on tracks. The food is richer and sweeter. The hotels are different. Petra says it feels a lot like India. We continue our pilgrimage in a new place. After a long sleep and a day wandering the streets we feel refreshed.

We procrastinated leaving New York. We didn't want to leave; we didn't want to stay. We thought about going to India for a rest. Then one day we bought a ticket to Lisbon. We wanted to stay on our path to Jerusalem. Afterwards we still debated whether to buy a ticket to India. But finally we decided to do that (if we wanted) after arriving in Lisbon. Now it feels comfortable to be in Lisbon. We know it would have been wrong to have made that decision before now. (We are trying more and more to make decisions only when it is time to make them, not before.) We feel ready to walk now and, besides, the last thing we would have needed is to spend another 12 to 15 hours in three different planes flying to India when we can rest a while here almost as well.

The main tourist street in Lisbon.

After four days in a hotel, we move from our hotel to a small apartment where we can cook for ourselves and spread out a bit. We wander the town on foot and by street car tram and just plain rest and avoid the rain. Our place doesn't have Wi-Fi so we search it out in the neighborhood. The apartment also has only one little heater in the kitchen. It's cold sometimes.

Lisbon trollies.

One day, we walk north from the cathedral to the main bus station beginning our walk to Santiago de Compostela, our next major destination. It feels good to start even though we are going to rest a few more days. The Portuguese have marked the path well in Lisbon with the yellow arrows of the Camino de Santiago. We don't know what the marking are like in the countryside, but it would be hard to lose our way here in Lisbon. What a change after finding our own way all across the America, suddenly we have arrows every block telling us where to go. No more looking at maps or dead reckoning or plain old guessing. We just look for yellow arrows to point out the way. As long as they are there, we have one big task totally off our minds. And when they are gone, our guide book is in hand to enlighten us. We only walk. In life we don't often have the arrows to tell up where to go. But it's enjoyable now and then to let someone else point out the way. We'll worry about flooded paths and useless arrows when we get there.

Yellow Camino arrows point to Santiago and Blue ones to Fatima.

In addition to the yellow arrows pointing to Santiago, blue ones point to Fatima. Many also walk the *Camino do Fatima*. Until just before Fatima both point the same way. North of Fatima they point in opposite directions.

It's too warm (not by much) to snow in winter in Portugal but it rains a lot this winter. One day someone tells us that it rains mainly at night. We watch it and sure enough the rain usually ends by ten or so in the morning and doesn't start again until around five. We have a walking window.

Heading north

On the 27 December we head north following the yellow arrows. We're now pushing only the bicycle trailer cart. Petra's doll carriage finally gave up its ghost in New York. She sent it to our storage at my brother's in Woodstock, Illinois.

We stop at a hardware store that first day and buy a couple large pieces of plastic. We make a cover and a liner for the cart. Together they keep our baggage quite dry through many heavy rains.

We quickly discover these yellow arrows don't always lead us along passable routes at this time of the year. In mid-morning we walk a couple kilometers (1.2 miles) out a path along a river only to be forced to turn back. Bicycles and four-wheeled motorcycles have made a mess of the path, digging deep mud holes that we can't pass with our cart. We end up back-tracking and walking the roads the rest of the day. We try to walk the marked paths the rest of the month in Portugal. Mud and water often make the paths impassible. So much for yellow arrows to guide us.

Go where?

Rain falls in bathtubs full that first night. Lightning and thunder crash through the night. Our room is damp and cold with only a tiny electric heater. The tile floor and walls actually have water on them in the morning.

I lie in bed awake most of the night thinking about the rain and the mud holes and the spray from trucks along the road. I figure we are destined to become mud pies whether from walking on paths or from being splashed by passing cars and trucks on the road. There's no way out. I am ready to quit, ready to go back to Lisbon and make different plans. Why go through this when we don't have to? I am miserable.

As we wake up in the morning I say, "Let's quit and go home."

"What? We just walked all the way across America! You want to quit after one bad night here? I'm not quitting."

Then she adds, "Besides, most of the rain is only at night. Even if a big rain comes while we are out walking, there are a lot of bars along the way. We can easily stop for coffee until the rain is over." I stretch and have to agree. It's nice that we seldom both have down days at the same time.

The forecast is calling for rain for the next ten days. I have a new birth of the pilgrimage this morning. I realize again that rainy weather is as much part of the pilgrimage as the beautiful days.

I say on our blog, "So it takes us a few extra days to get to Santiago as we sit out some rain days here and there along the way. We will neither melt nor freeze. Be patient, listen, feel, and learn. That's what this pilgrimage is all about anyway."

I'm glad this is not our road.

The next night we stay in a well-heated hotel room that can drive off some dampness. But heated hotel rooms are few and far between in Portugal. Most are cold and damp with, at best, a small, plug-in electric heater or house heat that is turned on at five and off at ten or eleven, hardly enough to keep out moisture, let alone keep the room warm.

In the next few days we begin learning the habits of the weather spirits in Portugal. Most rain does fall at night and what falls during the day comes in short downpours with lingering light drizzle. It's like little thunderstorms though sometimes it doesn't thunder. Big clouds approach. They dump on us for ten or fifteen minutes and move on. The air then clears for a few hours until the next cloud appears. Then everything repeats. We are usually lucky enough to be near some structure (barn, stand, shed) to shelter ourselves.

On the way to Santarém, we suffer some of these storms. We hide in a barn once and beside a shed with the second. Petra gets quite sick. We take a bus the last two-thirds of the way to town.

2010 arrives

In Santarém we celebrate New Year's with a huge fireworks display at midnight to begin 2010. The next morning we walk through a door in the city wall, down a weedy path off the city heights, and head north across the broad Tejo River flood plain.

The path takes us through these neatly planted trees.

Later in the day we cross a river spilling over the road. We wade through a hundred yards (110 meters) in two-inch-(50-mm)-deep water. I like the cool water (shoes and socks off) but my bare feet don't appreciate the rough asphalt. We are still walking roads because the Camino is often flooded here in the Tejo River Valley, the flat breadbasket of Portugal. When the river heads off to the northeast in a few days we will be able to get off the roads and back on the Camino once in a while.

In Entroncamento we stay in a modern, well heated hotel with a spacious room. Petra is not feeling well again. She has been under the weather since before Santarém. Now her back is bothering her, particularly when she tries to get up from bed. We stay here for three days. At one point she says, "I am homesick for the U.S." A German, homesick for America? It's true!

After Entroncamento we take a train part of the way and walk the last few kilometers into Tomar, the medieval Templar capital in Portugal. Petra is not feeling well yet so we take another train 110 kilometers (68 miles) to Coimbra and rest another couple days. There we befriend a South African couple, Rose and Nelson Silva, at their restaurant.

They say this is a Roman road.

Death

We don't spend much time haunted by death on the pilgrimage. But death is potentially here as we walk a third of the way around the world.

It would surely not be true if I said the thought of personal death doesn't surface from time to time. After all, we started this walk on my 66th birthday and I am walking through my 67th and most of my 68th year. And we often walk along roads and over paths that most would identify as "dangerous." As a healthy 66-year-old I confess death crosses my mind now and then, but never threateningly.

It surfaces one night in a dream as we walk through southern Portugal. I record the dream as follows in my notes:

> I was worrying about our possessions and what would happen to them in storage back in Paso Robles, California, where we started. Someone in the dream tells me, "Why are you worrying about these things? You cannot take them with you where you are going." Or was it, "You don't need any of these things where you are going"?

> In the dream I understand the previous statement as a clear prediction—a pre-announcement—of my imminent death. I was thinking, "Wow, you actually *are* told before you die."

As I awake, this gives me such a peace and strength that I can easily *feel*, from a *gut* level what I know intellectually, that I am here to live a while then die. The dream helps me to calmly walk a particularly dangerous stretch of always-dangerous Portuguese roads. My attitude is, "If it is my time, I'll go no matter what I do to cause or prevent it." I saw my task, then as I wrote it in my notes, and now as I see it sitting here writing it again, is to live bold and not in fear. There is no need to fear when you know in your mind, heart, soul, and gut that your death will happen no matter how you try to prevent it.

I must live knowing an end will come around some hidden corner whether I am looking for it or not. There are many corners to look around and horizons to look over. Death will only come at the last corner or horizon. So why sit trembling looking for death, waiting for it to find me? Don't shake and quake. Celebrate the time I have in joy and when I find death around a corner, welcome it knowing I rejoiced in the time I have had to live.

What is behind death's door, death's axe, death's casket? We don't know. We can only live what we have well and let death or its partner provide whatever may or may not be next.

Albergaria a Velha

This is our evening hotel and restaurant experience in Albergaria a Velha. It is only one night, a typical night, if anything be that. Every night in Portugal is different. But this one gives you a feel for what it is like as we walk north.

We walk down a steep road dug out of the mountain into Albergaria a Velha. High rock and dirt walls flank both sides of the road as we drop into the village below. Once down we follow an old road between what looks like equally old houses. They touch forming a canyon-like path, a smaller version of the one we just came through off the mountain. A faint sewer smell irritates our noses as the cobble stones make themselves felt through our shoes.

Entering a traffic circle, we approach a man parked on the sidewalk. "Do you know where the hotel is?" Petra asks in an attempt at Portuguese (It's a difficult language).

"It's up this hill. Follow the road straight. Cross the railroad tracks. Go some more and it's on the left." Then he repeats the directions a second time as the Portuguese often do to make sure you understand.

We start walking. It's getting dark. The rain that held off all day begins to drizzle. We get out our umbrellas and keep walking. The rain gets heavier. We take refuge in a bus stop. I go behind to relieve myself. Just then a train passes. It's good that it's almost dark.

When we begin walking again, a car passes. It's the guy from the circle. We walk several blocks more looking for the Casa de Alameda based on a picture in the guidebook. Suddenly, the circle guy is back. He speaks from behind parked cars at a doorway on a tiny sidewalk. "You are here." Wet and in the dark, the hotel doesn't look like its picture. We could have walked by.

He unlocks the second half of the tall two-door entrance and opens it so we can bring our cart in. We enter an old room. A bar sits in front to our right. The ceiling almost disappears into the darkness above. Sounds echo. Our helper tells the bartender we want a room and makes his departure. Thanks.

The steps squeak as the bartender climbs them and disappears into a dark corner. Soon he returns followed by another man, the hotel owner. We repeat that we are looking for a room with two beds and heat. "Yes, come with me." He speaks English, a welcome change.

We go back out and down the street a couple doors. Inside, he removes a barrier on the steps keeping his dog out of the hotel part of the building. He takes us up a stairway. I can barely see as I make my way up the unevenly carpeted stairs. We turn and walk down a corridor. The light he turns on is almost no help for seeing our way. We enter a set of doors, cross a landing, and go through more doors. Two halls later, he opens a room door and turns on a light.

It is your basic old hotel room only a little larger than its contents: high walls, small twin beds, a wardrobe, shuttered windows, a harsh overhead light, another no-less-harsh light on a night stand between the beds, one chair, and a cold feel. In fact there's not even a hint of heat on a night when the temperature is hanging just a few degrees above freezing. It feels as though there has been no heat in the room for a week or even weeks. Like so many Portuguese buildings this one feels colder than the weather outside.

"Do you have an electric heater?"

"We have heat in the room." He points to a small radiator sitting under the windowsill where it would give more heat to the window than to the room. Then he points out another radiator in the bathroom. Both are small.

"But there is no heat coming out." Petra said.

"I will turn it on now when I go down."

We retrace our steps through the tangle of halls. Once downstairs we agree to put our cart in the entrance hallway. We go back to the bar, bring the cart out into the now steady rain, push it down the street and into the hotel, tuck it into a corner, take out our bags, and tackle the maze back to the room.

The owner returns and says the radiators are on and assures us that it will soon be warm and cozy. As he leaves we know it will never be so; it might warm a bit but it'll never be "warm and cozy." The pillows feel like they are full of ice and the blankets are frosty as a pile of snow and so is the mattress. This says nothing about the cold walls and floors and bathroom tile. Those little heaters will not make this room cozy in the 12 hours that we are here. But this is the only place in town. This is our stop for the night.

We open the beds, set them up with our sleeping bags and the extra blankets we find, wash up (at least the water is warm), and breath a bit in preparation for a cold night.

Resigned to our fate, we return to the bar and restaurant. The dining room is a huge room lined with large wine barrels. Several people are eating and drinking at long tables. A large portable heater, the only heat source, stands in the center of the room. Petra leads us to the empty table next to the stove and pulls the table even closer to the heater.

The waiter takes our order, goes over to one of the wine casks, draws a pitcher of dark red wine, and returns it to our table. I like it. I never have been able to describe wine tastes and suspect that even if I could, many would either not understand me or not agree with my assessment. That said, I enjoy the heavy, slightly sweet flavor with a hint of some fruit. Later the waiter opens a bottle of wine from a back shelf for another customer. Petra asks, "How is that different from the wine we have?"

"It's the less cheap wine. This one costs 3.50 Euro ($5.10). The one in the barrel costs only 2.50 ($3.60)." *Cost is the only difference?*

We try the "less cheap" variety. I prefer the cheap one. I like that hint of fruit. Petra likes the other.

Petra follows her legume soup with lamb and potatoes. I eat delicious grilled squid that are cooked to perfection; there isn't the slightest rubbery consistency that often comes with squid fried in the United States. As often is the case in the smaller towns, the portions are huge for the price.

We return to our room full and ready to take on the cold. It doesn't take long to wash, shower, and get under the covers by just after nine. Though Petra gets cold, I sleep well and never am cold even though the heat goes off around 11:00.

In the morning we are up and on the way to a bar for breakfast by 7:30. Another night in a cold hotel is over. Even in big hotels with heated rooms, the lobby and public areas are seldom heated.

Broken axle

A week later on the way into Oliveira de Azeméis our cart breaks an axle. I ask for help in our hotel. Their driver takes us to a bicycle repair shop where they machine a new one using the good one as a pattern. When the shop owner brings the cart back the next day, he asks if we want a new idler wheel for the front. Ours is about wear out. He brings one from a baby carriage shop in an hour warning it will not last long. It lasts till Arles, France, where we stop using the cart. It is still in fine shape then. Thanks for the repair and for recognizing the front wheel problem.

The drive to the repair shop is frightening. Portuguese drivers look crazy from the side of the road. They look and feel worse from inside the car they are driving. We have a wild ride across town. Thanks for the help anyway.

The rain continues. In the evening we go looking for a restaurant. It starts to rain. Then it pours. We take refuge on opposite sides of the street under store porticoes. The wind whips the rain in sheets through the streets. I stand back up a couple steps at a door. Finally, it lets up enough for us to continue our search for dinner.

O Porto

We leave São João de Madeira Oliveira in light rain and heavy overcast. After following our yellow arrows faithfully for around an hour, they disappear. Well, at least we don't see them any more for a while. In our peewee Portuguese we ask a couple women for directions. "Go this way up to the National then turn left."

A "National" (like a US highway: ex. US 30) is a highway with much traffic. We go that way but refuse before arriving. We prefer light traffic when an alternative exists and there is a warren of side roads here. Thinking we can find our own way back to the arrows, we follow a sign to Santa Maria do Feira. According to the guide it's on our path.

After another hour we stop at a bar (café) just outside Sta. Maria. The waiter tells us the path passes Sta. Maria three kilometers (2 miles) to the east. He speaks good English and gives us directions to get to the village of Malaposta which *is* on the path. I should know from the name ("Malaposta"="bad place") it isn't going to be easy.

We lose ourselves in a coup-de-sac before 15 minutes. So we cross a ditch and walk along the National after all—it has a wide shoulder making the traffic somewhat tolerable. Finally, we stop in another bar and then a hotel to get more directions. In the hotel I realize we have walked the last kilometer southwest, the opposite direction from where we want to go. It's almost impossible to keep track of directions when the sun is not out and the roads are constantly winding. As you can guess by now we have neither a detailed map nor a compass. We were depending on the arrows.

Talking to the hotel clerk, I spot the clock. It's 12:54. We have been walking for more than four hours and we are less than four kilometers (2.5 miles) from our starting point. We are aiming for Grijó, 20 kilometers (12 miles) from our start. And Grijó is still 14 kilometers (eight miles) from O Porto. We have been walking in circles!

As we come out of the hotel, Petra spots a woman at a bus stop across the National. Petra leads me over and asks the woman where a bus is going. "To Porto, express." The labyrinth we have been walking has lead us here just in time for the next bus when the chances of making the original destination without a lot of effort are few. The rain and wind are once again angry. We decide to celebrate my birthday in Porto instead of on the road walking there.

The bus comes. We tie the cart into the baggage hold under the seats. As we enter the autovia (freeway) we passed a sign, "O Porto 30" That's kilometers (19 miles), a long walking day. In an hour we're checked into a hotel in O Porto. We don't arrive walking, but in the way of our pilgrimage on this particular rainy day.

Petra gets dizzy in the hotel. It's hard for her to lie down or move around without getting dizzy. She gets on the internet and finds information about a rather common illness where pieces of calcium float around in the inner ear. She finds exercises to help it and after a couple weeks it's gone.

An old wine boat on the Douro River in O Porto, the home of Port wine.

We stay around a while in O Porto. On the next day, my birthday, it's dry enough to take a city bus tour. We enjoy our time in the hilly city. We rest and wander.

We leave O Porto slowly, walking two days north along the Atlantic with its huge Pacific-like waves pounding the coast. Each night we return on the metro to our O Porto hotel. We avoid two hotel searches that way and extend our stay in the pleasant Pensão Grande Hotel Paris.

Douro River in O Porto.

Back on the road

A freighter on the Atlantic.

Sangre do Peregrino

On our first night away from Porto's hotel, we stay in São Pedro de Rates at our first refugio (pilgrim's hostel) in Portugal. We also meet four other pilgrims, our first in Portugal.

Settled into the refugio, we go shopping at the store across the street. Petra makes a large pot of pasta in the kitchen. When a Brazilian couple arrives on bicycles, we share it with them. They share their wine and food they bought at the store. They toast us with the "Sangre do Peregrinos," the "Blood of Pilgrims" as they call their red wine.

The Brazilian says, "The Camino is really only 30 centimeters (one foot) long, from here to here." He points, first to his head and then to his heart. It is indeed that internal journey that we need to take in order to really benefit from our Camino experience.

As we finish eating, there's knocking at the closed door. Two Koreans have walked here from O Porto (38 kilometers-24 miles) when they couldn't find the refugio in the last town. They were too shy to ask where it was. They arrive in a downpour with neither umbrella nor rain cloths. They knock on the door to be let in. They are 18 and 23, youngsters out for an adventure to find out what to do with their lives. They don't even have a map. They tell us that they were afraid of bears and wolves as they came through forests on the way here.

We have no more food. Petra gives them my umbrella and they go to the store to check in and get some food. We all have a fine evening talking before settling into our sleeping bags on beds in rooms with more than a little mildew created by the cold, damp Portuguese winter.

A couple nights later we stay in a private hostel, Casa Fernanda in Lugar do Cargo. Fernanda and her husband Jacinto are wonderful hosts. He cooks a fine chicken stew for dinner and serves breakfast in the morning. We really enjoy our stay. But Portugal's dampness is never far away. Fernanda's house is only four years old yet already heavy, black mildew marks the window frames and wall corners.

Ponte do Lima

Six days out of Porto we walk into Ponte do Lima. The days have been short, 15 and less kilometers (nine miles). Until today most days have included some rain. But today is a gem. The sun is bright, the sky deep blue, and the wind light from the north. The forecast calls for eight more like it. Today's walk is a real joy even though we forgo walking a couple Camino sections due to mud and rocky surface with washed out ruts. The weather is so clear we can see far in the distance and the traffic is light.

This road with its walls is tight and its paving blocks are hard to walk on. Many Portuguese roads are like this one.

Tonight we are in a wonderful, clean, new refugio in Ponte do Lima. It has no heat, but it is otherwise a delight to be in. Ponte do Lima is a splendid little town on the Lima River. The town is full of tourists walking around and enjoying the plazas and the medieval and roman bridges over the river.

As we leave in the morning, our *hospitalero* (our host) advises us not to try the low-lying portions of the Camino because they likely have too much water for us to navigate with our cart. He tells us about an alternate road. We take it at first but decide to try the Camino anyway only to get bogged down. Back to the road.

We wind our way up a lazy country road into the mountains. When the path for going back to the Camino comes, we skip it thinking it is a false sign coming too soon. After a while we realize our mistake but we are then a couple kilometers beyond the branch. We opt to continue up the road. In the end we walk over a 400 or 500-meter (1,300- to 1,650-foot) pass with wonderful views along the way. The sun is bright and the wind cool and delightful. Water runs in the ditches everywhere. We eat lunch in a small restaurant with a broad panorama just below the pass. We can even see the Atlantic on the distant horizon past the mountains.

Ponte do Lima's Medieval and Roman bridges.

Close to the end of the day we pass a goose chasing a pig across the field. For whatever reason he herds him homeward!

Today is indeed a delightful mistake.

Leaving Portugal

Portugal has not been totally friendly. It has often been a test of our wills to continue. Rain, mud, water, cold and damp hotel rooms, and mildew permeated our passage north. Only in the past week has the sun forced its way through the clouds to give us a warmer welcome. We suffered various minor sicknesses and I thought about quitting after our first day on the path.

Now the sun finally shines brightly our last days in Portugal. I think it is trying to make peace with us. Even with the cold and rain, Portugal is a positive experience; maybe it's positive *because of* the rain, cold, mud, and mildew. But my inclination today is to stay away from Portugal in the winter in the future.

The cold and dampness taught us to go slowly and choose our steps well, to take our time, to rest, to take a bus or train now and then, to observe and walk with the weather. Like Missouri last June, Portugal has tested our wills to continue. We have passed the test and are moving forward. We feel great.

We interact far less with the people in Portugal than in America, partially because of the language, and partially because with so many other walkers here, we are just part of the background, like in New York when everyone else was pushing carts. We disappeared into the background there too.

Even more than before, we walk in the Now. We appreciate Now. We celebrate each step and breath as if it were our first—or last. Now is what we have—not tomorrow, not yesterday.

One month after beginning our pilgrimage walk in Portugal we sit in Valencia ready to enter Spain. Santiago is only a week north. Tomorrow we take our first steps that way. Here we come, Spain!

Crossing the Rio Miño

Tui, Spain, across the Miño River from Valença, Portugal.

We cross the Miño River into Spain on 28 January.

Spanish Camino markers announce distances down to meters to Santiago. The route changes so often that it would be a huge task to keep them current. So we take the distances shown with a grain of salt.

Other markers tell us our route also lies over a Roman road, the Via Atlanticas. I suspect it

continues into Portugal but I don't remember seeing any signs identifying it there.

Learning from Nature?

At one point we navigate a long section of path submerged two inches (five centimeters) in water. Before we are done we carry our backpacks on our back and our cart in our hands. We walk a hundred yards (91 meters) through the weeds beside the Camino on a bushy, makeshift path created by necessity. At the end we sit resting on a stone watching a stream, the destination of all that water in the path.

I think about the excess water we have just put up with and all the rain that has been producing floods in Portugal and the rest of Europe this winter. Then I have an Aha! moment.

I think about old lessons and tales that have told us from youth to learn from Nature and the order in Nature. But order doesn't exist in Nature! It's not there! Nature does almost everything in excess, seldom in moderation, and never orderly. Too much! Too little! It rains till floods overflow rivers carrying the excess to the next river and the sea. It doesn't rain for months in other places creating deserts. Snow storms close down big sections of the country. Storms tear down trees and buildings. No rain and too much sun make deserts. Volcanoes and earthquakes devastate vast areas. Oh, there are some calm times, some moderate days. But we read about the excesses almost every day. We live with it.

And trees produce thousands more seeds than will ever produce trees. Animals and man also produce huge quantities of seed, most of which can and never will be used to create new animals or men.

Nature's norm is excess, not moderation. So all those old school things that told us to learn from nature turn out to be telling us to be a little excessive rather than judicious and conservative!?

While we are at it, think about the story of the turtle and the hare. The hare may tire himself and not make the end of the race as fast as the turtle. But what happens when they cross a busy road. The hare has a lot better chance of dodging wheels than the slow turtle.

And this says nothing of maxims like, "The early bird gets the worm." What happens to the early worm? I guess the maxim assumes we are the early bird and not the early worm.

Nature's lessons must always be interpreted. But the moderation of Aristotle and Plato are not in nature, anywhere.

What's it mean for our pilgrimage? If we are to listen to Nature, it's telling us be a little excessive once in a while. Risk being hurt. Risk doing grand things. Risk. Live on the edge. The old philosophers' words about moderation wash away with the flood waters.

Hot springs

In Caldas do Reis Petra finally finds a hot spring to soak in. For so long she has been trying to find one to no avail. Even though she has to settle for a little basin outside the bathhouse, she is delighted to get her feet wet one day before Santiago. The bathhouse is closed for remodeling.

It's not a very big one, but Petra has finally found a hot spring.

Santiago

In midday 2 February we come over a hill to our first view of the cathedral of Santiago. We still have a steep valley between us. But one of our primary physical goals stands before us.

As we traverse the valley, I complain loudly that the pathway is in horrible shape. Why do they send us down such a circuitous route? What is the Universe trying to teach?

Our first view of the Cathedral of Santiago.

Standing in front of the Cathedral of Santiago.

Two hours later we are standing in the square in front of the cathedral 392 days (284 of them walking) after leaving Paso Robles. We have walked from our front door to Santiago, 3,976 miles (6,441 kilometers), at 14 miles (22.7 kilometers) per day.

To the end of the world

After four days rest in Santiago, we head for Finisterra and the sea, the source and end of life. Finisterra, the "end of the world," is the farthest west point in Europe. Until the discovery of the Western Hemisphere, the Europeans thought this was literally the end of the world.

We leave our cart and the bulk of our possessions in Santiago taking only the things we are sure to need. It is refreshing not to be pushing and pulling the cart along the path and over rocks. We walk remembering how we walked here twice before in 2003, once mostly alone and a second time later in the year as we were getting to know each other.

Walking out of Santiago, like walking in, is down and up steep rocky paths. Later we balance ourselves with our sticks on narrow strips of dirt as we walk around mud holes. Leaving the cart in Santiago makes our passage a lot easier as we labor through many watery and stony mazes. These mud holes and rocks mirror life. We have to find our way through some messy and difficult paths in life. That doesn't mean that life is not good. It only means that sometimes we have to work at it in order to enjoy the beautiful times. We have the rough times to contrast with the smooth–to make the smooth more intense.

The Cathedral as we head west to the sea.

Negreira dinner

The first night out of Santiago finds us arriving late at a hotel in Negreira. At nine we are the only two in a large a room sitting at a table in the middle of many others arrayed for a 10:00 pm banquette. Two waiters serve us. It's a unique dining experience.

4,000 mi. (6,480 km.) – February 7, 2010

The second day starts sunny but deteriorates into clouds and then rain. We walk on fewer paths and more open back roads. The walk from Negreira used to be 36 kilometers (22.3 miles) to the next refugio in Olveiroa but a few years ago they built a new refugio half way between them to cut down that long distance. We arrive at the new refugio as light rain begins to fall. The owner is not friendly as he shows us the place. Mildew has already taken over and no one has taken a broom to the floors for a while.

The rain is coming down stronger. Olveiroa is still several miles over a mountain ridge. I am dead tired and not inclined to leave, though I don't want to stay either. Petra is ready to go. We head down the road under our umbrellas tilted into the wind to keep as dry as possible.

In and out of the rain

After a few kilometers the rain becomes steady and it is getting darker. An equipment shed offers shelter. We take it and wait for the rain to diminish. It doesn't. We aren't going to find that hotel listed on a sheet of places to stay off the Camino either. Petra goes to the farmer across the road and asks him to call the hotel. Its listing says it has a pilgrim-pick-up service. Half an hour later the hotel owner arrives with his Mercedes. We go for a long 12-kilometer (7.4-mile) ride around the mountain and in half an hour we're sitting in a warm, dry hotel room. The walk path to the same hotel was four or five kilometers (2.5-3 miles) *over* that quite high mountain. As in life, it is good to ask for help when you need it–hard as that is for some of us (like me).

Often we look too far ahead trying to anticipate what will happen when we get somewhere or do something. This is an ongoing theme with us both. We know we are better off when we try to live in the Now and deal with what's happening as it happens. We can deal with the future even the near future when we get to it. The next day I am getting tired in the middle of the day. Petra is ahead. Instead of just walking where I am, I keep looking at that long steep path going up forever in front of Petra. I'm not happy. Then Petra turns. Aha! The path turns. We don't have to climb that steep path. I wasted energy worrying about a walk I never would have to take instead of just walking where I am and turning or not turning when I get to the point of doing so.

The road looks like a tough climb until Petra turns. Don't look too far ahead. Try to stay in the Now.

The sun is shining brightly today. We walk through rolling mountains on mostly smooth paths to the Atlantic. Along the way we stop at a bar we visited almost seven years ago during our first Camino. That time we played with a little dog, Perla. She is still welcoming pilgrims and "bringing them into the bar," as the owner says. She must feed Perla extra for doing her duties as her prices were 20 percent higher than most other bars along the Camino.

Our Lady of the Snows

In mid-afternoon we arrive at the little church of Nuestra Señora de las Neves (Our Lady of the Snows). We have visited it a couple times before. A chapel with an ancient altar and crude statues stands on the side of a church. The place always feels holy and simple, so different from the cathedrals in the cities. I suspect the excessively warn objects (statues?) on the altar were holy to the Celts and that the Christians only baptized them. We stay half an hour regenerating our spiritual selves.

A shepherd with his dogs in the highlands of Galicia near the Atlantic.

The last day we walk under clear, blue sky from Cee to Finisterra along familiar paths and around villages along the Atlantic coast. For a while we walk separately. We have been walking together pretty much 24/7 most of the way from California and want to be alone for a while. After a few miles we meet by accident and walk together again.

Finisterra

We haven't been to Finisterra (Fisterra) since late 2003. It's emotional seeing some places again—Maison Blanche where we stayed a month, the beach we walked so often, the town, and Cape Finisterra. The cape is a mountain forcing its way into the ocean, the beginning and end of life. We stood there and symbolically ended one life and began another at the end of our Camino in 2003.

Late in the evening we stand together at the zero mile marker at the lighthouse on Cabo Finisterra for a photo just as I did six and a half years earlier.

After three days enjoying the town we take a bus through several picturesque villages along the Atlantic coast back to Santiago and put the pilgrimage on hold for a month. We fly to Germany to celebrate Petra's Mom's 80th birthday. But we don't really put the pilgrimage on hold; our time in Germany is only a non-walking phase of the pilgrimage.

Walking through the fields of France.

SPRING 2010

After celebrating Petra's mother's birthday and visiting several friends in Germany, I am ready to get back to the walk. It's mid-March and spring is here already. Petra is going to stay another month and rejoin me later. She says, "I have walked the Camino three times and don't want to walk it again now. Besides, we need some time off from each other." I agree. We have been together day and night, 24/7, for the last 14 months consulting each other on almost every detail and decision. This is a good change. She will go on her fasting retreat in Germany and I on my walking retreat along the Camino.

Camino de Santiago

The Camino de Santiago (The Way of St. James), it is an ancient pilgrimage route across northern Spain to the grave of St. James the Greater, the Apostle, in Santiago de Compostela. It has been around for 1,200 years. Over 150,000 walk it every year taking 30 to 35 days to do so. It offers places to stay every ten miles (16 kilometers) at most.

The main route across Spain is known as the Camino Français (the French Way). This begins in St. Jean Pied de Port just inside France, crosses the Pyrenees, and then goes on to Santiago de Compostela via Pamplona, Burgos, and Leon. The Camino Français is 535 miles (866 kilometers) long.

The Camino Français is joined in Puente la Reina (de Navarra), south of Pamplona, by another route starting at Somport Pass on the French border north of Jaca. Both routes are fed by other walkways coming from all over Europe. Three major European routes feed St. Jean and one Somport. We are headed for the European route that feeds Somport Pass, the Chemin d'Arles, the Camino of Arles, also known as the Via Tolonese.

2010 is a Holy Year, a year when St. James feast day, 25 July, falls on a Sunday. Pilgrims get special blessings for walking in a Holy Year.

The numbers walking have been increasing yearly through the last decades. In Holy Years the number of pilgrims is much larger than other years. Ultimately more than 272,000 make their way along the several Camino routes into Santiago in 2010. More than 238,000 arrive on foot. See page 340.

The Camino is an international pilgrimage path. One night I eat with an American, a Belgium, and a German, a few nights before with another German and before with a Check. I also talk with Koreans, Japanese, Italians, Spanish, Israeli, French, Hollanders, Swedes, English, and Canadians. The interesting thing is that English is the lingua franca, the language that most have in common, the major language that this polyglot mass uses to communicate with one another.

When we finish our pilgrimage, we will have walked 5,321 miles (8,620 kilometers), almost exactly ten Caminos. You who have already walked the Camino can begin to feel just how far we have walked (See map on p. 331).

Walking East

I am about to walk the same Camino Français (the French Way) that I walked in 2003 and 2004. This time I'll walk eastward away from Santiago. You can read about my first encounter with the Camino at WalkingWithAwareness.com.

On March 11 I fly from Frankfurt Hahn airport in Germany back to Santiago to continue walking east, to get "On the road again...."

Before I leave the next day, I have last minute things to do in the city: attend the Pilgrims' Mass at noon in the Cathedral and watch the huge sensor swing smoky across the church; say "Good buy" to Santiago the statue, Santiago the bones, and Santiago the city; buy a new watch (with yellow Santiago shell on it); stop at an optometrist and have my glasses put together again; stop in the official Camino office and make sure our personal credentials allow us to stay in refugios across Spain (they allow us, though westward walking pilgrims have priority); buy tooth paste, bananas, and a corkscrew (Petra has our only corkscrew); and put the cart back together again (I stored it disassembled). (How's that for a long English sentence, Petra? Almost as long as a good German one?)

This large sensor is about to swing from roof to roof across the church. It's part of the pilgrim ritual of the Cathedral of Santiago.

I head east around noon only to get lost before leaving Santiago. I'm walking against the normal westward Camino flow. The arrows point you *to* the city. You have to infer where they are coming from by watching how and where they are painted. It is a different task from just following the arrows forward as we did through Portugal. At least a lot more pilgrims are walking in 2010. I can use them as guides. They show me where to walk when the arrows don't.

In the first evening, I sit in the cafeteria of a *refugio* (a pilgrim hostel along the Camino, it's also called an *albergue*) on Monte de Gozo, the Mountain of Joy. Pilgrims coming from the east for the last 1200 years have had their first view of the Cathedral of Santiago from here. So the name, the Mountain of Joy; they were joyful that they had arrived so close to their goal.

Walking against the traffic, even with many on the road, I am not in contact with anyone for a long time. It's a good way to be alone while being among many—when you want to do that. I count those fellow travelers headed for Santiago the second day: 16 bicyclists, 48 long-distance pilgrims, and 71 day pilgrims, 135 in all. The long-distance pilgrim has a backpack and the day walker doesn't (See p. 340 for more pilgrim counts).

The next day the sun shines brightly. The wind blows lightly. Birds sing everywhere. A few flowers show themselves. It is a beautiful day to walk.

The Camino in Galicia. I have to backtrack on this section when I hit impassable mud patches in the next valley.

In the evening I want to go to a new private refugio in Santa Irene but it's closed. So I settle for the noisy Santa Irene refugio on the road where I stayed in 2003. The next place is 15 kilometers (9 miles) up the road and it is already four when I get to Santa Irene. At 3 kph (2 mph), my average speed that day, that's five hours away. So here I am and here I stay, like it or not. Though far from the best, the refugio is livable. The windows are closed through the night keeping out most of the traffic sound. The dead air is not all that dead even though we are five in a room fit out for six.

As I walk into the Ribadiso refugio mid-afternoon the next day, I stop and rest beside its calm river and sit and write in the sun at its inviting restaurant patio. I linger and in the end stay for the night.

Second broken axle

Even though many pilgrims are walking, only six others stay with me in the small refugio in Hospital de la Cruz on the fifth night out of Santiago.

On the way into Hospital I miss my turn to the refugio. When I realize it, I take a shortcut across a field. The mistake gives me some extra work. As I bounce through the field, suddenly my cart's right wheel falls off. Another axle has broken, like in Portugal in January. I slip the remainder of the axle and the wheel back on the cart and make my way into the village. I find no place to fix it in Hospital.

The next morning I walk the 13 kilometers to Portomarín reinserting the wheel with the broken axle every now and then. In Portomarín a repair shop sends the good axle to Lugo to a machine shop to use as a key to make a new one. It's done in a day.

My feet are doing well. Walkers always talk about their feet. I noticed a couple weeks ago in Germany that the condition of my feet is directly related to stress: when stress is up, they hurt. What kind of stress? Worry or fatigue. I realize that all I have to do is remind myself to relax and they start to hurt less. It works. This morning on a tight place along the road, I am walking fast and hard. My feet hurt. I notice it, slow down, breathe a bit, and soon I am no longer noticing my feet.

Fording a stream

Near Sarria I arrive at a creek crossing. Large rocks are set neatly across the creek forming a nice bridge ... if you are walking with your goods on your back. But they are neither big enough nor close enough together for the cart. I carry the contents of my cart across the sandy rocks to the far side. As I begin to carry the cart itself, a farmer watering his cows nearby offers to help. Together we teeter our way from rock to rock and get the cart to the far side. *Muchas gracias, amigo.*

The Camino follows many old roads roughly parallel to existing highways and byways. One path is fine for walking. But the cart can't pass mud holes I can walk around. I walk back a mile and then walk the highway a few miles before rejoining the Camino.

The Moor slayer

Just so we don't forget that Santiago is more than the apostle who converted some of the people of the Iberian Peninsula, many statues remind you that he is also known as the Killer of the Moors, Matamores, who led the Christian Spanish kings in their fight to drive out the Moors between the eighth and 15th centuries.

Santiago the Moor Slayer, Matamores, on the building across the square in front of the Cathedral of Santiago.

Fog teaches again

As I walk out of the refugio in Triacastela a couple days later, a blank, white wall a hundred meters (110 yards) away faces me, fog. I want to go back in to wait for it to clear off so I can see in the distance. I am about to climb the huge mountain toward O Cebreiro. I want to see it, to enjoy its beautiful scenery. But I restrain my reaction to wait realizing that the Universe has something to say to me with the fog. This is the day I'm given; this is the day I am going to take. I go forward.

I decide not to pull the cart up the muddy, stony Camino path. Instead I walk the regional highway. I can't even see a block up the street as I start. But I can see far enough that I am sure the cars can see me in time to avoid running me over. I swing the cart behind me and began to pull it up the hill.

As we walked to Rome in late 2006 we had a similar encounter with the fog. That time we continually looked for a town that was supposed to be ahead of us. It didn't come. We looked forward trying to see beyond to where we would be sometime in the future, all to no avail. In our book *Germany to Rome in 64 days* we say:

> "We're stuck in our immediate present, in our Now. Petra realizes that the fog is telling us that we have to look at it and pay attention more to where we are than where we want to be later. We have to live Now, not tomorrow. It's not a new lesson. But today a new teacher, the fog, retells it. Everything in the Universe has something to tell us. We only have to listen."

And today the fog is back to tell me a similar story. Live where you are and don't look too far down the road to see what is there. But this time it also has a second reminder: What is so clear today may not be tomorrow. The opposite is also true: What is not clear today may be entirely clear tomorrow. The world hides and reveals itself as it wills. What is enlightenment yesterday or today often is only confusion tomorrow. The fog plays tricks now. A tree appears. It disappears. It reappears. It lapses into a state of is-it-there-or-not. So it is that the enlightenment I had another time fades in and out today. It is like walking a labyrinth when one time you are so close to the center goal only to be thrown all the way out to the edge far from the center on the next turn.

The fog plays hide and seek a while, it totally covers me. It drizzles making me walk in the present and feel the rain, just walk. Then it shows me the whole valley covered with clouds, sun, and green pastures. It plays with me into the afternoon.

This fog is like a dream from long ago where I am standing on a hill looking at the road ahead and below. That road goes through valley after valley and over hill after hill. Each valley is full of fog; each hill clear. I interpret this to be telling me that there are many valleys where I will feel lost but the road always comes out again into the open and I will know just where I am. All will be clear again. If only I could remember that when I am in one of those foggy valleys.

This walk is to be walked. Its meaning at times dwells behind curtains of fog. I don't always know why I am walking. This morning's fog slows me down to look at nearby flowers, to enjoy the walk. It allows me to stop when I want to stop, to not be afraid of not covering my "required" 20 kilometers.

A typical Spanish village in the valley north of O Cebreiro.

Lost

A day later I stop in O Cebreiro for a noontime coffee and sandwich. I am ready to walk down the deep valley to the east. Someone tells me the Camino has a problem, "Walk forward and take the first road to the right rather than taking the Camino." I take the first road. It turns into a farm path that leads me steeply down to a barn. Then it becomes grassier and less traveled. I think I am taking a path to get my cart around a bad part of the Camino. Then scrub brush is growing in the path. By now I am far down and sure that the Camino is to my right. So I walk steeply down through a field and find a traveled path. *This must be the Camino.* This new path continues down. Farther on it becomes a creek. *I am not in the right place. The Camino is not here.* O Cebreiro is a long way back up the hill. In fact, by now it is invisible since I am deep in the valley. I'm not a particularly happy camper.

It's time to go back up to find where the Camino really is, even if I have to go all the way back to O Cebreiro. I start. The path is steep and full of rocks and little bushes. I tug and drag the cart up less than a step at a time. I sweat. I stop often to catch my breath. A long way up I discover that where I joined this lower path, it doesn't continue up. I must have turned the wrong way when I came out of the field. I hadn't; both paths end. So it's back up the field of short grass. I take my backpack from the cart and put it on my back to make the cart more maneuverable. I continue shuffling up the field half a step at a time dragging the cart. Finally I get to the original path struggling through the bushes again.

By four I am back on top. It was 1:30 when I started down. I am tired. I put my pack in the cart and look farther along the road for that "correct turn." It is only a few yards/meters beyond. It is well marked and clearly the place to go. But I am tired by now, exhausted actually. I get a room for the night in O Cebreiro and sleep a while. When I get up I have cramps in my fingers from dragging and holding the cart so tightly.

I take the correct path the next morning. It's far *above* the one I was on yesterday. It isn't difficult. The few steep and rocky places are no match for yesterday's bushes, brambles, and deteriorated pathways. I should have suspected things were wrong a long time before I got so far down. But I didn't and the experience isn't so bad.

To stay or not to stay

I have always liked Villafranca del Bierzo; so when I arrive this time, I stop even though it's only 2:30 and I have walked less than 14 kilometers (9 miles) as I arrive. Actually I argue with myself for half an hour: Should I stay or go? It's only a short 10 kilometers (6.2 mi) (three hours max) to the next town. I have no impassioned answer; so I stay.

I see the San Francisco Hotel as I walk into the main square and know, even before I decide to stay, that it is my place for the night. I am going to stay with St. Frances. When we, as pilgrims, stop for the night, we get a stamp in our "pilgrim's passport," a card with such stamps used as an entry ticket into the refugios. San Francisco's stamp is especially well made with a half-tone rendition of Saint Frances. Most stamps are often quite simple, line-draw efforts; they are seldom half-tone.

We had several pilgrim passports before we ended out walk. This one begins with Somport Pass on the Spain-France border

Snow

March 26 brings cold wind and snow to my path. Light drizzle begins as I leave Molinaseca. The drizzle and the sun alternately come and go as I climb almost 1,000 meters (3,280 feet) on a road over the mountains. The views on the way up are great but I am really waiting for the view from the top where I made a movie of thousands of flowers when I walked this way in 2003. But when I get there today, any movie would have recorded only white. Heavy snow and wind meets me on the top.

The snow doesn't let up. Then at one point late in the afternoon I hear one huge thunderclap followed by an especially heavy dump of snow. Interesting, I have never been in a storm with only one thunderclap. Today there's only one.

Just before that thunder I meet a group of around a hundred school kids walking up the road from their bus to see the Cruz de Fero, the Iron Cross. They stop and talk and several have their picture taken with me. Ah! The enthusiasm of youth!

As I walk down into Foncebadón, an almost ghost town, the snow falls almost in a white-out conditions. When I see the Hostel Convent, I think it's closed and I'll have to opt for the private refugio, if it's open. I am a little anxious and quite cold. I'm not feeling like walking several kilometers to the next town. But the hostel is open and I get a room with heat and a restaurant downstairs. I'm happy to be out of the cold and even happier to have an Ethernet connection here on a remote mountain side.

A Foncebadón dog

As I enter the Hostel Convent, I met one of the dogs of Foncebadón. He only sniffs me out. The dogs here have taken on mythical proportions. They are said to haunt you, demanding you face your deepest fears. Paulo Coelho's, *The Pilgrimage* and Shirley McLane's, *The Camino* have some hair-raising stories of these dogs.

The next afternoon, I walk past a small refugio in Murias de Rechivaldo. Something pulls on me. I walk back and talk a while with the *hospitalero* (the guy running the place). We hit it off. I planned to walk forward but I stay. He, his fellow *hospitalera* (the woman equivalent), and I talk until late in the evening on our path through life and many spiritual subjects. It is no one-way street; we all profit from each other's insights.

Palm Sunday

As I walk into Astorga Sunday morning, I hear heavy, brass-band music. In time, I catch up with the end of a parade. A band pounds out dirge-style marching music. Beyond the band a huge float with palm trees and statues carried by 80 people swings from side to side.

The Palm Sunday float in Astorga.

Christian literature tells how the people of Jerusalem welcomed Jesus into Jerusalem on Palm Sunday as they would welcome a king, with palm and olive branches and leaves on the road beneath him. On the following Friday they crucified him.

I have stumbled on a parade celebrating Jesus' entry into Jerusalem that day, Palm Sunday. The ones carrying the float wear heavy capes. Pointed hats cover their heads and faces. As sinners, they wear them to hide their identity. (Only much later did the KKK copy these religious hats to cover their identities in the southern US. The hats were religious first.)

I walk beside the parade as if I am part of it. It moves very slowly. Everyone steps from foot to foot swaying side to side in time with the music. I walk beside and then ahead of the band and then the float. I stop to let them pass. The music and drums are slow and deliberate and loud. It resembles a funeral march even though it is supposed to be celebrating a triumphal entry. I continue forward walking in step with the band. My eyes are full of tears.

Entering Jerusalem

I realize this ceremony is truly reenacting Jesus' entry into Jerusalem 2,000 years ago. I realize we will be physically walking into Jerusalem in a year or so. I realize the two entries are one and the same entry. All flows together and floods my heart. More tears flow. I let them flow. I let who sees them see them. These people and I are entering Jerusalem symbolically this morning. Petra and I will entering Jerusalem physically later in the year.

The drummers of Astorga.

I sway from leg to leg to the pounding drum cadence as I pass and re-pass the huge float. I walk through the Astorga's streets from the north to the south and back north to the Cathedral. I am entering Jerusalem this morning. I am emotional and totally into the experience.

The parade lasts for better than two hours. I'm so happy that I fell on this celebration. But I suspect I didn't *just* fall on it–the Universe had a lot to do with lining us up.

The meseta

Before Sahagún an icy, cold wind beats at my back left quarter most of the day. But it's an easy walk in the flat lands of the meseta, the plains of Spain. Few trees grow naturally here. But someone has planted them along the Camino. Save for a few trees near scarce creeks, the trees along the path are the only ones I can see–a string of trees stretching backward and forward to the distant horizons. It's easy to feel alone out here. I can understand why some walkers choose to take a bus across this stretch of the Camino. For me the Meseta is a great place to get in contact with self, just like in the vast deserts and plains of America, but the meseta is considerably smaller.

The path across the meseta with only grass and trees to keep you company. This is a 2003 picture. The trees have grown little since then.

In Sahagún I take a rest day just because I want to take a rest day–no rain, not tired, just want to stop a bit, to sit down a while, to wander in place, and write a little. I walk to the edge of town and then back into the center. I find a huge market going full tilt. Stalls line no less than seven or eight blocks. Walking is a shuffle with much bumping. You want it? You can buy it. I get some fruits, vegetables, and nuts for my dinner later. And I find some thick cushioned socks. It's time. My old ones have warn so thin that they give me little cushioning any more. At one point a short downpour sends masses to crowd under porticoed store fronts and merchants to putting tarps over their goods. It's over in four minutes.

A few days ago the wind broke my umbrella. As I walked through Mansilla de las Mulas, I bought a new one, not the best, but the best I can find. The day before Sahagún wind bent one of its spars already. It's neither big enough nor strong enough. So today I'm looking for a stronger and bigger one. I find only small ones.

Mountains north of the meseta.

First cuckoo

April 5 at 12:36 is an exciting time. Five kilometers (3 miles) west of Carrión de los Condes I hear my first cuckoo this year. For you in the U.S. where they don't exist in the wild, the cuckoo sounds exactly like the clock version. We used to listen to cuckoos throughout spring in southern Germany. Since his unique call is a lure to snatch a mate, it becomes silent after spring. The cuckoo was a special bird for me when I walked the Camino in 2003. I had never heard it in the wild before. There I heard it often. It became and remains a call Petra and I use to locate one another when we become separated. We, "Cuckoo!" and wait for an answer. It works. Now the cuckoo is back with me on the Camino.

Total change

As I approach Frómista, I knew I am going to pass a place where, in 2003, I took a picture of the road. There was a medieval pilgrim cross and a road sign saying 475 kilometers (290 miles) to Santiago. I was impressed that I had already walked 250 kilometers (155 miles). At the same time I was apprehensive that I had to walk so far yet. There are more than a few changes. The sign and cross are gone, replaced by a huge interchange with a new super highway that wasn't even here in 2003. The middle of the path in 2003 had many pillars marking the way (like the picture on the next page); they are all uprooted now. In a word, the place is totally different! The world changes.

Nineteen pilgrims walking west on the Camino west of Frómista.

I stay in refugios in Boadilla del Camino and Castrojeriz. Both are restful and quiet. All refugios are not created equal. Some give you ample space, a place to sit, tables for writing and eating, comfortable beds, circulating air, and friendly hospitaleros — some are actually rather nice. Others are quite basic offering few amenities. These belong to the former variety.

Flowers are still scarce in early April. Only dandelions and some little white daisy-like flowers are in bloom. This is a far cry from the hundreds of different flowers that inspired and excited me as I walked the Camino in May, 2003.

The distances between places and the height of hills I climb feel a lot less than they were in 2003. I suspect a lot has to do with being more in shape than I was then. And now I know a lot more about walking one step at a time and stopping to rest than I did then.

I remember many fewer young and middle aged people in 2003 than I am seeing in 2010. Now the age groups are more equally represented. No age group dominates.

The Internet is available many places along the Camino. When the place I am staying doesn't have Internet or Wi-Fi, I can often pick up an insecure network from someone else nearby. But the latter has its risks. The network can disappear without warning as it does for me a couple times in Castrojeriz.

Dinner on the steps

I stay in a packed refugio in Hornillos del Camino. It is a hot evening and the bunk beds are close together. The kitchen has room for no more than six to eight people to sit. We are many more than that. Not to worry. There are steps outside the refugio in front of the church though they're not well shaded. Many sit there.

A mobile store arrives at the steps. It sports all manner of food— olives, nuts, cheeses, breads, candies, prepared salads. I buy something for dinner. The kitchen is cramped so I retreat to the steps and find some shade and space for my elbows. As I finish my salad, olives, and bread, the hospitalero comes up and says, "You can't eat out here on the steps. You have to eat inside, in the kitchen."

"Why? The kitchen is full."

"Because you will spill things on the white steps and make stains." A rather feeble reason since all the other steps around are a uniform gray. You would think they would like the new white steps to blend in with the surrounding steps and pavement eventually. Oh well. It's their steps. Nonetheless, I'm still a bit miffed. After checking out the kitchen once more, I return to complete my meal on the steps before retreating to the bar across the street for a glass of wine.

In Burgos I rest a couple days. I also shop for shoes, wash clothes, and walk around to see sights. I enjoy the 65-degree (18-C.) sunshine, which would have been really nice had I walked. But I need the time off after seven days walking. My feet and back tell me so.

The first two times I visited San Juan De Ortega I was uneasy both times. I slept on a crowded floor the first time and in a cold dorm the second time and I just didn't feel good with the atmosphere. So the long walk from Burgos to San Juan was to revisit old daemons. They were nowhere around. I had a wonderful evening and enjoyed the people I talked with. One couple, Michel and Catherine, invite Petra and me to stay with them in their home in Bizanos, France, when we get there. We do. The stigma of San Juan is gone. I am at ease.

I walk rather deliberately and with little relaxation to Belorado, and on to Santo Domingo de la Calzada to meet Petra. I have a goal and a deadline and I walk less in the Now as I execute the steps that take me somewhere else than where I am. I could have had Petra meet me in Burgos as well as here, but I felt I wanted to walk these steps alone, especially to San Juan.

Petra returns

Petra rejones me in Santo Domingo de la Calzada. I have walked some 384 miles (622 kilometers) in 28 days while Petra was in Germany to fast, rest, and to visit friends.

While I walked alone, I chose not to shave. We are happy to see each other when Petra returns. But there is work to be done. Find a barber. In an hour I am clean faced and ready to walk with my lady.

Steve

As we walk east the first day together in a month Petra asks, "I wonder if we will meet anyone we know on the Camino? Remember how we met Steve in 2004?"

Steve, now 72, is an American Petra met as she walked her first Camino in 2003. We met him with his friend again as we walked east on the Camino in 2004.

Now this very evening we stay in the comfortable, new refugio in Azofra. While we eat Petra says, "He looks like Steve over there!"

"He does."

She gets up, walks over, and stands in front of him, "Steve?"

"Yes?" There he is! The Universe sent out messages this afternoon to get us thinking about him beforehand so we would be looking. Tears come to our eyes.

We tell each other what has happened to our lives since we last met in 2004. He lived with a friend in France most of those years. That's over now. He is walking the Camino one last time for nostalgia before returning to the western U.S. to do whatever is next in his life. Buon Camino of life, Steve.

As we walk the rest of the Camino we meet no one else we knew before, only Steve.

By Torres del Rio, we are walking forward at our 18 to 20 kilometers per day rate (ca. 12 miles). Weather is holding mostly well with cold wind in our faces now and then. Tonight we have a wonderful meal with a wonderful view of the mountains and village around us. Petra is the cook. The refugio is the place.

Cuno

The next day we meet Cuno, a pilgrim on the road for most of the last 17 years (that's right, **17 years!**). He went back home to Germany to try to work again in his carpenter career last year. He couldn't. Now he is back on the road. When someone asks him how he can do this for 17 years, he answers, "You have the watch. I have the time."

Cuno shows us Noodle.

Cuno is on his way to Jerusalem just now. But I suspect he will arrive later, a lot later, than we arrive. We walk together for half of a couple days and camp together one night. His tiny dog is *Noodle* because she likes spaghetti; but Cuno doesn't think *Spaghetti* is a good name for a female dog.

In Los Arcos Cuno plays his flute in the afternoon in a doorway next to the church on the Camino. Noodle sits on his lap helping to soften those passing by and to attract women pilgrims. That's Cuno and Noodle's work. As Cuno dines in the evening at someone's invitation, he tells me he did well this afternoon.

4,500 mi. (7,290 km.) – April 23, 2010

In two days, we are in Estella still around 180 kilometers (110 mi) from the French boarder moving slowly that way. The weather has heated up a bit. Except for drizzle today, we have seen little rain for some days. The flowers have finally made their presence known and the grain fields are green. We even see our first red poppies today. In a couple weeks they will be carpeting the fields. We are taking the day off, just to sit.

Petra stands on the top of Puente la Reina, a bridge built by the queen for pilgrims in the 11th century.

As we walk through Puente la Reina (Queen's Bridge), we stop to look in on the refugio kitchen where we met seven years earlier.

Eunate

The hexagonal Templar church at Eunate.

We stay east of Puente la Reina at the refugio at Eunate, a small hexagonal church attributed to the Knights Templar. It is a place of special spiritual strength for both of us.

Tradition says that when you walk around Eunate's courtyard three times without your shoes and then walk into the center of the church, you will get some insight. For me the walk on standing-on-end stones is anything but comfortable. But the insight I get is worth the discomfort.

Eunate's courtyard with its punishing stone pavement.

Petra describes her walk around the chapel like this:

> I think about my first time in this chapel in 2003. I received an important insight after walking around this chapel. I am ready for another insight for this long pilgrimage to Jerusalem. I start walking barefoot on the stones. Every step is painful. I feel a strong desire to reach the chapel's entrance quickly to get inside and off the stones. Near the end of my second circuit I realize that when I walk much slower and when I walk every step with awareness, then the pain of the little stones is totally gone. Even more, when I try to embrace every stone with the soles of feet, every step becomes a massage. A little later I feel that this walk around the chapel is my life and the entrance on the west side of the chapel is my death. Death comes after three circuits, whether I walk fast or slow. I start my third circuit walking very slowly. Every step is connected with my breathing and in slow motion. If I walk every step of my life or of this pilgrimage with total awareness, the stones along my path won't hurt. I am in the Now and enjoying life and pilgrimage right in the moment. The

longing to get to the west entrance is gone. I can enjoy every step. Just before reaching the west entrance, the symbol of my death, I am contented and ready to go inside because I am in peace and joy with every step of my last circuit.

I hope I can transfer this insight to my life and walk every step with joy and without rushing. Death comes at the west entrance whether I run or enjoy a slow walk through life. Rushing I'll have less experience, less depth, less awareness, less peace and joy.

That's it. I have the choice. I received this insight and it is good, it helps slow us down on our path to Jerusalem. This insight will be with me the rest of my life as a continuous reminder to be and live in the Now.

A fellow pilgrim in Eunate refugio tells us, "I climbed the corporate latter but when I got to the top, I found it was leaning against the wrong wall." At 38, he quit his lucrative job with a world-class company in Germany and took to the Camino to discover his next steps. We enjoy talking with each other.

Eunate's refugio accommodates only eight. They provide dinner and breakfast and a contemplative environment and ask only for whatever you want to give as a donation. Eunate is a good place to stop.

Earlier we stayed at a refugio we can contrast with Eunate. At that place they also serve dinner. But they are only interested in filling bellies and getting the preparation done efficiently. They serve the same food every day because the pilgrims "are always different." And the hospitaleros don't eat with the pilgrims. In contrast, at Eunate the food was prepared with care and the hospitaleros eat with the pilgrims. They feed the stomach but they do not forget the spirit also.

Every refugio is different. Some barely pass as places to rest and others are almost luxurious. Only a few provide food as these do. When we walked seven years ago, municipalities along the way provided most refugios. Now with the ever-increasing number of pilgrims many private refugios have popped up.

We have been questioning whether to continue this pilgrimage. It's not only Missouri's heat and Portugal's cold dampness but the day-in and day-out monotony of it that sometimes gets the best of us. What is the point? Why are we continuing? A week ago we thought of only walking as far as Eunate because of its spiritual importance. Now we are walking forward, at least a week or so into France to see what it is like. But this theme of stopping continues to come up as we keep extending our goal a little farther again and again.

A bracelet

In Monreal we stay in the Casa Rual Etxartena when the refugio is too crowded. The woman of the house makes bead bracelets and connects their use to Eckhart Tolle's exercise to help one have positive thoughts. You use the bracelet like this: when you have a negative thought or say negative things, you move your bracelet to your other arm. The object is to not move the bracelet. When you succeed in not moving it for 21 days, your life will be profoundly changed. I must say that even accomplishing that for a day or two is a positive thing for me. I find it also helps a lot to heal negative actions soon after you commit them, especially when two or more do the project together. Get a bracelet, any will do, and try it.

Foz de Lumbier

The next day we take an alternate route and stay in a mobile home in Lumbier. The following morning, our path takes us along an old railway bed through the *Foz* (Canyon) of the Lumbier River. It is only a mile or so (1-2 kilometers) long but an exhilarating change from the mountainsides and valleys we have been walking. We enter a tunnel and emerge in a deep canyon. Trees cling to sheer walls. Flocks of vultures sit on the cliff tops and soar in circles high above. Bird chatter and the sound of rushing water fill the air to the complete exclusion of the auto and truck sounds we usually constantly endure as we walk. At the other end of the canyon, we enter another longer and darker tunnel and emerge from the canyon back in land like before we entered the first tunnel. It is like we enter another world, like we are on some science-fiction starship entering and leaving some space warp. We knew nothing of this *foz* as we arrived in Lumbier the night before. Thanks for the experience, Universe.

Later in the day we stop at a nondescript truck stop for a sandwich and are treated to a delicious new creation: anchovies and tomatoes along with fired onions and eggplant on a hard bread roll. You never know what you'll be treated to along the path.

In the succeeding days we pass through deep valleys, high hills, and higher mountains and experience cuckoos, flowers, sun, wind, a little rain, and 80 kilometers (50 miles) of paths. We labor over a rocky mountain and walk down a long valley parallel to the Aragon River to Jaca, the end of traveling east for a while. We pass through Undues de Larde, Ruesta, Artieda, Mianos, Arres, Puente la Reina de Jaca, and Santa Cilia de Jaca, all tiny villages.

Berdún or Lhasa?

Berdún below the Pyrenees on the Aragon River.

As we walk down the Aragon River Valley the village of Berdún sits like a crown on a hill across the river on the far side of the valley. With the snowcapped Pyrenees in the background it looks like a Tibetan city, a bit like Lhasa actually, like the traditional pictures of the Dalai Lama's castle in Lhasa. We stayed in Berdún as we drove along the Camino in the fall of 2003. When we tried to walk from there we got totally lost and ended up in the Aragon River.

After buying warmer clothes in Jaca for the mountains, we head for Somport Pass in the Pyrenees. As we turn north the weather also turns north. The wind is cold and it's supposed to snow today. We are at only 820 meters (2,700 feet) in Jaca but the pass is at 1,632 meters (5,250 feet). We expect more snow up there. The temperature hangs around freezing, not exactly my expectation for May.

Near the pass we stay in Confranc Estation at the Albergue Pepito Grilio, Little Cricket. The owners travel to the Himalayas often. The walls are covered with pictures of the mountains. We have no idea that, as we look at the pictures, we would be in the Himalayas in a year, but we were.

The next day we walk over Somport Pass in the middle of the day. Snow sits deeply on the mountain sides. It's only a little over freezing and the light wind is biting. It's May 7, 2010; the day Mike started the Camino de Santiago the first time in 2003.

Chemin d'Arles

We have arrived in France. No more daily searches for smoke-free bars and restaurants. We are in France where all are smoke-free. Most in Spain are not.

We are about to begin walking the Chemin d'Arles also known as the Camino de Arles or Via Tolonesa. This route is the traditional route that fed into the Camino de Santiago at Somport pass after coming across southern France from Arles south of Avignon. See map on page **Error! Bookmark not defined.**.

Pyrenees

Trees showcase their new, virgin-green leaves. Yesterday's fierce wind is nowhere around. Only light breezes move the crisp air. It's a day designed to make me want to continue walking a long time. We walk 16 kilometers (ten miles) down into France.

High rocky peaks of snow and ice tower over us.

Borce

We stay in a six-person refugio in Borce. A small untraditional chapel stands next to it. Its altar has a tower with hundreds of lighted and colored glass pieces in place of a traditional altarpiece.

France is, well, French. So they have their own names for lodging. Here are the ones mentioned later in this section:

- A *hôtel* is like a hotel in the rest of the world.
- A *gîte* is a private home or municipal place for one to stay. It can be a dormitory like the refugios in Spain or a room like any hotel. *Gîtes* also sometimes offer evening dinner and breakfast for an additional price. *Gîtes* are for everyone. You

do not have to be a pilgrim to stay in them like the refugios in Spain.

- A *chambre d'hote* is like a B&B in the U.S. or Canada.

We continue down the Aspe Valley deeper into France. We are not walking fast. It is too beautiful to do that. There is much to absorb. Besides, what is an extra day or two in a pilgrimage that will ultimately take two years? We are really enjoying this part of the walk. None the less, the 1,200 meters (3,900 feet) we come down from the pass in the first couple days along the road takes its toll on our calf muscles, especially Petra's. We are not used to walking down so much.

Looking back toward the border from Bedous, France.

Next?

After Oloron St. Marie, though I try hard to stay in the Now and enjoy the walk, my mind wanders again and again to what we'll be doing and where we'll go when we stop this walk in a few days or weeks or months. I enjoy the flowers, the trees, the fields, and the rain. If we decide to end the pilgrimage in Pao, so we do. If we walk all the way to Arles, we do that. I want to stop. I don't want to stop. We want to stop, yet we don't want to stop. It's our walk and when we are ready, we can stop.

Three dogs

Before Lacommande we are walking a little used road in a forest. We pass couple houses and a house trailer. A car blocks part of the road.

I hear scrambling on the other side of the car. Petra is a little ahead. Suddenly, three growling dogs showing their teeth rush out clearly intent on doing me bodily harm. They keep coming. In less than a couple seconds I have to do something. What? I remember someone once saying you can scare a bear by making yourself big and yelling really loud. *Maybe it works with dogs too? If it doesn't....*

I take a deep breath, grimace my face, show my teeth, stretch out my arms, and let out a profound roar, a growl-roar from some dark place deep inside me. I have never heard such a sound come out of me. They all stop dead in their tracks, one only inches from my leg. It works. I am relived. Just then I hear the owner call the dogs off from behind the car. He apologizes and I walk away with a little less blood in my legs. Curiously, I was never afraid. I didn't have time to be afraid. I could only react. That is the only threatening encounter we have with dogs on the pilgrimage.

A lady and her donkey

We endure a short but intense rain and sleet storm an hour before we come to the four-person pilgrim *gîte* at the church in Lacommande. The drizzle continues. After we get settled, a woman, Elizabeth, comes into the compound with her donkey. She has come from north of Arles and is headed for Santiago.

Elizabeth and Petra eating breakfast.

After spending all day walking, she spends more than an hour feeding her donkey, setting up a fence, and generally getting her donkey settled before she comes in and prepares her own things for supper and the night. She repeats the same routine in the morning. And she does this day in and day out as she walks west, three or four hours a day. To me that's a lot of work just to have an animal carry your pack. Ok, I know, the donkey is a companion too.

We hear from Elizabeth a long time later after she has safely returned home, also with the donkey.

Michel and Catherine

In Bizanos, near Pao, we stay two nights with Michel and Catherine at their home. I met them in San Juan de Ortega, Spain, last month when they invited us to stay as we pass through. We have long discussions with them about the pros and cons of stopping or not. Stopping is an ongoing theme in France. Thanks Michel and Catherine for your input and for the home for two days.

We have already left the big mountains and have descended to the foothills—we see the high Pyrenees from a fine walkway in the city.

A ballpark

From my notebook written in Bizanos:

> As I quit studying to be a priest 38 years ago, my bishop told me I need a ballpark as a base for telling my story to the people. This afternoon standing in a church by an altar here in Pau, I realize that, that "ballpark" today is this pilgrimage to Jerusalem. "The people" are all those we speak to along the road encouraging them to seek and follow their dreams. They grow and I grow.

While we lived in Paso Robles we couldn't get people to come to our seminars and slideshows on walking and following their dreams. Once we began this pilgrimage, they appeared. We have our ballpark and people are interested.

Foie gras

On the way to Montesquiou we pass a beautiful château. They have a *chalêt*, a cabin with beds for sale. We think about staying. Its prices are reasonable and it looks like a fun place to spend the night. But we booked another place last night. So we walk a couple more kilometers and check into Le Ferme des Grisettes, a goose farm.

The goose farm turns out to be a mixture of good French food, French wine, and French farming, all offered for a reasonable price that includes dinner and breakfast. Our dinner comes with goose and several different versions of *foie gras*, the fat goose liver the French love so much. Before dinner the farmer takes us and the other guests, a French couple, to the barn and shows us how they feed the geese to make *foie gras*. They stick a tube down their throat into their stomach and inject them with a liter of ground corn and grease three times a day to produce the abnormal livers. To my way of thinking, that grows geese with diseased livers. The French love to eat sick livers? I like neither the taste of foie *gras* nor the way it is produced, but we have tried it.

French countryside.

Barran

The next night we stay with two other pilgrims in a municipal *gîte* in the small village of Barran. It is a simple place on the upper floor of a building in the middle of town, four beds, a table, chairs, and a stove. We all shop at the store and cook up a big pot of stew and eat it with bread and wine. Tonight we spend time with fellow walkers over a common meal. We cook, eat, and sleep all together in the same room.

We have had big dinners in the *Gîte* and *Chambre d'hote* the last two nights and now tonight again. If we keep eating like this, we'll have to walk faster and longer to keep the weight off.

Barran city gate.

Barran is a medieval village complete with city wall, water-filled mote, and swimming swans. And the church has a steeple that looks like a corkscrew. We are really enjoying this part of France with its high, rolling hills with young grains and trees stretching as far as you can see. Churches and the ruins of castles peek up through the trees on the ridge lines. And the Pyrenees lay along the horizon to the south.

At the Hotel du Lac in L'Isle-Jourdain we stay a couple nights on a lake resting in an almost empty hotel. In fact we are the only ones in the Hotel the second night. When we leave they gave us a bottle of *Chemins de Pelerins 2007* wine, Pilgrim Camino wine.

Barran and the Pyrenees.

Canal du Midi

We take a train 41 kilometers (25.5 miles) from L'Isle-Jourdain to Toulouse where we wander most of the day visiting the cathedral and finding a good French dictionary. Then we walk to the Canal du Midi and head southeast. The Canal du Midi at 240 kilometers (150 miles) is part of a canal system that runs around 500 kilometers (310 miles) across southern France connecting Bordeaux on the Atlantic with Béziers and Sète on the Mediterranean Sea. If you have a boat you can travel the entire distance.

A port along the Canal du Midi

Petra walks the Canal du Midi

We walk three days on the towpath along the wide Canal du Midi.

Sleeping on the canal

We leave Toulouse down the canal not knowing where we were going to stay in the evening. As the day advances we check out a couple hotels and pass. Then we notice a *chambre d'hôte* tied along the canal. It's a canal boat. Intriguing. We check it and decide to stay. In the end it's not our best decision. A pricy dinner is extra but not up to French standards. Things aren't totally ship shape here, but that's part of a pilgrimage too. After going to bed, Petra moves to a different room when light sewer smell invades our room. It's an OK first and last experience on a canal-boat *chambre d'hôte*.

The trees along the canal reach high and to the center of the canal forming huge flowing pointed arches over the water. The trees and canal are more majestic than the ceiling in the cathedral in Toulouse.

Parting waters

At one point we come to the parting of the waters. For a canal to work it has to have a water supply. For the Canal du Midi it is the *Rigole*, the feeder canal. The water comes down the *Rigole* from the mountains to the canal where some water flows south to the

Mediterranean and the rest north to Toulouse. Think of it as the top of a hill. The locks in each direction let water to a lower level as they move boats up and down to the next level they want to travel.

The Rigole *waters the entire canal. It isn't very impressive.*

Claud and friends

In Castres we visit three bicyclists we met earlier in Oloron de St Marie. Two of them pick us up in the early afternoon and take us to their place. They are mechanics. Today proves to be a French eating experience. We go to the house of one. All three cyclists are here with their wives and a full meal is prepared and ready. We have appetizers, meat, potatoes, and the trimmings, cheese, and desert. And, yes, wine too. And for the whole meal they talk about food they have had, what they are eating, and what they will eat next week. This is all part of the French way of dining.

After we rest and talk, it is time to go to Claud and his wife's place, where we will stay tonight. Someone says we will have a "small meal." We are full and protest. "It'll only be a little bit." That "little bit" turns out to be almost as big as the first layout. We eat and drink enough for half a week today. And following French tradition, the conversation is again food. Thanks much, ladies and gentlemen. This was a good introduction to French culture.

A peaceful road in southern France on a sunny afternoon.

After a week walking mainly small mountain and valley roads, we stay three days in a mobile home in St. Gervais sur Mare to rest and sit out a bout of rain. A couple days later we happen on La Palombe a fine hotel and retreat center while walking a remote mountain road. We stop in for a coffee and the woman running the place invites us to stay for the night. We stay that night and the next. The stay is free but the restaurant costs more than our normal budget allows. Together the free room and higher-than-normal food costs even out in the end. We enjoy the stay. Thanks, Margaret.

Cherries

We have been eating cherries as we walk the roads this month. Many trees hang their ripe-cherry-filled branches over the road asking to be eaten. One day in early June someone just pruned a tree and left the branches and many cherries on the ground. We each eat more than a quart before we move on.

We arrive in St. Jean de Fos 11 June after walking over a mountain into a newer and drier environment. Though it rains late in the afternoon, the vegetation here is more dry-climate-like with smaller and thicker leaves than what is on the other side of the mountain. The air even smells drier.

After establishing ourselves in our *chambre d'hote* in St. Jean, we walk a few miles up to St. Guilhem-le-Désert viewing the narrow and deep Heraut Canyon along the way. The town is mostly an oppressive tourist trap. The rain comes back and the bus isn't running today. We hitchhike back to St. Jean.

5,000 mi. (8,100 km.) – June 12, 2010

A Montpellier triumphal arch.

We'll stop

Stopping the walk is never far from our minds in France. We've said that before. We sit on a bench on the way into Montpellier and decide to stop the pilgrimage in Arles. Having made the decision, we still waffle for a few days.

In Montpellier we stay in the hostel Saint Roch, a huge baroque castle. We are the only ones on a floor with many bunk beds, a kitchen, dining room, and large lounge. We have a castle to ourselves! We enjoy this stop.

As we leave Montpellier we begin to see more and more huge fields of flowering lavender. The land becomes flat.

This building behind our refugio in Montpellier is not what it looks like at first glance. Except for the tables in front and the middle-level windows at the right and middle, this is a painting, entirely a painting.

No room but ...

The sun is not always with us here. In fact as we walk into Le Cailer and enter the La Manadiere Hotel a huge downpour begins. But they have no room. They call around and find a place miles away. That doesn't help us. More phoning.

The woman running the place suggests we eat dinner first. She seats us next to the kitchen in a room with a glass roof. We eat a fine meal complete with ice cream cones at the end. As we eat the rain pounds on the glass above and smiling waiters and waitresses scurry past loaded down with plates of food. I think I will remember this surreal evening as a truly French experience for many years.

After dinner we are surprised when the woman in charge announces that our room is ready. Though the room small it is far better than going back out into the rain. It turns out that a group of school girls has booked the entire hotel tonight under the condition that no one else stays in the hotel. Some negotiations went on with the chaperones while we were eating. They decided we could stay.

The next morning we leave town through a long dark tunnel of trees. Tree-lined roads are everywhere in France but this one is particularly dark and dense. It is a rather spooky walk actually.

Petra walks through a French tree tunnel leaving Le Cailer.

Beyond the trees as we walk up to a bike path. A car pulls up and two guys get out. As they remove their bicycles, a little goat jumps out. He prances over and bounds onto a bench next to Petra who is now sitting. She pets him and he bounces off. The bikers say, "Hello" too and pedal down the path followed by an awkwardly running kid goat.

Petra's joy of walking

Petra's impressions of the walk so far:

> I walked so many miles with deep joy out in nature with the elements, touched by the rain, wind, sun, dust,

fragrances, and the vast open land of the western U.S. I can still see myself walking down roads in the west and feeling so small in that wide-open land and yet so connected with the spiritual world.

Every morning started with a ritual evolved after meeting and talking with many different people along our path. In this ritual I said thank you to all the people we had met and made them part of our pilgrimage. By the end of our walk, quite a number of people were in the ritual.

Breathing deeply and walking with awareness was a focus of the walk. Walking along big roads was a challenge in the beginning. Staying in the Now and embracing the joy of walking made it possible to walk with joy. After a while little causes me to complain about cars, trucks, noise and other things that are part of the world that we are all living in. I find it is easy to be in peace in the solitude of pure nature, but to be in peace walking on a busy highway is far more a spiritually challenging moment. One time I was walking down a busy rush-hour highway. I had a hard time enjoying the walk with all the traffic noise and fast cars. After a while I discovered a little creek on the left as I walked. The creek was meandering through the countryside. In spite of the road noise I could even hear the water trickling. I discovered it was my decision what to concentrate on: on the creek or on the busy road. I always have the choice to see the beauty. After two or three months I was joyous even with unpleasant encounters. Walking became mediation.

One question that people asked us often: "Do you carry backups, like extra shoes or clothes?" Walking with all you need for right now is walking without backups. We don't have room for backups. Backups are for the non-nomadic world. Walking across America and Europe was clearly nomadic. I used to say: "I am working on remembering my spiritual backup." That is, my belief that all beings are connected and that the Universe will provide all things when we need them. Finding a doll cart in the desert was first the answer for Mike's back pain. Second, it was a long-term solution for taking care of our body joints on this long pilgrimage. It came when it was needed.

The joy of walking is also connected with feelings and insights that came to me while I was walking. In the desert, for example, deep roots help the Joshua tree to survive and even flourish in the desert environment. Walking through the Mojave Desert with many Joshua Trees made me think about how deep my spiritual roots are. How could I deepen them to live well and even flourish in difficult situations in life?

Walking in the strong spring winds of Arizona and New Mexico was a new experience. I had never before encountered such a force. At first, I had no idea how to react to the wind without getting exhausted. The wind frightened me. I prayed that it would stop or at least decrease. Only after a Native American told me the wind is a deep cleansing agent that blows out winter's debris did I realize it was time to send prayers with the wind to all beings. Only then was I more at peace with the wind. The force and sound of the wind was good for praying and purging all unnecessary thoughts from my head. It was cleansing my mind! No thought had a chance to find a corner to hang onto in my head when the wind blew like that.

I felt connected to the trees along the roads and paths across America. With all the cars the trees have little chance to say hello to us human beings or the other way around. I liked greeting a tree and saying thank you for being there, for giving us shade during a hot summer day or shelter from rain. It was a great joy to see the first spring green and the first tree in blossom at the Rio Grande in New Mexico after walking miles in the desert. I was so thankful for that. I could understand why the early Spanish wanted to live at the Rio Grande.

The joy of walking comes also from movement under your feet; with every step you move forward. Moving forward and breathing in and out become one. If your breathing is deep and calm, the walk is joyous and light.

Someone told us, it takes 12 months to renew all the cells in your body. After walking 12 months my body was all walking cells created with a lot of oxygen, wind, sun, rain, heat, prayers, and deep and intensive conservations with people along the way. This is a reason that after walking a while you become one with the walk.

On a long pilgrimage one has no choice of the "best" walking season. Nirvana is where you have no choice. Each season has something in store for you. Missouri's humid summer heat was difficult to walk through. At the same time the heat cleansed our bodies with much sweating. In Germany I often went to a sauna and paid to get the same effect. My experience is that every situation has more than one side.

The steady walking movement and the deep conversations with each other and with the people we met helped my physical and spiritual flow. I felt peaceful and joyous with what I was doing. After entering Europe this flow decreased. The deep conservations were missing because I don't speak Portuguese.

The rain was heavy. The food was heavy. I felt heavy. Portugal was a different part of the pilgrimage. Portugal was both a challenge to deal with and a temptation to end the pilgrimage. Portugal's mildewed, cold, and damp housing made me question whether I still felt the urge to walk the pilgrimage to Jerusalem. I was sick three or four times. I felt homesick for the U.S. I wanted to go back. Was it really important to walk forward? The only thing pulling me forward was Santiago de Compostela a major milestone along our path to Jerusalem.

As we arrived in Santiago de Compostela in Spain, I felt the pilgrimage was done for me. We had planned a side trip to visit my mother in Germany to celebrate her 80th birthday. As I met with German friends during that break, it became clear that I needed a longer break. I wanted to fast. I was overloaded with experience and happenings. I had to take time off. After a month Mike went back alone to continue walking. It was good to be alone, fasting and renewing my walking spirit.

Mike and I met a month later in Spain and continued walking toward Jerusalem. There were things to see along the path, but even though I had taken off two months, I was less in tune with the walk than I was in America and before Santiago. At that point, walking the pilgrimage became mechanical for me, almost like I was doing a routine job.

Things change from Spain to France. France was light and bright with spring flowers and virgin green. We loved the landscape, the flowers, and the little French villages. We enjoyed the people we met. The walk again became delightful and I enjoyed walking even though it sometimes felt mechanical. The other part of the pilgrimage, having no home, no kitchen, and no friends to meet was not an easy matter. Yes, we met people and we talked, but less deeply than before. I missed my social community. As we stopped in Arles, we had been one year and 5 months on the pilgrimage. Most people have a social community. On our walk in Europe we had no such community. In the U.S. we talked with many people and shared our story of life. There was an exchange of life experience and wisdom. The Camino de Santiago has a pilgrim's community. This is helpful in many situations.

If you go on such a long pilgrimage, you are mainly alone or with your partner. You meet people, but you are separated from your social community. On a pilgrimage you leave your home community. On the path nobody knows you longer than a few days; so you get to know yourself. This experience taught me, that a home and a social community are important for me.

In France we were around 2/3^{rds} of the way to Jerusalem, a time when many questions and crises occur in a pilgrimage. In France we walked forward out of commitment and, like in life, sometimes we walked through difficult situations to grow without knowing how we would grow. But we questioned ourselves more and more in France. Why we are walking to Jerusalem? How can we stop the pilgrimage? What is the end of the pilgrimage? Do we want to stop only when we are sick or one of us dies? What would the other one do if one were to die? For both of us it was clear. We would continue to walk the pilgrimage to Jerusalem alone after a while.

Before we started our pilgrimage, I had many romantic ideas about life on the road. I had never thought that a two-year walking pilgrimage could be too long for me and full of its own challenges.

Time to stop

As we approach Arles on June 19, we have already decided to end the pilgrimage. We take an "official" end-of-the-pilgrimage picture along a little-used road a few miles from Arles.

We are so sure we are going to stop that we post the text below (without strikeout) on the WalkingEast.com journal. But all is not so much in stone. We still waffle. Fifteen hours later I modify it (striking out text) as shown. We have been thinking and talking about this since Spain. We thought we had a decision. But now we have other solutions and perhaps we will be continuing. We leave the post online to let our readers know that we are not always sure what is going to happen even the next day as we walk east.

> ~~We have ended our pilgrimage here in Arles. We will be returning to the US soon.~~ It has been a great 500+ days. Wow! It has really been 16+ months and we have walked over 5,000 miles (8,200 kilometers). Now it's time to rest and digest for a while. ~~We leave the Alps, Italy, Greece, and Turkey for another day.~~

We walk into Arles 19 June, exactly seven years after arriving at Finisterra at to end our first Camino de Santiago pilgrimage.

We look up Paul and Babette, the writers of the *Lightfoot Guides to the Via Francigena* and *Via Domitia* (pp. 267 and 341). We find they are out on the trails gathering information for their upcoming updates and for the new *Guide to the Via Domitia* (not written at that time).

We stay in Arles a while. Looking over a map of Arles one day, I discover a Rue Metras! *It isn't a long street.* It's in a dark corner of town along the river. But here it is. It is even in what I thought was our Anglicized version, Metras vs. Matrau, which I thought was the French version.

One afternoon four days later we sit under big trees in a square. The sun is bright. The shade is cool. The breeze is gentle. The temperature hangs around 77 (25 C.). The night is just as beautiful. It's a fine time to be here. But there is an overriding call to go to the mountains for a while. After so much discussing and so many 'yeses' and 'nos' in the past several weeks, we have decided to stop the walking part of the pilgrimage for now.

An Arles café near our hotel.

Encounters on the road to Jerusalem

Edison Lake from our campsite.

SUMMER 2010

A retreat in the Sierras

The Sierras? They aren't in France. They're in California. Yes.

We are going on retreat in the Sierra Nevada Mountains of California for two or three months. Even walking is too fast for us now. We have to stop, to sit, and to see what the Universe wants to show and tell us.

We book the flight to San Francisco, go to the Mediterranean at Adge (near Béziers) for a week and stay in a mobile home, and then fly to Germany to visit Petra's mom before flying to California.

On 23 June in Arles on the blog I ask: "Will we ever arrive in Jerusalem? We don't know. It's important that we recognized the original call and acted on it. The journey is and has always been the destination. We have walked 5,000 miles (8,200 kilometers). We can take on the last 3,000 or so miles (5,000 kilometers) sometime in the future—if we ever do."

We have stopped to digest what has been happening. We have fallen into many habits and ways of doing things that are draining our excitement. It's time to revitalize the pilgrimage…or to stop it.

When we get to California, we stay a week with friends Helga and Alex on the coast near to where we started walking a year and a half ago.

We stop at our storage to pick up and drop off some things. We are amazed that clothes still smell like they were washed only yesterday. California's dry weather should continue to keep things fine in the storage for another year and a half or more.

Our camp site at Mono Hot Springs.

Edison Lake

We rent a car and head for the Sierra Nevada Mountains first staying at Mono Hot Springs to soak in the hot water before moving up the mountains to Edison Lake at 7,500 feet (2,285 meters) to set up camp. We are between Yosemite and Kings Canyon National Parks just below the John Muir Trail, a section of the Pacific Crest Trail that goes from Mexico to Canada along the crest of the Sierras. Tree-lined mountains topped with bare rock surround us on three sides. It storms only once while we are here and that is more thunder than rain. Standing in the sun, we bake; in the shade we are decidedly cool. But the temperatures are only in the 70s (22-25C.).

Edison Lake.

Though we leave a few times, this is home for 25 days. I take bi-weekly trips to the lowlands to resupply but Petra spends most of her time here. We drive 20 miles over a primitive mountain road to a mountain pass a couple times to use the telephone. Ours doesn't work at the lake.

It is a good place to reflect on where we have been, where we are, and where we are going. We can take long walks on little used mountain paths, bathe naked in the lake (bit cold for me), and just sit in our new and necessary 12 x 12 (3.6 m x 3.6 m) screen tent to avoid the day's flies and evening's and morning's mosquotes. Petra cooks on our alcohol stove using our bear box as a table.

Speaking of bears, they are through the campground almost nightly though we only hear them. The only one we see walks harmlessly through another campground below Mt. Whitney in late August.

Petra resting on Edison Lake.

"5,000 Miles"

We eat and get minor supplies at the informal Vermilion Valley Resort at the west end of the lake. Besides offering services to those visiting Edison for fishing and camping, it caters to the hikers on the Pacific Crest and John Muir Trails. Jim, the owner, on hearing we have walked 5,000 miles sets up our tab with the name "5,000 Miles" and nothing else. He doesn't know who we are other than Petra and Mike. We pay for everything at once as we leave. We eat at their restaurant and set around the campfire talking with others one or two nights a week.

On 6 August on the web journal I report, "When will we return to Arles? Today we don't know when or if we will. Our time here in the dry, fresh air will tell us. We'll decide when it is time to decide."

Petra walks John Muir

One of Petra's aims in coming here is to walk on the John Muir trail alone. On 6 August, two weeks after arriving, she heads up the trail into the wilderness.

While Petra is gone I walk, bath in the lake, and sit in the screened-in tent reading, meditating, and writing, just like I was doing before she left. When I decide to heat something, I remember Petra has the alcohol stove; what to do? Then I remember I can do it the old fashioned way, with a smoky campfire. Petra asks why the pan is black with soot when she returns.

Old tree trunks crawling into the lake.

Essay on wilderness

One day I am sitting in the tent watching lizards and chipmunks come in under the tent, run around, and then go a little wild trying to find a way back out when they realize I am here too. I write the following in my notebook:

> What is it that is so great about wilderness like this? What makes people want to come here? Why are outdoor pictures often "beautiful"? The mosquitoes eat you up in the morning and evening. The flies eat you the rest of the day. Rodents badger you for your food. Bears come in the middle of the night to eat whatever you have left out. Storms are heavy. Winters are deadly. That calm and peacefulness is deceiving. Living here is difficult without some of society's goods.
>
> We have made houses, villages, and cities to protect ourselves from the wilderness. Why do we want to go back to the wilderness? Perhaps, these houses, villages, and

cities have become so complex and noisy (and nosey) that primary simplicity is totally gone and we crave its return without realizing that it includes many difficult things that we left when we first came out of the wilderness. Do we really crave a return to simplicity from that complexity and noise?

A few hours later I put it in different words:

Why is it a beautiful view standing on a high place or sitting in a plane looking over a vast panorama? Is it because it looks so simple? You cannot see the mosquitoes and other troubles?

At one point in time we moved together into houses and villages for protection from the elements, animals, and insects. The togetherness brought its own problems and annoyances. We found living together required rules so we wouldn't infringe on each other's independences. Rules led to societies that led to tribes that led to states. Some don't like or follow the rules. The simple jobs of hunter-gatherers are divided and individuals specialize in only a small part of one job or supporting job. Life becomes complex. We have to protect ourselves from the rule breakers in our group and in other individuals-towns-tribes-states; police, jails, and armies enter the picture. In addition to the protection, we can now more easily take from other individuals-towns-tribes-states. The noise of society reigns now. Now the wilderness is indeed again appealing.

Petra's return

Petra enjoys her time alone above 10,000 feet (3,050 meters). When she doesn't show up at our designated rendezvous the fourth evening, I decide to eat at the Vermilion Resort. The people there are concerned. There's a certain healthy fear of the environment here; but I know Petra. She just wants to enjoy another night alone in the wilderness. And sure enough, she comes back the next afternoon. She reports she is so happy she went.

Wandering

After 20 days in the Lake Edison area, we drive around to the east side of the Sierras, the dry side and drive up US395 to Bishop and Mono Lake. We like this side better than the interior valley on the west. We camp below Mt. Whitney the highest mountain in the lower 48 states at 14,494 feet (4,419 meters).

We wander a while taking in Yosemite, the Pacific Coast from San Luis Obispo to Berkeley, and Lake Tahoe.

The walk is back on

We mull over many logical scenarios of what to do next as we wander the Sierras and California. As we sit in our motel in South Lake Tahoe September fifth, enthusiasm wins out over logic. With the measuring stick of excitement and enthusiasm, a meandering pilgrimage wins hands down over staying and settling down a while. We are just a lot more excited about returning to the walk than looking for a place to live in the US. Our pilgrimage is not done.

As we decide to return to France, we resolve to walk more relaxed with more emphasis on walking east easily than worrying so much about how far we go in a day, where we will stay, and whether to book a bus or train. And when we feel like walking for an hour, a day, or days down separate roads to experience different things separately, we will do it. And we decide to shed the cart to open up foot paths we have been unable use while pushing it before Arles. This also gives us a little freedom to walk once in a while alone with our own backpacks.

From Lake Tahoe we return to Paso Robles to get some dental work done. Then we go back to Lake Edison for a final six days before visiting Helga and Alex again in Atascadero. Then we leave for Germany and Arles.

Petra on the Alta Via. Water has eroded much of it away in several places.

FALL 2010

We are entering our eighth and last season of the pilgrimage. It's late September. Summer was rest time on the other side of the world. Now we are back in France ready to meander east.

Via Domicia

During our time in California we changed the emphasis of our pilgrimage and its name from "Walking East" to "Meandering to Jerusalem." We are still walking but no longer are we going to walk the direct path we have been walking. Now we intend to follow the path that draws us, whether it is on foot or in a bus, train, car, or boat, whether it is east, north, south, or west. When we come to a crossroads, we will decide which way to go and it will not always be the shortest way to Jerusalem. We want the journey to be more the destination than it has been before. That is our aim today.

We arrive in Arles in the late afternoon 29 September, my saint's day, St. Michael's. The temperature is 75F (23C.). The wind is light and the sun bright. Wonderful!

Babette and Paul

We visit with Babette and Paul, writers of the *Lightfood Guides to the Via Francigena* who live in Arles. We have communicated long via email. But it is great visiting face to face. We learn a lot about each other and they share their knowledge of our route east into Italy. They are working on the *Lightfoot Guide to the Via Domicia* the link between the Camino de Santiago and the Via Francigena. This is the route we will be taking walking from Arles to Genoa and beyond (See p. **Error! Bookmark not defined.**). The book is now available at their Pilgrimage Publications web site (See p. 342). Thanks for everything Paul and Babette.

The Meandering begins

We walk along a long Roman aqueduct leaving Arles. After much traffic, we get to a little-used road (N33a) where walking is more comfortable. Petra is expecting a path. She is not a happy camper. In time, after crossing the Canal de Vallée, we head off east on a nice walking path (marked with yellow markers). A short time later we change our destination for the day deciding to go to Paradou saving several kilometers in our first exercise of meandering. And it is a beautiful walking path.

When we arrive in Paradou, my feet, now carrying 33 pounds (15 kilos) that I am no longer pushing, are tired though not as much as I was expecting. We stop at a *chambre d'hôtes* that is a bit too expensive, but we stay in deference to my complaining feet.

Supper is bread, sausage, cheese, olives, grapes, and red wine in our basic blue room with greenish trees and red sun setting outsjde the window. The room is a "dark" setting to Petra but a pleasant to me.

Day one of our new meandering pilgrimage is over and we already have made an in-route change.

It will happen

We are drinking coffee in a pleasant city square waiting for a bus, yes, a bus to take us forward to a walking path. We are practicing our new meandering agenda, no longer sticking to "walking as much as possible" as we tried to do before Arles. Today is the day to deviate. The sun is bright, the wind light, the temperatures in the middle 70s (23 C.); the smell of coffee and bread fills the air. People, cars, trucks, and birds entertain our ears.

The bus doesn't come. We wait half hour. It's not coming; so we begin to walk. The next bus is an hour away. I don't want to spend the better part of a nice day waiting for a bus. Petra, impatient with me, isn't happy and wants to be alone. She suggests strongly that we walk separately. "How will we get together tonight?" I protest.

She answers, "It will happen."

I take off down the marked path, a little-used paved road—without saying "good bye." Petra told me so later. In time, I cross a mountain ridge and am heading down past olive trees into the next valley. At the end of the path, I quickly find the route markers (now even Santiago markings) and head up a four-wheel-drive path through a valley and over another mountain ridge.

I enter the village of Aureille around four. The next bus east isn't coming till seven and I'm not ready to sit around for three hours. I think Petra has taken a bus here earlier and would be walking ahead of me by now. So I continue down the path knowing I can make it's six kilometers (3.6 miles) before that 7-o'clock bus gets to the next town. When I arrive and don't find Petra, I catch the bus to Salon in Provence and find a hotel room after checking out four other hotels.

Once in my room, I immediately get on the internet to get our long-distance calling card number for France. (We have only one cell phone.) With the number, I call Petra and get no answer. Within a minute the room phone rings. *Who's calling?* I thought, *Petra didn't have time to listen to my message with the phone number.* It is **Petra**!

Back at the original bus stop where we parted, Petra followed me after deciding to see how the path was while she waited the hour for the bus in the original location. In the end she decided to continue walking and forget the bus. She enters Aureille a few minutes after I left and decides to wait three hours for the seven o'clock bus. Her feet tell her to do so. She takes the seven pm bus from Aureille to Salon at the same as I take a different bus to Salon from the next town.

Petra is waiting for a phone call from me beginning at five. When I don't call after she arrives in Salon, she decides to find a hotel room. She checks out four places also. As she finally registers in fifth hotel, the owner-clerk asks her what she wants to eat. Like me, she says, "Couscous."

Then seeing her backpack he says, "I could connect you to another walker and you can eat together. He is walking to Rome."

Surprised, Petra says, "That's my husband!"

He isn't at all convinced. "Married and walking together and you don't know where he is?"

"We are doing an experiment."

"But it can't be him; he has a different last name."

"Mike Metras?"

"Yes."

"My husband."

With a big smile he says, "Call him. Call him now."

She tries, but at the same time, I am on the room phone calling her.

A moment later I hang up; she dials me again and we talk.

The Universe is guiding us again! We come back together without working at it. "It will happen," Petra had said earlier.

In the end it is just as good that I didn't call because it gave the Universe a chance to guide us through our intuition to the same hotel in a large town filled with many hotels. Wonders continue!

The couscous and wine were great! We stayed in separate rooms because the hotel clerk wouldn't refund Petra's credit card charge, the only gray spot on a wildly wonderful evening experience.

Where's the tent?

When I begin to pack the next morning, I notice that the tent is not tied to my backpack as usual. Panic! I still have the ticket to the bus so I find their phone number on the internet. It's Sunday morning; they're closed.

Maybe I lost it before I got on the bus. We take a bus back to Eyguières where I began my ride the night before. We walk back up the path where I had rested and might have left the tent. No tent. We walk farther. No tent. We walk back into town. No tent.

A bit about the tent. It's light and strong. We have used it in many places, once in a huge thunderstorm on the Mississippi, and Petra twice set it up above 10,000 feet (3,050 meters) in the Sierra's. It's valuable to us.

Now we can only wait for Monday morning. We spend the rest of the afternoon walking the crowded village streets of Eyguières in one of the biggest flea markets I have seen in a long time. Everything is for sale. It looks like they have emptied their houses of goods accumulated over the past fifty years. We even looked for the tent in case someone had found it and were attempting to sell it.

The next morning after breakfast, I head to the bus office. A long line of monthly-ticket buyers greet me at the door. When my turn finally comes, the woman calls a couple people, gets the bus line number (10), and gives me the name and number of another company, the one I was actually on. I call. He will call me back in 15 minutes. Petra has the phone. I call her. No answer. I return to the hotel. No call. Frustration! How are we going to get the tent?

But Petra's read is that there is another way to attempt a solution to something like this: sit and wait for the right moment instead of action, action, action. Point well taken. I slowed down.

On a hunch or a last-ditch attempt, or is it at the prodding of the Universe, I go to the bus stop. Wonder of wonders, Bus 10 is here. It is time for his morning stop where I got off the other night. And the *same driver* is driving. When he sees me he points to the luggage rack over my seat. Voila, the tent. It's here.

We celebrate two nights later by camping in our returned tent. Thank you, Universe.

Walking east of Aix en Provence.

Abbaye Saint Hilaire

As we head for an Abbaye Saint Hilaire where we're planning to stay for the night, we are expecting to stay in a true abbey since it's on our maps. When we get to the abbey we walk around it and realize it is not occupied save by rodents and insects. It is a ruin. Our Abbaye Saint Hilaire turns out to be an inexpensive and clean hostel on a vineyard. They even make us some sandwiches because their restaurant is closed and the closest place to eat is a too distant several kilometers.

We have a pleasant stay. We are the only ones in a place with room for twelve in two-person rooms. Being alone gives Petra the license to find the breaker and turn off the noisy ventilation for the entire place. We have the window open and a quiet night.

As we leave in the lingering fog the next morning, thousands of wet spider webs sparkle like crystals in the morning sun. In a year and a half, this is the only day we are treated to this show.

Good signs

The route of the Via Domicia, the route we are following, between Arles and the walkways in Italy is quite well marked in France mostly with stenciled yellow shells. They are well placed as long as they are with us. And they are well placed whether you are walking toward Rome or Santiago. The paint is fresh enough that they could have been painted only a few weeks or days before we pass.

Villa Saint-Camille

We're resting today, 13 days out of Arles. We're just short of Cannes on the Mediterranean and staying in a religious hotel, Villa Saint-Camille, a nice place with full pension and a balcony overlooking the Mediterranean, all for a very reasonable price, a special price for pilgrims. We'll return if we are ever in the area again.

Côte d'Azure

The tourist season is winding down so the numbers of people that crowd this *Côte d'Azure* (the *Rivièra*) in the summer are much smaller. We are enjoying our time walking along the Mediterranean. But Petra has walked closer to the water than I. Earlier today she happened on a path right on the rocks along the coast. I managed a half a mile before I chose to return to the road. It was pretty with crashing waves. But it was also on steep, narrow paths both at water level and several yards (meters) above the water on jagged rocks.

A lot of the world's money has crystallized in the mansions and palaces and marinas along the coast here, especially from Nice to

Monaco. And tourists are drawn here too. But that splendor is a bit too much at times.

Most roads give us a shoulder to walk on. When the traffic is particularly heavy we take busses.

Cannes is a too much of itself, not interesting. On the other hand, Nice is quite nice for a big city. If we were staying around for a while, I would like to spend more time exploring its streets. Monaco is not at all interesting—too many huge boats in the harbors, too much money in the streets.

Tomorrow we leave France after walking through Menton. In the past few days we have walked and taken several local busses traversing the mountainous *Côte d'Azure* (the *Rivièra*) from Fréjus to Menton along the Mediterranean. It is a beautiful meeting of water and land.

So now it is on to Italy, our seventh country. We passed through our sixth, Monaco, in a couple hours this afternoon.

Menton

Today we walk through beautiful Menton among runners in some long-distance run.

A plaque in Menton announces that you are standing on the Rome-Santiago Chemin de Compostelle, the Way of St. James, the Camino. We are a long 1,890 kilometers (1,167 miles) from Santiago—we have covered ground to get here. And only 750 kilometers (467 miles) separate us from Rome. GR 653A is the French name for this walking path when one is just walking and not on the Camino.

We stop at a *boulangerie*, a bakery, on the border and buy our last French croissants, croissants that will forever remind me of the best of French foods. It is interesting that the French make wonderful croissants and poor coffee. And on the other side of the border, the Italians make poor croissants and wonderful coffee. That difference is immediately apparent as you cross the border. Different cooks, different recipes, and different ingredients make the difference.

Petra and I stand at a Menton, France, marker on the road between Rome and Santiago. We have 750 kilometers (467 miles) to Rome.

The marker next to us in the picture above.

Italy

We enjoyed France. But as we enter Italy we hope for better beds and bigger hotel rooms where we can relax a bit. The room we had in Menton didn't even have a chair. I had to sit on the bed to write our journal post–or go outside where it's now getting cool in the evenings.

The road leaves France and goes through a mountain at the sea to get into Italy. We walk a narrow path around the mountain and over a railroad to get back to the road. Then more paths, the road again, and a couple tunnels. We follow an old roadway-now-path around a half-mile tunnel only to find ourselves far above the road on the other side. We climb down through a fence, and walk the railroad before getting back to the road.

A short time later we spot a sign to the B&B Acqua di Mare, our place for tonight. We stay in a beautiful room. It has a couch and a large bed. Luxury! And the breakfast cappuccino was Italian. Great!

It's another fine day on our meandering to Jerusalem even with the rain that dogged us from two for the rest of the day.

In the morning we see a sign now identifying the path from Rome to Santiago as the "Via della Costa," the Coast Road.

A messenger

We are on our second day in Italy along the Mediterranean on a bicycle trail. It's late in the afternoon. We are looking for a place to eat and a place to stay for the night.

We have already passed on at least four hotels and as many restaurants. None feel right, even to me. The process is really taking "too long" for me. We are testy with each other. Our words are loud and not very friendly.

We are getting to the far side of town. Maybe we'll find no more hotels. We sit on a bench to cool down and discuss what to do next.

An Italian woman comes up and asks, "*Scusi*, (Excuse me,) I heard you speaking English. I think you can help me with this translation."
"Si?"

"Can you help me with this?" She shows us a folded, blue letter quickly. I can't really read anything.

"'Don't be angry with the conditions.' What does *condition* mean?"

"Situation. *Situatione*."

"*Situatione, si*, situation. 'Don't be angry with the situation.' *Grazie*."

Petra looks at me. I look at her. We are taken back. An angel appeared right in front of us and told us, "Cool it. It isn't worth getting all riled up about." By the time we recover from the shock and look up again, the woman is gone, lost somewhere in the sparse crowd walking on the bicycle path.

Her message is loud and clear. Thank you, Universe, for the blunt reminder to be gentle with each other, especially during trying times.

The Alta Via

On our fourth day in Italy, we begin walking on the Alta Via dei Monti Liguri, a long path on mountain trails paralleling the arc of the northern Italian coast from Ventimiglia to La Spezia. We have walked the coast a week and now we will do the same in the mountains. We took a bus up from Savona last night to Altare where we are catching the path this morning. You can learn more about the Alta Via dei Monte Liguri at their web site. (See p. 342)

We walk the Alta Via three days on paths between 500 and 1,200 meters (1,640 and 3,950 feet). As you can imagine with those numbers, we climb up and down a lot. The first day out of Altare is a long up followed by several long downs and ups ending in one treacherous and long descent back down to around 500 meters (1,640 feet). It's so steep that we hold onto trees like monkeys to keep from slipping down the muddy, rooty path. It was work. Good thing the cart is at Petra's Mom's house.

We end that day in the town Giovo Liguri in the Albergue Liguri, a large, old hotel, the only place we knew of in the village. We find another the next morning on the way out of town, but it's no match for the Albergue Liguri—we make a good choice without knowing it. We are only five people in the Liguri. But the restaurant makes us a fine dinner all the same.

The next day is a heavy work day, more than 800 meters (2,600 feet) up and up and up. The path is often full of rocks washed free by water coming down the same paths we are walking. Most paths were once stone paved roads (or paths), but they have but long since eroded to stone stairways up the mountain side. We have little we can do except concentrate on the next step, let alone steps. We see little beyond the rocks, the mud walls, and trees. On top we come out to a forest of microwave relay towers surrounding the place we want to stay. We refuse to put ourselves in their electromagnetic umbrella and walk another few kilometers to the Pra Rionido Refugio where we have a cool night with a warm-hearted, young family trying to make an ill-kept-up place into a nice place of rest. We enjoy them and our night in their home. Thanks.

Nirvana

The stay at Pra Rionido was a case of Nirvana. Sometime after the pilgrimage is over, an Indian Swami, talking on another subject, said that *Nirvana* is *no-choice*. I remembered our nights of going through hotel after hotel and restaurant menu after menu looking for the "right" place to sleep or eat for a night or two. For me *Nirvana* is the times that we walk into a village with only one hotel and one restaurant—no choices or rejections to be made those nights. I'm happy. I was happy last night.

Yesterday trees blocked our view. Today there are no trees but fog blocks our view. We still see nothing at a distance. The road is much easier to walk today. The Mediterranean is not to be seen far below. Only later in the day can we finally see a few far views.

If you are going to break a leg these paths are where it would happen. They are treacherous with stones and leaf-covered holes. But then when you are on paths like these, you are much more cautions than you are on a normal, flat path.

As we arrive at our chosen albergue, its rooms are closed for the season. But the owner gives us a ride down to the next town. What a ride! The mountains plunge from the road to the sea. He said that this place is the most steep and high descent in all of Italy.

Failing to find a place to stay in the mountains, we catch a quick bus down to the outskirts of Genova (Genoa).

Genoa

We arrive on Genoa's far west shoreline. We take a city bus a few miles east. After searching the streets for better than an hour for a place for the night we settle for the big, old Pegli Hotel Mediterranee. We stay only one night and then move across town to the accommodating Hotel Acquaverde near the train station and a huge statue of Christopher Columbus. When it isn't raining heavily, we wander the back streets in and behind the port and get to know the city of Columbus and seafarers going back to Roman times.

Where next?

In the Genoa area we are at a fork in the road. We have been back walking for less than a month and the whole time we haven't taken our mandate to meander too seriously. Or have we taken it too literally? When a river meanders it searches out the easiest route and follows it. Are we working too hard to find the easy route? Or do we want something else?

At this junction we could go south to Rome and continue to Bari or Brindisi and sail to Greece. Or we could go across to Venice and Trieste and walk down the Dalmatian Coast to Greece. In Italy we know the language. It's easier. We don't know Croatian or Albanian or any other language that can pop up along the Dalmatian Coast.

Petra checks out ferry companies out of Venice and Trieste for routes down the Adriatic Sea to ports south as far as Greece. But then she finds a container ship that goes from Trieste to Hypha, Israel, three times a week. Petra calls and finds it is only about 50 Euro a day. We could take that and then walk from Hypha to Jerusalem — are we missing something in between?

I know we would get forward by walking the Balkan Coast but I'm a little ill at ease about my scanty knowledge of it. But then that is a challenge too. Remember Portugal. But Portuguese at least has a little similarity to Spanish. And then Turkish is down the road that way too. If we want to walk to Jerusalem and not sail, we have to live with a lower level of communications.

But then we'd really like to first stop at a wonderful restaurant, La Volpara, in Ponzano Superiore above La Spezia.

If we go through Italy we'd likely then take a train from around La Spezia to Rome because we already walked that in 2007. Otherwise we'd go up the valley toward Venice (on foot or in a train).

So let's walk down the coast to the restaurant and put off the decision of where to go till then.

The pilgrimage changes

Not wanting to walk a long distance through Genoa's streets, we take a train to Sestri Levante 26 October and rest on the coast after getting a room in the Hotel Marina in the middle of town.

Sunset at Sestri Levante's Silent Bay.

The next morning we head south for Moneglia along an established path between Genoa and La Spezia.

The sun is bright and the air in the mid-70s (24 C.). We're walking south of Sestri Levante on a high path in the mountains above the Mediterranean.

The path begins wide and easy to walk. Then it gets narrower and the mountains more steep. Finally we are walking a cow-path-wide line on the mountainside, still easily. Petra is walking in front.

She asks me how I am doing with the narrow, steep-sided path. She is concerned about my fear of heights.

"I'm doing well. There's a lot of undergrowth below. I can see it clearly. If I fall off, the bushes will catch me before I fall ten feet." I am thinking about the steepness but brush it off. Without the bushes below me, it would be a different matter. I would be a lot less at ease.

The fall

The path has become loose, dug up by *cinghiale* (wild pigs) searching for food in the soil. Petra's right leg slips off the path. She starts to fall. Her left leg sticks in a hole in the loose soil. The backpack's weight carries her down the mountain far enough to twist and break her left leg.

I hear a loud crack like a wet twig snapping. She doesn't move. "I think I broke my leg…. I broke my leg." She doesn't want to accept it. She knows the pilgrimage has changed in that second. "No. No!" She knows it will take months to heal the leg. There's no way to go back to walking soon.

I remember in an instant her other broken leg 13 years earlier. That time she lay on the mountainside while her partner ran down the mountain for help. Now it's my turn. We have no signal on the phone. We are far from any road. A helicopter is the only rescue option.

I take off my backpack and help Petra as much as I can. She doesn't want to be touched at all because her leg is hurting so much. She is under a tree, invisible to any helicopter flying over so I put our yellow flag on a nearby stone where it can be seen from above. In retrospect, that flag is rather small and unlikely to be seen. In the end it isn't needed.

Going for help

I leave my backpack and head half running out along the path. It's no less steep than before but now I have a different determination. I have a vital task. I'm no longer remotely afraid. I walk steep sections of the trail over narrow, rock paths as if they were open roads.

Petra fell on a path back in a valley high above the road. We're on a mountainside about midway between Sestri Levante and the small village of Moneglia. The only way to phone is to walk out of the valley we are in and call at the farthest extended point of the trail.

I get to the first extended point. No signal. I find a stout stick to replace the one I left near Petra. I walk faster and sometimes run. At the second extended point, still no signal.

After half an hour I get a signal at the third point. I try to call 112, the emergency number. No ring. 118, another emergency number is also silent. So I call 115, the fire department.

I have been practicing my speech as I walk. "*Mia donna a rota la gamba.* (My wife has broken her leg)"

"*Dove?* (Where?)"

Now my Italian is getting to its limits. "*Sulla montagna.* (On the mountain.)" But I can't tell him that it is on this remote path.

He hangs up on me!

I call back immediately. This time he hands the phone to someone who can speak about as much English as I can Italian. I manage to tell him what happened and generally where Petra is. I say they need to take her out with a helicopter.

Then he tells me to return to Petra; they would come. I insist I have to come with the helicopter to show where Petra was. I'm coming out to Moneglia.

Waiting

Meanwhile, Petra is preparing herself for what she knows from experience will be a long wait. In very slow and deliberate movements she props herself up with her backpack so she didn't have to hold herself from rolling down the mountain. She uses my umbrella to drag my pack closer and take out my sweater and coat to keep herself warm. The ground is damp and cold in the shade of the tree.

As she lies under the tree not moving, she watches and listens to the birds singing, perhaps to her. Then she hears a hunter's dogs and someone shooting. Bullets slash through the tree. The dogs come near. Petra's afraid they will touch her leg. A hunter comes. Petra says, "Call off the dogs! I have a broken leg."

He calls them off.

"*Come Stai? Come fatto?* How are you? What happened?"

"I broke my leg."

"Are you sure?"

"Si" "I'm cold."

The hunter cuts open a plastic bag (for the pig he was hoping to shoot?) and puts it over Petra like a blanket. He gives her his gloves.

Even though she knows better, Petra's biggest wish is that no one will move her.

Back on my trail, I talk with a couple others on the phone as I make my way to Moneglia. After getting lost once, I finally step off the path onto a driveway entrance. I call again to report I'm out. They say they'll send the ambulance now that they know where I am.

"*No, no, no aqui. Mia donna non e qui. E sulla montagna. Bisogna helicoptra. E due hora de aquí.* (No, no, not here. My wife is not here. She is on the mountain. It's two hours away.)" Or that's what I'm trying to say.

Then a voice from behind the fence calls out in English, "Do you need some help?"

"Yes, please."

The house owner comes out and uses my phone to tell my story to whoever is on the other end of the phone.

The Carabiniere

Soon the unneeded ambulance arrives followed closely by the chief of the Carabiniere, the state police. They all get out, the chief talking to someone on his cell phone.

I repeat that I don't need help here, that Petra needs it two hours back up the trail. I tell them as best as I can where she is and that I can point her out from the helicopter.

The chief is a two-fisted caller. Before one conversation is done the second phone rings. Then he goes back to the first and calls someone else.

Finally, he decides to take me to the helicopter pad up on the mountainside by the freeway above the village. We get into the car and race up winding streets, the siren wee-whooing all the way to a concrete square a couple miles (three kilometers) from where he picked me up.

We wait half an hour or more. Nothing happens except for another bundle of phone calls using both phones. Then he says, "There's someone with your wife, a hunter."

Then word comes that the helicopter is with Petra and will not be coming for me.

Rescue

At the accident site two men come down from the helicopter. One gives Petra morphine. "I felt a rush of cool painlessness surge through my body," she recalls later.

Then they wrap an inflatable cushion around her leg. But it is old and stiff and consequently extremely painful. When they use a hand pump to pressurize it, the morphine did little to disguise the moving pressure and pain.

They put her on a narrow board and into a bag, preparing to lift her to the helicopter. Then they carry her out to where she can be picked up. But the path is narrow and the four men (another hunter joined them) have a hard time carrying her. They tip her on her side so they have room to walk. Petra's problem is that they tip her onto the broken-leg side and she is in horrible pain.

Later Petra says, "I wanted to scream but I knew it was hard for them to walk and that screaming wouldn't help. Earlier when they first came, I screamed when they were moving my leg and one of then just said, '*Tranquila*. Be calm.' I knew this move was going to be short so I didn't scream."

When they get her to a place where they can take her up, one holds a rope on the ground while they raise her. But the rope doesn't keep her from spinning, only from swinging a lot. Again she says later, "The spinning along with the feeling from the morphine was making me want to vomit. But I decided I was not going to make a mess so I didn't."

In the helicopter it is very cold. Someone puts his coat on Petra to keep her warm. One rescuer holds her hand and keeps eye contact with her for the whole flight. "I could feel so much love in his eyes."

While this is going on, the chief and I are talking back at the pad and I am able to give him a better location. "There are two long tunnels along the coast and Petra is just above where the road comes out of one and enters the other."

"Oh, the Grand Valley; let's go there now."

So we get back into the car and speed down to the tunnel near sea level and wee-whoo through the tunnel to the opening. The helicopter is circling high above.

After more phone calls, my chief says they have Petra and are on the way to transfer her to the ambulance in Moneglia.

Back in the car we wee-whoo even faster through the tunnel back to Moneglia and up to the helicopter pad. Again we wait, this time with the ambulance. Again phone calls. Again the tempo and volume of the chief's voice belies mass confusion. Finally he says, "*Vanno a San Martino in Genoa.* (They are going to San Martino in Genoa.)"

So, with no more reason to wait for the helicopter, the chief takes me down to the Red Cross station, the home of the ambulance and we part company. Along the way he says, "I'm sorry for all the chaos. It shouldn't be this way. But that's how it goes sometime." I thought: *No, Captain, that's the way it works in Italy.* What is important is that in the end it all works out well no matter how intense the chaos is. And it works out very well that day and the days that follow.

Now I sit in the Red Cross station at a table in a big meeting hall and realize that I am getting a bit cold without my sweater. It's in my backpack back on the trail. They give me a coffee and a coat and I wait.

"How do you want to get to Genoa? Bus? Train? Taxi? We can take you there for taxi fare. It's about 100 Euro ($140)."

"I would like that."

I sit while they talk on the phone and among themselves.

Then I ask, "What about my backpack? It was up on the mountain where they picked up Petra. Can you find out if it went with Petra or how I can get it?" That sets off more phone calls.

By now it is close to seven o'clock. The accident was around two fifteen and they picked Petra up between five and five thirty. I'm still sitting in the Red Cross office in Moneglia.

At last, someone comes in and says, "Let's go."

"What about my backpack?"

"We'll pick that up along the way."

We get into a many-seated van painted like an ambulance and head toward Genoa. Near Sestri Levante the van stops along the road. Soon another ambulance stops, takes out a backpack, and brings it to us. It's mine; rather, it's Petra's. They took mine with her.

While Petra was waiting to be rescued, she remembers how they didn't want to take a second backpack into the helicopter the last time 13 years earlier. She has the hunter, Mario, prepare the backpack and asks him to carry it out to the police when he leaves. So he does and now I have it. *Grazie*, Mario.

Emergency room

Petra is in a hall on a bed waiting for an x-ray. She wants to use the bathroom and to call me to tell me where she is and that she is alive. Everyone else has some family member or members to help him or her. Petra is alone.

She asks a nurse, "Can I make a call to my husband?" Nothing happens. She worries that I will not find her.

Then they call her name. She yells, "*Ecco mi.* I'm here." She is up a side hall. They find her and take her in for her x-ray. But first they have to take that plastic protector from around her leg. The plastic sticks to her leg. Much pain and screaming. Then an x-ray and back into the hall along the wall.

I finally arrive at the San Martino emergency room in the ambulance. The chaos is as high as that in American 1960s TV hospital shows. People and peopled beds line the hall. Some have bandages on their arms or faces. Many are talking, loudly.

One of the men from the ambulance collars a nurse and asks for Petra. Both disappear a while then came back and take me down to a drowsy Petra lying in a side hall. It was just after eight, six hours from the accident. We kiss and wait.

After a while someone calls out, "Petra." They find us and wheel her back into the examination room.

A doctor says, "You broke your leg."

"I know I did. How bad is it?"

"We have to put a pin in it."

"I don't want a pin."

"We put a pin."

"I want to see how bad the break is. I had a break 13 years ago. I know what I am talking about."

Seemingly miffed, the doctor leaves the room for a couple minutes before opening the doors and rolling Petra's bed to his computer where he has the x-ray on the monitor. It looks bad, a spiral break with several pieces. That twist did a number on both the tibia and the fibula.

"We'll operate Friday if we can. Otherwise, we'll have to wait 'till Monday." It's Wednesday night.

"You can go to your room soon."

We sit in the hall another 20 minutes before someone comes and rolls Petra to an ambulance for a rough ride up to the orthopedic building.

They wheel Petra into a room with one bed. Without asking they bring sheets in so I can sleep in the chair. They also bring food for both of us and then leave us to ourselves. They don't ask whether I am staying. They just assume I am and give us what we need. We aren't in an American hospital!

After a full meal, Petra lies back and gets ready to sleep. I try to sleep in the chair before getting out my mat and sleeping bag and lying on the floor.

It is 11:30 pm. A long day is over. I sleep soundly.

San Martino

The University Hospital "San Martino," *Azienda Ospedale Università San Martino,* the largest hospital in Europe, is associated with the University of Genoa. Petra is there with a broken leg.

Three doctors come in early to tell Petra her options and say they hope to operate the next day, Friday, to insert a pin in her leg. They convince her it is her best option, much better than plates.

Concerned about the single room the night before, Petra asks about it. A doctor answers, "In Italy it doesn't make any difference how many people are in the room. It costs the same."

She is soon sharing a room with a patient recovering from a hip replacement. And I'm out on the street to find a room for myself. I really appreciate it that they let me stay the first night with Petra.

Inserting the pin

At 10:00 the next morning a bandanna-covered aid ("my pirate," Petra calls him) wheels Petra into the operating room. They lay her on a cold table. They strap her arms down. Her good right leg is raised straight skyward. And her broken leg is bent sharply downward so they can work on it. She endures the next three hours in that position under local anaesthetic.

In concept the operation is simple. Insert a titanium rod down through the center of the bone, align everything, and anchor it on top and bottom. To do that they drill the top of the bone open, hammer the pin into place, measure to make sure it was the same length as the other leg and that the foot is rotated precisely in line with the leg. Then they attach the rod to the bone with one screw on the top and two on the bottom. Local anaesthesia allows Petra to hear and feel every tap of the hammer throughout her body.

When her "pirate" rolls her back into the room she is wide awake and annoyed with the cold operating room.

I massage some heat back into her good leg and back. And then she sleeps a bit. I smuggle a cream-filled *cornetto* (croissant) in for her supper since she is allowed only tea. She already had a big appetite when they brought her from the operating room.

It's interesting that with the broken leg she is just as alert as always. She just can't walk, a slight inconvenience for someone walking to Jerusalem.

She has no cast. They don't do that anymore. She and her doctors are surprised how much she can move her ankle and knee from the very first day. Nerves must not have been dammaged. Petra remembers how hard it was 13 years earlier when she had a cast and couldn't move ankle or knee until the cast was off 6 weeks after the operation. By then she had lost a lot of muscle.

The pain is heavy in the beginning. In those early days she expands her Italian vocabulary with *dolore* and *padella* (*pain* and *bed pan*). She is not very fond of either word.

Ecstasy

When she finally gets crutches four days after the operation, she is ecstatic to be able to go to the toilet on her own even though it's a tiring task to go that short distance. On the way she has her first view out the window.

The next day I take Petra for a ride in a wheel chair. She laughs uncontrollably and cries at the same time. It's ecstasy! Laughing. Crying. Loving. Happiness. It is so great for her to be able to move from the bed and go outside. We go down the elevator and out into the streets of the hospital.

Discharged

At eleven in the morning 4 November, six days after the operation, the doctor comes in and tells Petra she has to leave that day. There's no warning, just, "Here are your discharge papers." Petra argues to stay until the morning and he allows it at first. But not the head nurse. She comes in at 1:30 and says, "You have to leave by four. We need your bed."

It is blunt to say the least. They said nothing the day before to prepare us. I have been staying in different hotels and have none that day because they sold my room from under me. Before I realize we have to leave, I check out a place and find it is not ours. I am beginning to feel like Mary and Joseph with no place in the inn.

All that said about the abrupt discharge, we have to say that everyone was wonderful in the hospital. The doctors and nurses were very professional and personal. Everyone was so helpful. Though Petra didn't need it, there was a service I suspect one would only find in an Italian hospital. She even had nurse who would wheel her to a place where she could have an illegal cigarette, had she wanted one—which she didn't.

Finding a home

Rosetta, the woman in the room with Petra, calls a couple places and gets us a room in one. The doctor offers to get us a ride in an ambulance to the hotel so Petra doesn't have to endure the taxi ride. We wait for two hours for the ambulance to arrive. When it does, it's old and its shocks are gone. They sit Petra in a cloth seat that transfers every Genoa bump (there are many.) to her leg. By the time we get to the hotel her pain is much more than when she started.

The hotel room is damp and cold. After struggling up 15 steps to the room it is clear we are not going to stay. "I saw a big hotel on the way here. I want to go back there."

The understanding and sympathetic receptionist gets a taxi and doesn't charge us anything for our visit to his hotel. Petra says later, "The taxi was a ride on a cloud after the bumpy ambulance." The "big hotel" is the AC Hotel, a four-star hotel. We check in and stay.

Day's not over

My day isn't done. First I go out, buy pain pills for Petra, and bring them back. Next I take the bus to my hotel downtown for my backpack. After selling my room from under me this morning, the hotel holds another room for me and charges me 15 euros ($20.00) when they find I am leaving. That's OK. They could have charged me the entire 35 euros ($47.00) the room cost.

I return with my backpack to find that the hotel phone isn't working and our cell phone charger is still at San Martino. So I catch another bus and retrieve the charger.

By the time we discuss the phone not working with the hotel management, they are beginning to understand our overall situation. They switch us to a suite at no additional charge. We remain there for the ten days we stay in the AC.

This day has been a long. It feels good to go to bed.

For all its chaos, San Martino was a fine hospital. They did a great job repairing Petra's leg. We may even return to have the rod removed after it has been in for a year. Thanks for everything.

Recovery

The following recovery section, up to "Into the Promised Land" is Petra's rendition of our time spent between the hospital and beginning our tour in Cairo.

My life changed from one moment to the next. It changed from walking to lying and sitting with the broken leg elevated on a pillow on a chair. The damaged blood vessels rule the first part of recovery. If I put my leg down only for a few minutes to move somewhere, my leg hurts when it fills up with blood. The blood vessels can't pump the blood from the lower leg. For a while ice packs are my steady companion — ten to twenty minutes on the leg and then the same off. They help a lot. Thanks to Mike who gets so many ice packs. Even with the experience of my broken leg 13 years ago, this leg is still something to get used to. Every basic task, like using the bathroom, taking a bath, showering, or moving from one room to another is only possible with huge effort. When I was walking so many miles, I didn't realize how complex simple movements are. I had forgotten how it was 13 years ago.

I am lucky that I don't have a cast. In one week I am able to get into a bathtub while keeping my leg out. I love taking a bath and being in water where my body is light. I am surprised how quickly the healing process is happening. But in the end a serious broken leg takes a year to recover completely. I start walking with crutches four days after the surgery. It is a huge effort. Reflexes aren't working or they are slow. I am afraid to walk down hill. I walk very slowly. I am walking with full awareness.

Now, after 8 months, I am so thankful that I can walk. I can dance. I can run. I can sit on my heals in yoga and can walk down steps without holding onto something. I have my balance and strength back. The body is so wonderful. I am grateful for every little improvement. In November or December 2011 I'll get the screws and pin out of my leg. That's the final step, but I am not there yet. This is something to deal with later.

One day after I broke my leg I write in my diary: It was a brutal end to the walk; but it was the right end. I feel released and free again. The long walk to Jerusalem is over, but the pilgrimage is not. The time after the accident is for initial recovery. We don't know whether to go back to U.S. or to my mother in Germany. We have no place to go to in the U.S. We gave up our home before we began our walk. Germany and my mother's house aren't close to a real option. Winter in Germany is not good for a leg in recovery.

First home

Our first "home" after the hospital is the AC Hotel about three miles (five kilometers) from the hospital. Being that close makes it easy to get to the hospital. In the hotel I begin to move around more. This sounds like I am back on the walking path. Not at all; but I am able to move up to a mile 14 days after operation. The second evening in the hotel I have an appetite for Pizza. The Pizzeria is only across the street, a round trip distance of around 500 yards (460 meters). I step from the hotel, see the distance, and compare it with my strength. I have to admit that it is too much for me. I go back to room and Mike gets a Pizza to go. I have walked more than 5000 miles (8000 kilometers) and now 500 yards are too much. That's how I am.

A tour

On 11 November we clearly want to finish our pilgrimage in a different way. I find a tour on the Internet that will be in Jerusalem on Christmas. I feel strong enough to do it. I can see myself getting on a tour bus in Cairo on 14 December to ride *Into the Promised Land*.

Diamond in the pain

The first days in the hotel help me to see more and more the "diamond in the pain." Here my 7 November note from our blog:

> Hello to you all. I'm back at the desk. Thank you so much for all the thoughts, prayers, comments, emails, telephone calls, and…. It's getting better every day and I am surprised how good I am doing now. The heavy beginning pain is over, but sometimes I can't believe this happened because when I look back I see myself walking, walking, and walking. And now I am stopped. Walking and enjoying was the main thing I was doing. Now the main thing I am doing is resting, healing, and enjoying being together with Mike. To be together, holding hands, and loving each other more than before. We have a totally different life together and this is a great gift. In every

situation a great gift is included. The only thing you have to do is accept that nothing will be like before and not let the pain get into the way of seeing the gift, the diamond, in the misfortune. This is my experience in life. Like when a baby is born. So much birth pain is followed by great joy.

Walk, walk, walk

Fourteen days after the operation, they remove the staples (stitches) and take an x-ray. Then the doctor tells me, "Walk, walk, and walk and put 60% of your weight on the leg to help the healing process." The bone needs the stimulation of walking to grow better.

At that time I am still moving around with two crutches. The doctor then told me, "When you come back in 14 days for your final x-ray and checkup, I want you to be walking without your crutches." I can't see myself at all without those little helpers.

Second Home

To get started with the doctor's advice to walk a lot and to get in shape for our tour bus to Jerusalem, we have to move. Genoa has step hills and a lot up and down walking. This is still too difficult for me. We settle on Sestri Levante at the Mediterranean Sea. It has a long flat walkway along the beach and in the town. We move to the Centro di Spiritualità P. Enrico Mauri, a convent in Sestri Levante and stay for two weeks. Sestri Levante is the last town we stayed in before I broke my leg. I want to learn to walk again and Sestri's Mediterranean views, its fresh air, the helpful sisters in the convent, and Mike are all with me to help. Without Mike my recovery will not be easy.

Learning to walk

This is the third time in my life I am learning to walk—once as a child, once 13 years ago with my right leg, and now in Sestri Levante with my left leg. This is the place to start walking again, to heal more, and have less pain.

Giving up one crutch and putting more weight on my leg is a major step in Sestri Levante. Friday November 16 is the time for only one crutch. It is an interesting situation. Mike and I are walking into town toward the beach, a mile walk one way. While we are walking, a heavy thunderstorm moves in. I am walking very slowly. In these days it takes me an hour to walk a mile. Our normal pace is 2.5 to 3 miles (4 to 4.8 kilometers) an hour. Mike is still on 2.5. I am so slow that Mike decides to do some chores and afterwards catch up with me. I walk alone to the beach. It starts to rain; and it becomes heavier and heavier. Walking with two crutches and an umbrella is impossible. By the time the thunderstorm is on top of me with all its lighting, thunder, heavy rain, and wind, I reach the beach and take shelter under a big roof beside a kiosk. It's winter; the kiosk is closed and nobody is around. The storm catches Mike too so he doesn't catch up with me before I get to the beach. He takes shelter in a shop. His umbrella isn't enough to protect him from rain and wind.

Without an umbrella I am trapped under the roof. At least I can keep dry. I take the opportunity as a training time for walking with one crutch. It is an easy decision. I can't sit down; and I can't stand without moving because that would make my leg hurt a lot. I have to keep moving. First I imagine how I would walk with one crutch and then I try it. It works. I walk with one crutch while the thunderstorm is banging around me. I feel so strong and so blessed with the moment—the storm's high energy, my direct view on the Mediterranean Sea, and me on my personal quest to walk with one crutch. So I walk back and forth many times under the roof with one crutch. I walk every step with high concentration and I try to role on my left leg from heel to toe.

I enjoy at least one hour of the thunderstorm and training. But how will I met Mike again? It's still raining. After more than an hour it is time to go back to the convent for lunch in a warm dining room. At one point I see Mike far away walking by searching for me, but he never looks toward me at the beach here. I call him very loudly, but no response. He tells me later, he thought that there couldn't have been a place with an enough shelter for me at the beach.

Several Africans are walking around trying to sell me an umbrella, but I have no free hand to hold the umbrella. I still have to take care of my second crutch. This is only practice under the roof. The umbrella sellers are watching what I am doing. I ask them if they have seen my husband with a rainbow-colored umbrella. They have and they will tell him where I am. Thanks so much to the umbrella sellers for getting a message to Mike. After all that rain and training,

I am tired and hungry. We take a taxi back to the convent and eat a good Italian lunch.

A nearby friend

The world is small. While we are in Sestri Levante Mike finds a friend, Rosalina, from 40 years ago in Eritrea who lives in the town just to the north of Sestri Levante. We get together and walk along the sea and talk a lot. We even see a water spout far out over the water. Continue to have a good life, Rosalina.

Petra and Rosalina.

Healing waters in the third home

After being in the convent for a while I ask myself how I can help my leg's healing process. I know I love water and it has helped to heal me often before. The Italian island, Ischia, is famous for its healing hot springs. I find a resort and we book two weeks. Ischia's is on the way to Jerusalem. It is just off Naples, a train, taxi, boat, and taxi away. We make it even though the rides are long and tiring for me.

It's a wonderful place. Every morning and evening I go into the pool where a hot spring continuously fills the pool. The physiotherapist helps me a lot to get more confident about the upcoming bus tour. I get stronger and am less tired after exercising and the pain is much less. After one week in the resort I walk without crutches in the hotel. Outside on the road I still use one crutch for security and on uneven road surface and to stay balanced.

The Sorriso Spa and Resort on Ischia, a fine place to recover.

Petra practicing walking along rough Ischia surf.

We leave the resort 13 December to travel to Fiumicino to stay for a night before flying the next day to Cairo and to join our bus tour.

On the recovery journey we took every necessary step at its time. We don't plan anything. During this time I'm living very much in the Now and I enjoy being in the Now. I think the biggest blessing and gift that the broken leg gives me is the intensive time being in the Now. Especially the time with the strongest physical pain, I can embrace the pain when I am in the Now and with acceptance. I feel this is one of the gifts of the pilgrimage. This comes along with the humility that every plan, quest, or pilgrimage can take an unpredicted turn and it is enlightening to embrace the change. To be strong is one side of the coin. The other side is to be weak. Both sides of the coin have value. I have the chance to experience both sides of the coin on this pilgrimage to Jerusalem.

I never before thought that I could heal such a major injury without a home base—heal and recover on our way to Jerusalem. Every place we stay feels like a home for that time. This experience gives me the freedom and wisdom that I can heal in any house or place that I can call my home at the time.

Into the Promised Land

A bus tour was never in our plans. But it's time to adapt to the situation we have no control over. After al, this is a pilgrimage and pilgrimages demand things we sometimes have a hard time accepting.

As Petra mentions earlier, two weeks after breaking her leg, she turns from the computer and announces, "I found a bus tour from Egypt through Jordan to Jerusalem, *Into the Promised Land*." Eleven days later we book it.

It's a solution for getting to Jerusalem, but so out of character. Neither of us has ever taken such a tour in our lives save for a couple hours around a few cities. When it comes to longer bus tours, I can only think of the chaos of the 1969 movie *If it's Tuesday, it's Belgium*. I truly have no desire to take a bus tour, much less take a bus tour to finish our pilgrimage *walk* to Jerusalem. But with Petra's leg, walking is out. We talk about it and agonize over it. If we want to get to Jerusalem and see some of the Middle East, it's about the only open option left. It is a comprehensive tour including the Pyramids, the Cairo Museum, Mt. Sinai, Petra, and many biblical places in Israel.

Egypt

It's 14 December and we're on a plane headed for Cairo to begin our 12-day, whirlwind tour of the Middle East. A tour representative picks us and another couple up at the airport and takes us to a sprawling four-star hotel where we walk a quarter mile to dinner.

In the dining room a Sri Lankan physiotherapist asks Petra, "What happened to your leg. How is it doing?"

She tells him about our pilgrimage and her broken leg and now this tour and how so much has changed. "In my dreams I wanted to walk high and tall into Jerusalem but with my accident everything changed. Nothing is possible just with your own will. Everything is given you."

The Sri Lankan says, "Now with a leg in recovery and on crutches it's much more difficult to continue to Jerusalem than it is to walk with a healthy leg."

Petra understands him to be saying, "With a broken leg, the pilgrimage is even harder so you will learn more." This helps her give up the dream of walking into Jerusalem. It helps her accept that just because she wants to do something doesn't mean that she can.

Cairo

When our group gathers at the hotel the next morning, we are 23. Most are from the U.S. Petra represents Germany. Two are from Argentina and a couple more are from Canada. Our guide and bus driver are native and strongly national. In Egypt our guide even called the Arabs overlords: he is **Egyptian**, not Arab.

In true tour form we cram three blockbusters into the first day: Coptic Cairo, the Cairo Museum, and the pyramids. Each deserves at least four or five days. But a tour is just for whetting your curiosity. And that it does. We also have our mandatory stop at a curio shop.

We start out at the Cairo museum. The crowds are oppressive. "No pictures, please. Give us your camera." We squeeze our way between the people through room after room of ancient Egypt including the famous gold of Tutankhamen. I remember seeing that in Chicago when it toured the U.S. in the late '80s or early '90s.

Walking in the crowds of the museum was really hard for Petra. She was constantly fearing someone would bump into her leg.

After a couple hours and only a fraction of the museum, we are back in the bus heading for the Coptic section of old Cairo where we break for lunch. We sit at a long table and begin to get to know each other as we eat some local fare. Then we run in and out of a couple early Coptic churches before crossing the Nile and heading west to the Pyramids.

The pyramids

As we leave the bus at the pyramids, the guide warns us, "Be careful with the people wanting to give you camel rides here. They will over charge you. If you want a camel ride, we will show you camel drivers who'll give you a good price." As we progress along the tour in days to come, we realize that what our guide is really saying is, "Don't go to just any vendor. Go to ours so we can get our 20 to 30 percent cut on what you buy or spend." Merchants in Jerusalem said it was as high as 35 percent.

We get out of the bus and my jaws drop. We're at the pyramids!

The Pyramids of (left to right) Khufu (c. 2566 BCE), Khafre (c. 2532 BCE), and Menkaure (c. 2504 BCE) in the late afternoon sun with Cairo in the background. Khufu's is the largest. It looks smaller from where we're standing because is a more distant and on lower ground.

At one time all the pyramids were covered with smooth, bright limestone. It's been used in other buildings of Cairo and Giza over the millennia. Only a little (and that's not too bright) is still in place on the top of Khafre's pyramid.

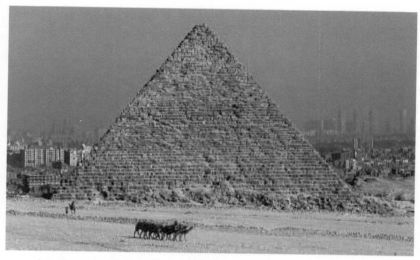

Mankaure's pyramid with Cairo more clearly in the background.

As I look closely at the pyramids, I can see the size of the blocks used to build these huge tombs, if they were even that. These stones are huge but we don't even have time to go over and stand next to them and feel their size. We have too many other places to go.

They found this boat disassembled and buried at the base of Khufu's pyramid. They think it was used to carry the Khufu to his burial. Then they put it here to carry him to the afterlife.

By the time we get to the Sphinx, the light is behind it. It would have been much better to have arrived before noon or earlier instead of late in the afternoon. But that is how it is. We could have spent days here at the pyramids. All we had was less than a couple hours. But even with so short a time, my tears flow a while as I stand in the presence of these 4,500-year-old monuments.

I remember being in Selinus in Sicily several years earlier. It flourished and died by 400 BCE when Rome was still only a tiny village. When Selinus was destroyed, it was already 2,200 years after the Great Pyramid was built. Now we are another 2,400 years after that day. Dust to dust man.

A reminder to trust

Back at the first stop, I give a few glances at the many camels carrying tourists. It isn't for me, so I return my attention to the pyramids in front of me.

Petra comes over and says, "Take a picture of me with this guy." She wants me to take her picture with a camel driver."

"No, he only wants some money."

"No, he doesn't. He said he doesn't."

"I don't believe him." I revert to my life-long mistrust of tourist-related vendors. I "know" he must want money.

"I believe him. Please, take our picture."

"No."

She goes back and tells him, "My husband thinks you just want money. They told us on the bus not to trust anyone here."

"We are not all the same. I want no money."

She returns and says, "He says he doesn't want money. Will you take our picture? I want you to do it." She has tears in her eyes.

I take the picture and they are happy. He doesn't ask for money. I go over and shake hands with him and we part with a smile.

I have just finished walking a third of the way around the world and have met no one but honest and interesting people. So many have trusted us and we them. But I choose not to believe this camel driver.

The driver reminds me to trust first, always. Only when trust is broken is it time to distrust. Thanks for the lesson.

Petra and the camel driver at the Pyramids

The Sinai

The next day we leave early for the Sinai to follow the route of the Exodus, the route the Hebrews took as they fled from Egypt to go to the Promised Land, just as we now were going "into the Promised Land." We make our way through Cairo's heavy traffic and actually see the Nile as we cross it this morning. Many half-completed apartment houses line the freeway on the edge of Cairo. Our guide tells us they are mostly illegal and below code. But they are filling a need for housing. Many are waiting for money to add more stories.

We head east past the airport and across the Eastern Desert. After a couple hours we drive under the Suez Canal and are in the Sinai.

Our first stop is at what tradition holds to be Marah by the Red Sea, a desert springs along the shore of the Red Sea, the site where the Israelites found the waters bitter. We both avoid the long line of Bedouin tourist shops and look out on the Sea where ships are waiting to head north through the Suez Canal.

Our next stop is Elim another desert oasis, the possible site where the Israelites found 12 wells and 70 palm trees as they continued toward the Promised Land. We spend half an hour walking among the palm trees and over the eroded land.

Elim. Is this the site of the oasis with 70 palms?

After another hour we stop at Wadi Feiran (Rephidim), the possible desert valley where the Israelites fought against the Amalekites. We stand on the slopes of Mount Serbal, the possible site where Moses held his arms up for victory at the end of that battle. Every place is only a *possible* candidate for the original location when it comes to locations from 3,000 or so years ago!

We pull into our hotel near Mt. Sinai in the early evening. Later we have a "traditional" Bedouin meal in a tent.

Climbing Mt. Sinai

At 2:30 in the morning some of us begin climbing Mt. Sinai. For obvious reasons, Petra stays back. But one of her crutches goes; I use it as a walking stick. The paths are steep and narrow. I'm glad it's dark so I can't see the steep down sides of the paths. Around 4:30, an hour before sunrise, we arrive near the top and rest in a tea shop for an hour before finishing the climb to see the impressive sunrise. I can even see the north end of the Gulf of Aqaba on the Red Sea.

I walk back down on a less steep path along with those who road camels up and down. It is a lot easier than the footpath up.

We barely have time to eat breakfast and put our things in the bus before we go to visit St. Katherine's Greek Orthodox Monastery, here since the fourth century at the base of Mt. Sinai. A friend did a vision quest near here during the time we were walking in America.

Jordan

After our quick tour of St. Katherine's, we are rushing off across the desert for the Israeli border at Eilat. We are inspected closely and bussed to the Jordanian border at Aqaba. The only formality in Aqaba is handing our passports to our new tour guide, Fadi. He has them processed *en masse*. They don't inspect our baggage. Soon we are in our Aqaba hotel, eating, and off to sleep to end the third day.

As we get up on this the fourth day, Petra announces, "I'm not moving. I'm staying here. This schedule is too fast. I cannot follow this timetable with my leg in recovery."

After a long discussion and soothing, she gets up and gets ready to go. But neither of us is happy with the pace or the timetable. We're going to Petra today. We'll live with the timetable — at least today.

Petra, Jordan

Since my college days I have wanted to visit Petra, the city. Petra, my lady, has had a similar wish since she first read about it when she was 13. On 18 December we walk into Petra. Before we married, I showed Petra a coin from Petra that I had purchased a few years earlier. That's when she first told me she wanted to visit Petra too.

Petra was the center of the Nabataean kingdom that controlled trade in the area from a few centuries before Christ until the sixth century after Christ when trade routes changed. An earthquake finally destroyed Petra and its elaborate system of aqueducts in the early seventh century. It was abandoned to the desert sands and only rediscovered by Europeans in the person of a Swiss explorer in 1812.

As we stand near the visitor's center about to enter the ruins of Petra, the city, I'm excited. Petra, my lady, is excited. Our life-long dreams are about to come true.

We have half a mile (one-kilometer) to walk before we get to the entrance. Petra opts for a horse provided by the park. She negotiates a tip and gets on. As I rejoin her at the entrance she says it was great letting her healing leg dangle as she road.

The entrance to Petra is down an ever narrowing and deepening canyon between sandstone cliffs. A channel is carved in the rocks on the left side of the canyon. This aqueduct brought water from the river at the beginning of the canyon into the city. It's now broken.

First view of the Treasury.

At places the canyon widens a bit only to close in again. After a half mile or so we get our first glimpse of the Treasury, the first tomb of the city. We get a little piece of a view between sandstone walls, that piece of a view I have seen in a thousand pictures over the years, some sandstone-colored pillars and flat rock. But now this is my live view, no longer a picture. A few meters farther and we see a sliver of the tomb. And then it is all in front of me, the Treasury in its ancient splendor.

The Treasury is an elaborate tomb cut out of the living rock. Most of the many monuments carved from these sandstone walls are tombs. The walls of the entrance to the town were their cemeteries. This one is called the Treasury because when it was first rediscovered in 1812; people thought the ancients had stashed treasure here. They shot at many statues and urns carved on the front hoping to expose that treasure. Nothing materialized.

We walk into another large tomb around the corner from the Treasury. It is only an empty room. It looks like we can walk into the Treasury too, but we're on a tour and you know tours, you can only take a quick look and run to the next highlight.

Mike stands before the Treasury.

Petra's leg is hurting. Walking downhill is still an effort. She wants to ride a camel and to give her leg a rest from walking. She solves both problems after negotiating a price with a cameleer (there are many to choose from) and getting on a big camel. She rides around showing off a bit and then sways back to the entrance proceeded by her gallant cameleer. She is clearly ecstatic. Now she wants to spend a month in the desert riding a camel!

After 500 meters (550 yards) or so the tomb-filled walls recede leaving a wide-open area for a street and huge plaza in front of some temples ruined by the seventh-century earthquake. The excavated square has huge, square flagstones. The stores and houses of the city sat beyond the square to the right and up a hill.

Beyond the plaza stand the remains of the temple dedicated to Petra's principal god, Dushara. The temple is a huge block of a building 20 to 25 meters (65 to 80 feet) high built with large, well cut stone. It's the only building in Petra more or less completely standing. I am impressed. It reminds me of a similar temple in Yeha in northern Ethiopia built around the same time to the Sabean moon god, Ilumqa.

Petra enjoys her camel ride in Petra.

The view back across the main town plaza from the temple heights gives an overview of a huge public space.

That's Petra! As I write this I am wandering the Internet looking for information to include. But if I don't stop, I'll have another book in this book. As with other pictures in this book, you can see more pictures of most of the things we talk about here on the Pictures tab of WalkingEast.com.

All too soon we are back in the bus and rushing off to Amman. Three days *might* have done justice to Petra, *not* three hours.

As we leave we drive through Wadi Musa, the town around Petra. It also looks like an interesting place to visit; but you know, the tour…. We have to come back to Wadi Musa and Petra some time, for no less than a couple weeks.

Passing through Wadi Musa, I discover that my Petra owns far more than she has been letting me know. Her name is on many businesses.

Amman

We only stop in Amman, Jordan's capitol to stay in a hotel. We have time for nothing else. I try to take pictures from the bus windows as we arrive in the evening and as we leave in the morning. Few work. But one does a fair job of recording a huge Jordanian flag flying over a neighborhood.

The next morning we leave Amman and head for Mt. Nebo where Moses got his chance to see the Promised Land before he died. But we can't see the land. Sandy air keeps us from seeing the few miles down to the Jordan River and across into the Promised Land.

The Jordan Valley north of the Dead Sea is green and there are several villages just before crossing into Israel on the King Hussein (Allenby) Bridge. It is easy leaving Jordan but an ordeal entering Israel.

Sheep fill the Bible. The Middle East is still full of sheep. We passed several huge flocks on the way down to the Dead Sea.

Israel

By two thirty we are at the Israeli border. We are bussed a long distance through a no-man's land to the customs post. No tour group guide meets us so we make our own way through what proves to be a two-hour customs and immigration ordeal. Thanks to Petra and a customs official, it goes better than it was beginning to feel like at the when we arrived. Our tour guide meets us outside.

For the next four days we rush from biblical site to biblical site around Israel, west, north, east, and south.

Joppa

From the Jordan River we ride all the way across the country to TelAviv-Joppa on the Mediterranean--maybe all of 62 miles (100 kilometers).

In Joppa we view early Roman ruins. Along the coast a huge storm has just exposed Roman-era ruins a week before we arrived. It had been buried under the coast since antiquity. Archeologists are working to protect a mosaic floor as we walk by.

In the same area, they found a stone engraved with Pontius Pilot's name. There aren't many stones around with his name. You can read **IVSPILATV** *clearly. The* **U** *was written as* **V** *in antiquity.*

Megiddo

At the ruins of Megiddo a statue of Elias stands swinging a wavy sword in the park where he led the Israelites in one of their many battles to take the land away from those who were there when they arrived. We must remember that the Israelites took the land from the indigenous at that time too. They often killed every inhabitant of the cities they took. Just read the Old Testament.

Nazareth

The divisiveness of fundamentalism is alive and well in Nazareth as it is in so many other parts of the world. A large Muslim billboard just outside the Christian Church of the Annunciation reads, "And whoever seeks a religion other than Islam, it will never be accepted of him, and in the Hereafter, he will be one of the losers. – Holy Quran." If only we could allow each other to live as we would like to live. Fundamentalism is widespread today. It's one of our worst diseases. It ranks with cancer in my book.

Tiberius

After staying overnight in Tiberius, we take a relaxing boat ride on the Sea of Galilee. No one got out of the boat to see whether they were good enough to walk on its water. Next we make a circle of several sites north of Lake Galilee and return to Tiberias via the northern Golan Heights where the Syrians liked to shoot down on the Israelis before the 1967 war when the Israelis took it from them.

We sit on a boat on the Sea of Galilee.

At Yardenit on the Jordan River, a minister who is part of our tour, re-baptizes several in our tour John-the-Baptist style, fully submerged. This place is not the traditional place of John the Baptist, but that place is in a security zone now so Yardenit is the surrogate.

Dead Sea/Salt Sea

We continue to flow through the Middle East at the rate of a fast mountain stream bouncing from ancient site to ancient site. It is good, interesting, and tiring. From Galilee we follow the Jordan River south to the Dead Sea where we stay for the night and take a dip in the Salt Sea as it is called here. The next day we head north and west into Jerusalem stopping at Masada and Qumran along the way.

Jerusalem

5,321 mi. (8,620 km.) – December 23, 2010

December 23 we came to the top of the hill east of Jerusalem for our first real view of the city. The temple mount with the Mosque of Omar and the old city lay in front of us with New Jerusalem in the background. The graves of centuries line the hill below us. We have arrived at the physical goal we set out for 23 months ago, almost two years.

Jerusalem after 23 months on the road.

We get out of the bus and look down over the graves in the Kedron Valley and across at the city fought over for more than four millennia. Petra has the choice to walk down the steep hill to the Garden of Gethsemane or to take a bus. She chooses to walk. She struggles with her leg. We walk back and forth down the street like skiers ski back and forth on a steep slope. It's hard. These are the last steps of our pilgrimage to Jerusalem. *It was a big journey.*

Western Wall

One day we stand back and above the Western Wall of the Temple of Solomon, the most holy place to Judaism. The Mosque of Omar on the temple mound just above is Islam's third most holy place.

The Western Wall of the Temple of Solomon (center right) is the most holy place to Judaism. The Mosque of Omar (top left) on the mound is the third most holy place of Islam. They both contribute to the complexities of solving the problems of the peoples of the Middle East.

Holy Sepulcher

Jesus' traditional tomb in the Holy Sepulcher.

Inside a box of a room in the Church of the Holy Sepulcher they say Jesus was buried. This said, all these places we see in Jerusalem were known only by verbal tradition for 300 years until the time of St. Helena and Constantine when the buildings were built around them. Another place outside the Damascus Gate, the Garden Tomb, Also claims that it is the place of Jesus' tomb. We visit many places in Israel with titles beginning with "The place where…." The exact place is neither important nor often *really* known. The reminder of what happened here somewhere some 2,000 years ago is the important thing.

We also remember that the current street level of the city is actually 20 to 30 feet (6 to 9 meters) above where it was in the time of Jesus. The difference in height is the due to the debris that has accumulated in the intervening 20 centuries, one to two feet per century.

Mosque of Omar

The Dome on the Rock, the Mosque of Omar from the roof of the Sisters of Zion Convent.

The Mosque of Omar, also known as the Dome on the Rock, stands on the temple mound, Mount Mariah, in Jerusalem. The rock is the place where Abraham prepared to sacrifice Isaac and where Mohammed ascended to heaven to meet Elijah and Jesus. It is a very holy place to both Islam and Judaism. The building is one of the most beautiful in the world, befitting of the place it stands.

Built in the seventh century after the Arabs captured Jerusalem, the Mosque of Omar is visible between many buildings as you wander the city streets.

The Mosque of Omar is a clear and visible symbol of the seemingly impossible obstacles that the people of the Middle East must overcome to arrive at a lasting peace. It is about land. It is about People. It is about religion. It is about holy places. It is about Jerusalem. It is about so many things. Someday? Someday! When it is time. *Inshallah*! God willing!

The Wall

A wall separates the Palestinian territories from Jerusalem. It surrounds Jerusalem. It is huge and visible from many parts of the city. When we get a chance to see it up close it looks like similar recent walls separating societies with its satirist graffiti.

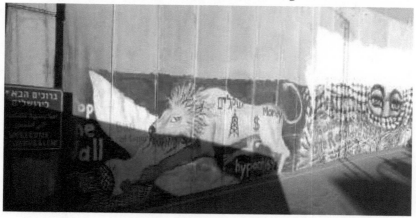

Next to the gate on the wall on the road to Bethlehem a fierce lion named "Money" has his mouth around a dove. An official sign next to it says in Hebrew, Arabic, and English, "Welcome to Jerusalem."

Bethlehem

On Christmas Day we are in Bethlehem. I have been estimating we would arrive next Easter for a long time. But Petra wanted to be here for Christmas. Her broken leg made it possible. In fact, without the broken leg we may not have arrived on foot at all. Within a month of our arrival uprisings flared up around the Arab world. I suspect walking anywhere in the Middle East would have been quite hard if not taboo.

Our initial entry into Bethlehem is less than auspicious. They tell us that because we are going into Palestinian territory, a Palestinian driver and guide have to take us. But we traveled through all other parts of occupied Palestine with our Israeli driver and guide. I don't know why it's different here. Reason has little to do with things in the Holy Land. So our driver takes us into Bethlehem and drops the bus at a huge souvenir shop, gives us some tickets for ten percent off, and tells us another guide is coming to take us to lunch.

We spend an hour and more in the shop. No one comes. We feel abandoned. Petra and I go out searching for a place to eat and find a small shop around the corner where we have some water and a falafel and a good conversation with the owner. Like us, several others wander off for something to eat too. Finally, two hours or so later the driver and guide float in from somewhere and first take those left to a nearby restaurant and then take us all to the Church of the Nativity.

We are at the Church of the Nativity Christmas day. We go in with the crowds and head for the crypt of the nativity. To see the traditional site of the manger, we stand in a long line and wait as it slowly moves us into the basement. In a small room with several monks standing around directing traffic, a multi-pointed star indicates the place of Jesus' birth. I barely have a chance to look at the manger. I want to take a picture. My camera is pushed down and I am pushed forward. I come. I see. And I am pushed on. There and gone so quickly. I have no opportunity to feel what is happening. I am only up the opposite steps and back in the church proper looking back at the curtain on the door. I wait for Petra, who is still in the crypt.

Petra's manger experience is much more profound:

> Christmas day at the church of Nativity means long waiting lanes to get down to the place where tradition tells is the manger where Jesus Christ was born. It's difficult for me to stand in line. My leg is still hurting when I stand too long. Finally, after half an hour, I'm at the entrance to the birthplace. I go down some steps with my crutch. A monk helps me. I see the birthplace marked with a star, the star of Bethlehem. There are so many people. I have no time to stand for a while at the star. I have a flashback of our entire pilgrimage walk. So much passes through my mind and heart in only a few seconds. I am rushed past the manger. I don't expect anything in this kind of rush. I leave up another set of stairs. Another monk helps me. While I walk up the stairs I feel a bright light energy flowing through my whole body. The flow of light is so strong that my heart opens up and at the same time my tears are flowing. I am crying in peace. I let it happen and at the same time I don't

know what is happening. I sit on a bench outside the crypt. More tears flow. I need time to recover. Suddenly in my inner eye I see Michelangelo's Finger of God in the Sistine Chapel. I just experienced the touch of God's finger! As long as I have known this painting, I have wondered what the meaning of the touching finger was. Now I have experienced the meaning. I am sure more than a finger touch would have "burnt me away". This is my Christmas light. With it all the pains of the pilgrimage where purified and washed away, healing in an instant, with a Finger Touch.

As we leave between the Church of the Nativity and an adjacent convent, we stand over a hole in the ground where St. Jerome is said to have translated the Vulgate Bible from Greek and Hebrew into Latin. No wonder he had such a bad temperament.

Palestinian wishes

As we cross the church courtyard, some youth hand us a Christmas card and small wooden cutouts and wish us a Merry Christmas. The card has a manger scene and the simple message, "Merry Christmas and a Happy New Year. Pray for the freedom of Palestine." Inside was the final stamp for our pilgrim's passport, "Christmas for all, Bethlehem, 24/12/2010." The cutout is a refrigerator magnet that says, "From Bethlehem to the world, a message of Love and Peace." The other cutout is a king with a gift in a house. The handout comes from the Palestinian Ministry of Tourism and Antiquities.

We are surprised to receive the gifts. We are so touched by their simple message. Our eyes immediately fill with tears. It is the climax of the entire pilgrimage for me, even more than our entry into Jerusalem. The pilgrimage has been an experience of peace all along the way. And now here in the center of clashes that have lasted millennia, the simple message, "Peace," shows its face again. We can be only emotional and grateful for the honor of being able to make this pilgrimage, and pray for peace here in the Holy Land too.

The tour is over

The tour is over on the 26th. So what's our final assessment of a bus tour like this? It's hectic. We arrive at a hotel late in the evening; eat later; bed later yet; up by six; breakfast; in the bus before 7:30. Then we stop at place after place only to be snatched away before we learn much, only to be taken to the next stop, again to be there for too little time. But they always have time to dump us at least one huge curio vender every day. The tour is too much like work.

Our Jordanian and Egyptian guides are quite knowledgeable, informative, entertaining, and can speak well. Our Israeli guide, though he may be just as knowledgeable, has a hard time getting his point across at times. At least we don't stop at every site on the itinerary. That would be far too much.

Would we take a similar tour again? One should never say never. But I suspect we would only go in extreme circumstances (as is the case this time). It is nice having someone else set up the lodging and schedule. And it is nice to get a surface introduction to the area, though we paid a high price in lost leisureliness in taking this tour.

Our Jerusalem

On our own, we tour the city more leisurely until 13 January living back in our small hotel mode first with the White Sisters just outside the Damascus gate and then at the Ecce Homo Convent with the Sisters of Zion on the beginning of the Via Dolorosa. The Ecce Homo Convent stands over the traditional place where Pontius Pilot condemned Jesus to death. The convent has a beautiful roof terrace overlooking Jerusalem. We spend a lot of time on the terrace.

The Holy Sepulcure and the roofs of Jerusalem from our Ecce Homo Convent roof.

While we are in Jerusalem we have some errands to do for people who asked us as we walked across America. We go to the Western Wall and leave the note from the Spanish woman in Truchas, New Mexico (See p. 59). While we are at the Western Wall we also leave the money the hotel owner gave us in Richmond, Illinois (See p. 148). From the roof terrace of the Ecce Homo we let the dirt Stan gave us in Baldwin City, Kansas, filter into the air above Jerusalem. (See p. 102). And we included all the people we encountered on our pilgrimage in our prayers in Jerusalem. We also send our several post cards to people we met along our pilgrimage.

One day we visit Oscar Schindler's grave outside the south wall of Jerusalem below the Zion gate. You likely remember *Schindler's List,* the Steven Spielberg movie of Schindler's epic saving of many Jews during the Second World War. His grave is covered with rocks. Other graves have a few rocks but Schindler's has little room for more. The rocks are a Jewish custom. Instead of leaving a flower to remember the person, they leave a rock, which lasts a lot longer.

We wander the city aimlessly meeting people in the street and in the convents where we stayed. It was a luxury not to be bussed around from here to there in rapid succession by the tour. In one shop, we drink coffee with a merchant and then are expected to buy his earrings even though we don't want to buy earrings. We drink coffee and tea at sidewalk shops and just watch the people going by. Petra poses next to a head of cabbage that is as big as her head. We eat falafel from small shops. We talk and play with a macaw hanging across from his owner's shop. We talk with a Palestinian bookshop owner. We're getting to know Jerusalem, the community.

With one crutch Petra walks up the narrow, almost-pitch-black, stepped alleyway of the Via Dolorosa at five am to attend the 5:30 am Mass in the Holy Sepulcure when less people are packed into the church. There were several changes of priest groups (Copts, Romans, Ethiopians, and others), each taking their turns at the holy places, none celebrating together. She uses the quiet time at the Holy Sepulcure to let our pilgrimage and our arrival time sink in, to see how we are not the same as we were when we started two years earlier, to just sit and be in the now. I do a lot of those things just wandering the streets.

Besides sitting and doing little tasks, we wander Jerusalem's narrow, dark streets until we leave 13 January 2011.

Sunset behind the Holy Sepulcure from Ecce Homo.

REFLECTIONS

Our pilgrimage is complete. So many things have happened. In this section we talk about the walk and the pilgrimage, and try to give some closure to the pilgrimage to Jerusalem.

Meeting people

Almost to a person, everyone we met was great. All were curious and ready to hear and help us. But more than just helping us, we helped each other; we had great times and exchanged life stories and dreams. With every meeting we received physical and spiritual energy and excitement. We were enthused. It made us happy and gave us extra fuel for the day's walking.

We even enjoyed the cops stopping us. They were only doing their duty. All were people just like the other people we met, curious and a pleasant addition to our day.

We are thankful to the many who invited us in to stay in their homes after knowing us for so short a time. Our Thanks page on WalkingEast.com names most of them in North America. But I got lax and never updated that page once we crossed to Portugal.

In America we interacted with many because we all spoke English. But in Europe, especially in Portugal, and to a lesser extent in France, it was harder to interact. We didn't speak each other's language. Petra and I had each other for companionship 24/7. We came through that quite well—to the disbelief of many. But Petra missed companionship with regular friends near her. I, more solitary by nature, was more able to overcome lack of regular friends nearby with e-mail contacts.

We are so honored that the Universe has assigned us to be ambassadors of dreams, to inspire others to think about their dreams. See p. 45.

Being a Nomad

We walked as Nomads, with a capital N. as opposed to nomads, with a lower case n. People walking a path like the Camino de Santiago are nomads. They leave their homes to walk for a few weeks and then return to their home. They look for places to stay and eat for a while, but somewhere they have a home. We, however, are Nomads, we have no home where we came from or are returning to. We live on the road.

After almost two years on the road, some tasks taken on when we became Nomads (night after night looking for place to stay, a restaurant, and the path to follow the next day) never became entirely comfortable. Mike always had a hard time with all three, especially the first two. Petra wasn't easy with forever searching for and deciding on the path to follow. Petra says it was I who never wanted to give over control of the map; that's why she did so little path finding, not because she didn't like the task. These three tasks were not insignificant.

And lest I forget, the task of washing clothes still stayed with us as Nomads. Petra assumed this task and I didn't argue.

Sometimes I think we wanted to only live in the Now and have these things magically take care of themselves. The ideal inn, p. 178, developed from our adventures in searching for a place for our heads each night.

Neither of us missed most of the things we gave up, like, paying gas bills, water bills, garbage bills, rent, car insurance, electric bills, internet bills, phone bills, taxes. We didn't miss having to buy gas for the car or watering the grass. And sweeping the sidewalk, the kitchen floor, or the back patio or vacuuming the living room, our offices, and the bedroom were not on our mind for the better part of two years.

At times, especially toward the end, we longed to cook our own dinner in our own kitchen.

Other than these discomforts, walking is soothing and invigoration. Being a Nomad is a rather appealing life style. There is something magic about having a new back yard and a new front yard every few hours, about walking endlessly to an unknown place—or just walking endlessly in the Now.

We reconfirmed that we can live with only a few things, the things that fit easily in a backpack. Yes, we have the bed at a motel and its chairs. But we carry a mat to sit on and a tent to sleep in almost everywhere also.

The walk

The 5,321 miles (8,620 kilometers) we covered was a vast distance. The lands we walked through were so big. We walked it. When we later drive over some of it in America, it was hard to believe we walked it all.

How did the walk change us? I now have a profound and absolute feeling in my mind and gut that a person—at least this man—can do anything s/he wants to do as long as s/he does it one step at a time and with the sanction of the Universe. Using the broken leg the Universe teaches one of our biggest lessons. Everything is given to you, even the one step at a time. Only if the Universe grants you the ability to walk, will you be able to walk. Everything is granted, is a gift.

We know much better now that we walk every distance, every hill, no matter how high, every valley, no matter how deep, only one step at a time. When faced with one of them we try to look at our feet and stay in the Now. We can take one step and then another and another until all add up to that long distance, that hill, or that valley.

The weather was always a factor. When we walk such a long walk, there is no question of not walking one or another season. Our pilgrimage spanned eight seasons. We took what we got when we got it—rain, snow, sun, wind, clouds. Though we groused at it and took off one entire summer season, we learned to adjust to what Nature dished out.

It was almost always comforting to know in the morning as I got up that I would be walking within a couple hours and for the rest of the day.

We said in the beginning that we would hear the call of the road to end the walk if it gave such a call. Petra feels at one point we did not listen too closely. She thinks it begged us to stop several times: in Brooklyn, in Portugal, in Spain, in France, especially in Arles. It was only the Universe breaking Petra's leg that actually stopped us. Was a two-year commitment for a pilgrimage too long? Were all those "beggings" really only *temptations* to stop? Was it good as it was? There was a big lesson to be learned with the broken leg.

The walk itself was a meditation, but after a certain time the daily routine and the walk became mechanical. The walk was an everyday practice and like any meditation it can become a routine without depth. [Does this also hold a lesson? That routine should also be practiced in depth in the Now?] The lesson of the broken leg showed, that it wasn't important to *walk* all the way to Jerusalem. But it was important to adapt to the new situation, to finish the pilgrimage, and to experience the lesson of being in the Now.

In the beginning one of our minor goals was to show one could walk from his/her front door in North America to Santiago de Compostela. We did that too.

The journey was the destination, most of the time. But we lost sight of that at times and spent too much time with the destination. This especially happened during the final "meandering" stage when we did a lot more worrying about the path and its destination than meandering.

Being in the Now

When I, Petra, now read my experience at Eunate, the Templar chapel in Spain (see p. 232), I can see the insight, or message, much clearer than at that time in Spain. Being in the Now, with every breath and at the same time knowing my death will come, makes my life full. While walking my three circuits around the chapel, I realized I can slow down and embrace the moment and then I will be more in peace when I die. My broken leg was such a moment in my life. When I was forced by the injury to be more in the Now and more aware and more enjoying the moment, then the pain disappeared like the pain walking barefoot on Eunate's stones. Walking or moving forward with the goal of Jerusalem and walking the three circuits around Eunate with the goal after the third circuit to reach the west entrance, my death, are similar. Both times I was rushing and was not 100% in the Now. Both times I was slowed down by pain and learned that while I am in the moment and breathing deeply, the pain will disappear and joy, happiness, and inner peace will arise.

The next stage in my life is to transfer the insights I gained from Eunate in Spain and my broken leg into my daily life. I want to avoid rushing through life. I want to be in the Now because death (the west entrance of the chapel) will come. In the end it doesn't change anything if I rush or fill my life with more than I can experience with full awareness. I must be fully aware of what is here before me in the Now.

So the beginning question: "Who will we be after walking this pilgrimage for two years?" still has no full answer. And we are not at all sure what we'll do next. But we do know more surely from the walk; we will live more in the Now.

We still like to walk, perhaps not in two-year chunks any more. But some day we will surely walk again.

Encounters on the road to Jerusalem

APPENDIX

This appendix section includes a potpourri of items that fit only here at the end of the book.

FAQs

Several questions come up often as we walk and now after it. So here are the quick answers to these most frequently asked questions (FAQs). The body of the book gives you the long answers.

- Is it safe to walk? *Yes!*
- Do you carry a gun? Aren't you afraid to walk in the open (without a car) …? *No! And No!*
- How are the people? *Amazing! Wonderful! We give each other strength and enthusiasm.*
- How are the dogs? *Accept for a pack of three in France, we have no problem with dogs.*
- How many pairs of shoes have you warn out? *Nine. See p. 338.*
- How long was this pilgrimage? Did you take rides? *6,322 miles (10, 242 Kilometers) in America and Europe. We walked 81.6%, 5,108 miles (8,275 kilometers) of that. See p. 334.*
- How far did you walk in a day? How fast? *13.3 miles (21.2 kilometers) average per day at 2.5 to 3 miles (4 to 5 kilometers) per hour. See p. 334.*
- How was it being together 24/7 for so long? *Quite well. The body of book tells you more.*
- Did you have backups like extra medicines, extra clothes? *No. If we need something we buy it or it is provided.*
- How much did it cost? *About the same as the cost to keep up a modest household. See p. 337.*

Maps

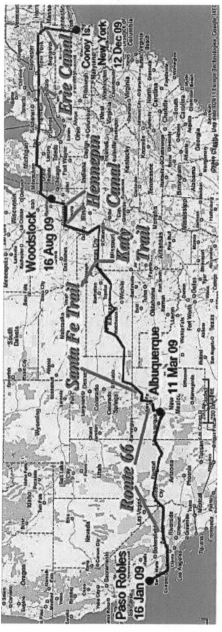

Our route across southern America.

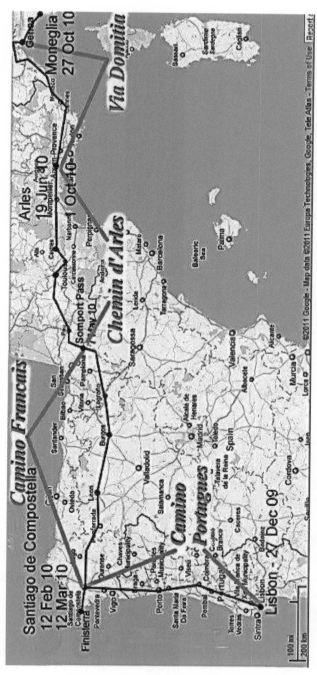

Our route across southern Europe.

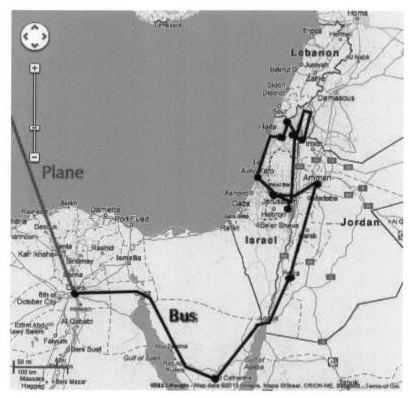

Our Middle East tour.

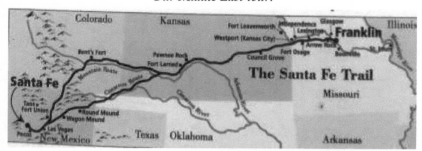

The Santa Fe Trail (from Dept. of Interior display in Franklin, Missouri.)

The Katy Trail (courtesy of BikeKatTrail.com).

The web of European paths that feed into the main Camino de Santiago, the Camino Français.

Our flag

As we prepare to walk across the America, we realize we will be a minority, a small minority, on the road. No one walks in America, except indigents and the homeless, or so one is given to think. In fact, as we get into the walk, we find that *few* actually walk the *open* roads, vagrants or not. We are almost always alone walking on road.

We are walking by choice, walking a pilgrimage. So we set out to make a flag to let the world know we have a mission, a bright yellow flag so we will be seen. We put it on our backpacks in the beginning and on our carts when we begin traveling with them. And it graces every new post on our web journal.

You can see it on the cover and scattered in the pictures throughout this book.

Two interweaved titles *California to Jerusalem* and *Walking East* flow together from top to bottom forming **California Walking East to Jerusalem**. *2009-2010?* announce our walk and our proposed timeframe, our best estimate as we start. It proves to be an accurate guess—we entered Jerusalem 23 December 2010. Finally *WalkingEast.com* announces our web journal address.

The pictures celebrate major destinations along our two-year route. The **bell** is the symbol of the **Camino Real** connecting California's eighteenth-century Spanish missions running from San Diego to north of San Francisco. We begin our pilgrimage along the Camino Real, walking between six missions.

Our next great pilgrimage stop is **Santiago de Compostela** in Spain, 3,976 walking miles (6,441 kilometers) down the road . Its symbol is the **scallop shell**. We have been to Santiago before and plan to walk into it again, this time from our front door.

The **keys** symbolize St. Peter's keys to heaven, they represent our **Rome** passage. We walked to Rome from our home in Germany in 2006-07.

The **palm tree** symbolizes our final destination, Jerusalem.

We are the **two pilgrims** walking forward with our backpacks though we pushed carts across America and half of Europe.

In effect, our flag identifies us and calls attention to the extent and length of our pilgrimage walk.

Our early version at the flag is a crude, iron-on attempt. The wind and weather quickly begins to tear off the iron-on design. My brother Marty has a great professional version printed for us on a yellow cloth background. You can see it on any picture of the flag on our carts after in Flagstaff in February 2009.

Our flag flies somewhere near us for the whole journey. It will hang on one of our walls now for a long time.

How far did we walk?

The first table below breaks down the walking statistics between North America and Europe. It tells how far we walked, road, and traveled over water, first in North America and then Europe. The second table combines the information of the first table into the total statistics for the walking portion of our pilgrimage. Percent walked is the percent of walking mileage divided by the walking and riding mileage. Water mileage is not factored into it. We also do not include any walking in Germany or in the Sierra Nevada Mountains. Though their walking is part of the pilgrimages as rest times, I have chosen not to include them in the walking pilgrimage statistics here.

	North America		Europe	
	Miles	**Km.**	**Miles**	**Km.**
% Walked	81.1%		83.6%	
Walk	3,593	5,821	1,515	2,454
Ride	835	1,353	297	481
Water	82	133	0	0
Totals:	4,510	7,306	1,812	2,935

Total Europe & N. America		
	Miles	**Km.**
% Walked	81.6%	
Walk	5,108	8,275
Ride	1,132	1,834
Water	82	133
Totals:	6,322	10,242

Because of Petra's broken leg, we no longer walked as before once we arrived in the Middle East. Because of that I do not give a separate account of our passage there. Instead this table gives you the total mileage for the entire trip including the flights over the Atlantic to Europe and over the Mediterranean to Egypt. As above, percent walked is the percent of walking mileage divided by the walking and riding mileage. Air and water mileage is not factored into it. The percent walked is much lower because of the number of miles driven in the Middle East.

Entire trip including Trans-Atlantic

	Miles	Km.
% walked	67.5%	
Walk	5,321	8,620
Ride	2,564	4,157
Air/Water	7,510	12,166
Totals:	15,395	24,943

Where did we stay?

We stayed in many different places along our pilgrimage. Here is a summary of those places. This does not include the days we were in the mountains of California in summer 2010 or the days we spent in Germany.

Type	Percent
Hotel	47.1%
B&B	20.5%
Private home	12.2%
Refugio	9.1%
Tent	5.4%
Marty's RV	2.7%
Mobil home	1.9%
Apartment	1.2%

How much did it Cost?

Our pilgrimage cost about the same as running a modest household. We can give you some approximate numbers that do not include the costs for the side trips to Germany or back to the US in the summer of 2010. Costs directly related to the walking (hotel, food, shoes, clothes, and the like) in the America (U.S. and Canada) amounted to around $92 per day or $8.73 per mile ($5.41/km). Similar costs for the walk from Lisbon to Petra's broken leg south of Genoa, Italy, were $94 per day or $10.65 per mile ($6.60/km). This latter number does not include the flight cost to and from Europe to America. We walked shorter distances in Europe giving the higher per-mile costs there.

These are the costs for two people walking and staying double occupancy the way we walk and stay. Your walk could be considerably different since your housing and eating habits can vary considerably from ours.

Some walk the pilgrimages in Portugal, Spain, and France with no money living on the gifts they receive along the road. Others on these routes stay only in hotels and eat only in "good" restaurants. You can see a broad range of possible costs. Along these routes we stayed in hostels (refugios) 40 to 50 per cent of the time and ate modestly. If you stay only in refugios and eat modestly all the way you could probably get by on $35 to $50 a day on the Camino de Santiago.

We received many gifts as we walked across America (See p. 180). These are not included in the numbers above.

Our shoes cost both of us about $0.25 per mile ($0.15/km).

Shoes

One day as we are preparing for this walk Petra says, "We should think about what we are going to do about shoes."

"What about them?" I am a bit slow.

"Well, we are going to need a lot of shoes to walk so far."

"I didn't think of that. How far can we get on a pair?"

Neither of us has a clue. I haven't thought of what kind ether. Another thing to research before starting.

Petra gets on the Internet and finds a shoe outlet in San Luis Obispo just south of us. We go down and hit them with many questions and come away with some answers.

Running rather than walking shoes are better for walking on roads. They have more cushioning and breathe better. The clerk estimates the shoes will last 600 to 800 miles (970 to 1,300 kilometers). That means that we need between six and eight pair for the 5,000 miles (8,100 kilometers) we estimate for the walk. In the end I average almost exactly 600 miles (970 kilometers) per pair for the various pairs I walk the insides out of. Souls often are still OK when the insides are done.

We both buy good running shoes the next day. Petra likes hers so much that she buys the same pair from the Internet time after time until they are out of production and no longer available. She has them shipped forward to a place where we are about to arrive.

Running shoes in Europe are really expensive. Our American outlet does not ship to Europe. So we have the outlet send the shoes to my brother, Marty, in Illinois. He then resends them to us in Europe. We save around $50 even with the double shipping.

As for me, though in the end I get the most mileage on that first pair, I never really like them much. So I buy different ones each time I buy new ones. Until the second-to-last pair I am not satisfied. Petra enjoys every pair of her shoes but some of mine hurt my feet more than they help.

One of the most frequent questions we get as we walk is, "How many pair of shoes did you wear out?" We each go through nine pair. I average 608 miles (984 kilometers) a pair. They cost me $0.12 per mile to walk in. Petra's cost about the same. Here's the breakdown of how Mike's shoes held up. We haven't given details for Petra's because the average comes out to about the same.

	Shoe Usage	5469*	8859	:Total
		608	984	:Average
Nr	Name	Miles	Kilometers	First used
1	Asics	844	1367	15 Jan 2009
2	New Bal. Running	640	1038	30 Mar 09
3	???	485	786	22 May 2009
4	Good running shoes	724	1173	23 Jul 2009
5	Dr. Scholl's	326	529	6 Oct 2009
6	New Bal. Walking	561	908	4 Nov 2009
7	New Bal. Walking	671	1088	8 Jan 2010
8	Spanish-Gortex	692	1121	10 Apr 2010
9	New Bal. Running	525	850	1 Sep 2010

* The mileage is more than the distance we walked on the pilgrimage because we included mileage we walked on the shoes in Germany and the Sierras also in order to get a true life span of the shoes.

Counted pilgrims

I count pilgrims several days as I walk against the flow on the Camino de Santiago during this Holy Year. Most numbers represent the number the pilgrims I meet in a two hours. Many people are walking!

Day (2010)	Pilgrims Met
4 April	156
5 April	93
6 April	192
7 April	105
8 April	152
9 April	136

People entering Santiago

The official Camino office in Santiago keeps statistics on the number people arriving in Santiago after having traveled at least 100 kilometers (61 miles) on foot, cycle, horse, or donkey. As you can easily see, the numbers of people jump during a Holy Year.

Year	Total	Walkers
2003	74,614	60,721
2004 (Holy Year)	179,944	156,952
2005	93,924	76,674
2009	145,887	120,605
2010 (Holy Year)	272,135	237,852
2011	183,366	153,065
2012	192,488	164,778
2013	215,880	188.191

Books

These are just a few of the books that come to the forefront as I write this book. It is in no way exhaustive.

Karen Armstrong, *Holy War: The Crusades and their Impact on Today's World*.

Pico Ayer, *Life of the Dalai Lama*.

John Brierley, *A Pilgrim's Guide to the Camino Portugués*.

John Brierley, *Camino de Santiago Maps*.

Paulo Coelho, *The Alchemist*.

Paulo Coelho, *The Pilgrimage*.

Phil Cousineau, *The Art of Pilgrimage: The Seeker's Guide to Making Travel Sacred*.

Brett Dufur, *The Complete Katy Trail Guidebook*.

Babette Gallard and Paul Chinn, *Lightfoot Guides to the Via Francigena and Via Domitia*.

Shirley McLane, *The Camino*.

Mike Metras. *Germany to Rome in 64 Days: Our Pilgrimage*. (Available at www.WorksAndWords.com)

Mike Metras. *Walking Live: Meditations on the Pilgrimage of Life*. (Available at www.WorksAndWords.com)

Elaine Pinkerton, *The Santa Fe Trail by Bicycle*.

Mireille Retail and Marie-Virginie Cambriels, *Miam-miam-dodo du chemin d'Arles + le camino aragonés : Chemin de Compostelle (GR 653) d'Arles au col du Somport, du Somport à Puente la Reina (Navarra)*. [Guidebook in French to Camino d'Arles]

Inez Ross, *Without a Wagon on the Santa Fe Trail*.

Links

The web changes rapidly. These may be outdated by the time you read this book. For this reason I have only added a few. You can quickly find most of the other places we mention in this book with a search engine like Google.com.

Our web sites:
www.WalkingEast.com
www.WalkingWithAwareness.com
www.WorksAndWords.com

Acoma Native American pueblo: www.acomaskycity.org

Alta via dei Monti Liguri:
    www.altaviadeimontiliguri.it/portale/it/aree_protette.wp

Camino statistics: www.jakobus-info.de/jakobuspilger/statik01.htm

Confraternity of Pilgrims to Jerusalem on Facebook

Kingsley, KS carnivals Heritage Center:
    www.kansastravel.org/carnivalheritagecenter.htm

Mariandale New York Retreat Center: www.mariandale.org/

Medina Railroad Museum: railroadmuseum.net/

Pilgrimage Publications: www.pilgrimagepublications.com

Poughkeepsie, NY walking bridge: www.walkway.org/

Sue Kenny: http://www.suekenney.ca/

Press articles

The following newspapers interviewed us at one time or another as we walked the pilgrimage. This list names the paper and gives a link to the paper. Use the link to search for an article that has our names. As the Internet is constantly in flux, some links may be no longer valid.

Our press page, www.WalkingWithAwareness.com/press.htm, has the full links.

Paso Robles Press (CA) on July 11, 2008 www.pasoroblespress.com/

Northwest Harold, Woodstock (IL) Daily News on 21 January 2009 www.nwherald.com/.

Hillsboro (KS) **Free Press** 12 May 2009 www.hillsborofreepress.com/.

Ottawa (IL) **Times** on 10 August 2009 www.mywebtimes.com/.

The Daily News of Greenville, Belding, and Montcalm Counties (MI) on 18 September 2009 www.thedailynews.cc.

Attica (MI) **Tri-City Times** on 7 October 2009 www.tricitytimes-online.com/.

The Rockford (MI) **Squire** on 8 October 2009 rockfordsquire.com/2009/10/08/.

Lapeer County (MI) **Press** on 11 October 2009 thecountypress.mihomepaper.com/news/2009-10-11/.

Sentinel-Review of Woodstock, Ontario, on 15 October 2009 www.woodstocksentinelreview.com/

The Daily News of Batavia, New York, 5 November 2009 thedailynewsonline.com/

About us

Petra and I as we reached the Atlantic.

For many years I wrote books to tell people how to use computer software. In my vacation time I traveled by car throughout the United States. I dreamed of traveling more distant paths at a slower pace. The mountains of Spain, Italy, and Greece and the Nile River called to me for many years. My earlier education in philosophy and theology called me to look more deeply into the soul of the path I was walking in life.

In earlier lives, I studied to be a Catholic priest only to opt out after a second try following four years in the Army. I served in Ethiopia, Viet Nam, and the U.S.

In 2000 I retired from technical writing to walk and write about more varied subjects. In spring 2003 I walked the Camino de Santiago across northern Spain to the Atlantic. While walking Petra and I met.

My passions include walking, writing, coin collecting, and encouraging others to be true to their hearts' desires.

Petra began her professional life as a hairdresser only to move on to the university in Berlin where she became an environmental engineer and worked several years as an engineer. She was running an agency for renewable energy in Constance, Germany, as she began her pilgrimage to Santiago from Constance in late December 2001. This pilgrimage changed her life in many ways. She quit her environmental engineering career and began a new life. Petra conducted workshops and gave slideshows about the Camino de Santiago and other pilgrimages. Since then she is helping others to walk with more awareness both along the physical paths and along their walk through life, the pilgrimage of life. After beginning a new life she deepened also her passion for shamanism and vision quest.

Since we met we have married and walked parts of the Camino four times again. We walked the Via de la Plata from Seville to Santiago in 2005. We walked from our home in Germany over the Alps to Rome in 2006-7 and across America and Europe to Jerusalem 2009-10. We have also spent several months in India. In our non-traveling times we have lived in Germany, California, and Santa Fe, New Mexico. We are currently in India.

Read the real-time journal of our pilgrimage to Jerusalem at *WalkingEast.com*. Visit us at *www.WalkingWithAwareness.com* to see what we are currently doing.

Have a long and joyous walk through life.

Mike Metras and Petra Wolf

Other books

We have written other books on various subjects:

- *Germany to Rome in 64 days: Our Pilgrimage* is a book describing our 64-day walk from out front door in Germany over the Alps and down the Via Francigena to Rome.

- *Walking Life: Meditations on the Pilgrimage of Life* is a book of meditations and photographs to help in walking our life path.

- *Sicily's Historic Coasts* is a book about Sicily, its history, and my month-long visit there in 2000.

- *Ethiopia: Travels of a Youth* is book describing people and places I visited in Ethiopia and Eritrea during the late 1960s while in the U.S. Army.

- *Money Meandering: An Introduction to Numismatics* is a book introducing you to coin collecting.

- *Axum: Coins and Places* is a video of coins and places associated with ancient Axum, a kingdom in northern Ethiopia.

Browse and order these books at *www.WalkingWithAwareness.com* or our sister site *www.WorksAndWords.com.* Refer to either of these sites also for information on how to obtain an electronic version of this book with color pictures.